a violent embrace

a violent embrace

art and aesthetics after representation

renée c. hoogland

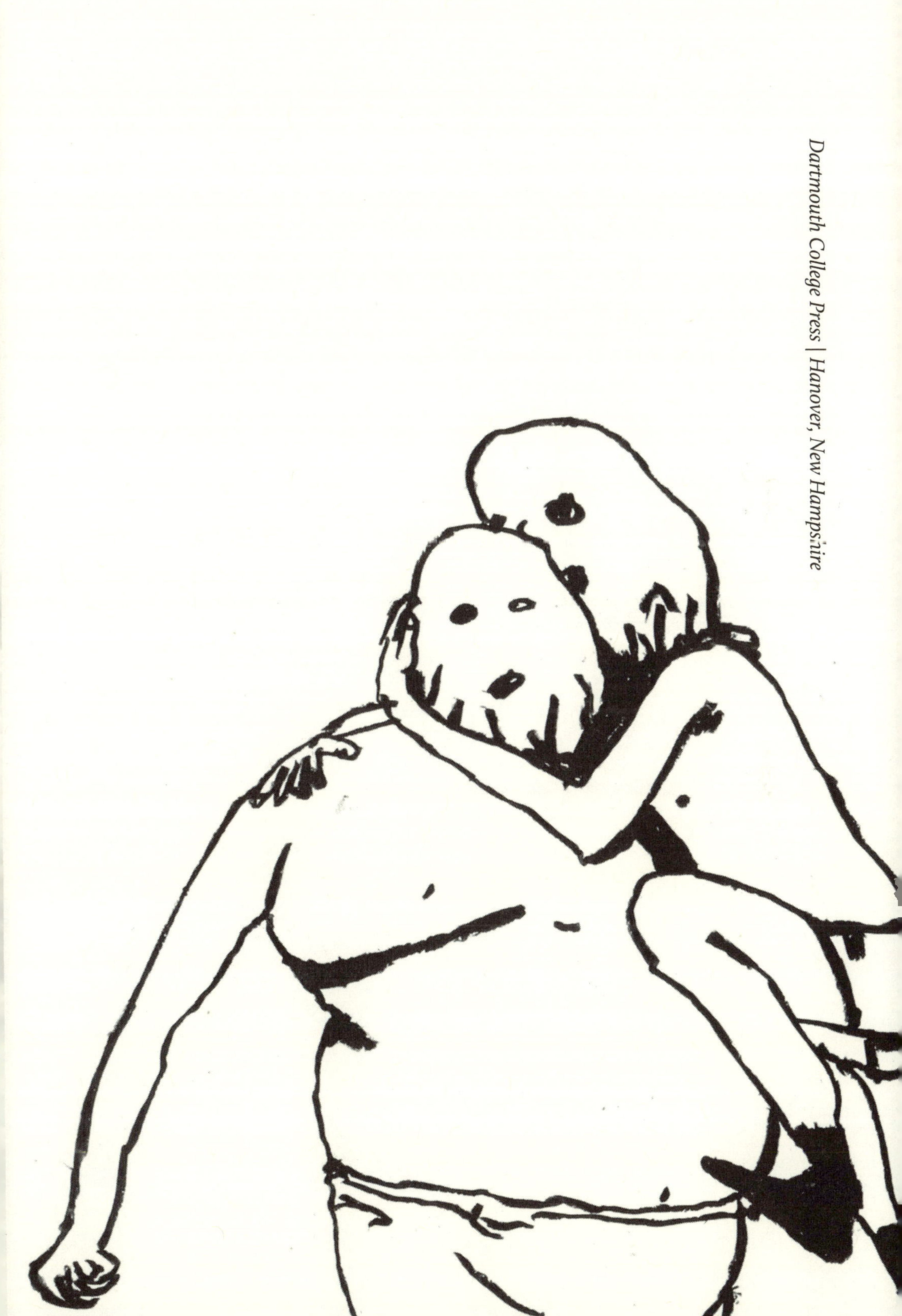

Dartmouth College Press | Hanover, New Hampshire

Dartmouth College Press
An imprint of University Press of New England
www.upne.com
© 2014 Trustees of Dartmouth College
All rights reserved
Manufactured in the United States of America
Designed by Mindy Basinger Hill
Typeset in Calluna

University Press of New England is a member of the
Green Press Initiative. The paper used in this book meets their
minimum requirement for recycled paper.

For permission to reproduce any of the material in this book,
contact Permissions, University Press of New England, One Court
Street, Suite 250, Lebanon NH 03766; or visit www.upne.com

Library of Congress Cataloging-in-Publication Data
hoogland, renée c., 1960–
A violent embrace : art and aesthetics after representation /
renée c. hoogland.
pages cm. — (Interfaces: studies in visual culture)
Includes bibliographical references and index.
ISBN 978-1-61168-490-2 (cloth: alk. paper) —
ISBN 978-1-61168-491-9 (pbk.: alk. paper) —
ISBN 978-1-61168-492-6 (ebook)
1. Art—Psychology. 2. Aesthetics. I. Title.
N71.H66 2014
701'.17—dc23   2013018744

5   4   3   2   1

for marijke

contents

Color plates appear following page 112.

acknowledgments

The larger part of this book was written during a sabbatical leave from Wayne State University—for which I was and remain grateful. Additional material support was provided by the English Department at Wayne State University, which granted me a Josephine Nevins Keal Fellowship during the summer of 2012. My thanks extend to Hilary Ratner, the vice president for research, and Wayne Raskind, dean of the College of Liberal Arts and Sciences, also at Wayne State University, for support toward copyright fees, the color insert, and the preparation of an index. Many, many thanks to Richard Pult, my editor at UPNE, who has, simply, been great throughout. Finally, I wish to express my sincere gratitude to the many artists who have allowed me to reproduce their work, often without requesting a copyright fee, and several for providing me with the images themselves.

These are the easier thank-yous. Much harder to define and to articulate is my indebtedness to the individuals, objects, and circumstances that, over the years, inspired my thinking and eventually compelled me to write this book. Some of these influences are too elusive to be traced. Others stand out, so I will forgo any attempt to be inclusive and mention only the most immediate objects of my gratitude. In the first place, I wish to express my thankfulness to amazing artist and my life partner Iris Eichenberg, who, besides much else, not only taught me to look (at art and at other things), but also forced me to write about what I saw, thus enabling me to find a voice I did not know I might have. Thank you, Konstantina Karageorgos, Susan Bernstein, Deb Al-Najjar, and Heather McGill, for the joys of your friendship and the delights of your agile minds. Three of my friends and colleagues in the English Department at Wayne State—Steven Shaviro, Scott Richmond, and Jonathan Flatley—have been great interlocutors over the past few years and lovely supporters in many other ways as well. My dear friend and colleague Kathryne V. Lindberg was there for me, in her myriad singular ways, when I first arrived in Detroit. I can only express my profoundest regret that she no longer is. Many other colleagues and, indeed, so many of my students at Wayne, especially the grad students in my Comparative Media seminar on "The Image," have helped me along in a variety of ways—my thanks to you all. Finally, I am grateful to Herman, Fritz, and Otto, for their alterity, their love, and their companionship.

I dedicate this book to Marijke Smalbraak, my all-time mentor and longtime beloved friend, without whose beautiful mind, generosity, integrity, and care, I would have done little worth (my) while—scholarly and otherwise.

* * *

Earlier versions of a portion of the introduction appeared in *Teaching Visual Culture in an Interdisciplinary Classroom: Feminist (Re)Interpretations of the Field*, edited by Elżbieta H. Oleksy and Dorota Golańska (Utrecht: ZuidamUithof Drukkerijen, 2009). A shorter version of chapter 6 appeared in *Wide Screen* 4.1 (2012). An early version of part of the conclusion originally appeared in "The Matter of Culture: Aesthetic Experiences and Corporeal Being," *Mosaic: A Journal for the Interdisciplinary Study of Literature* 36.3 (2003).

abbreviations

*Parenthetical citations of the following works
are abbreviated after first use.*

AI Alfred North Whitehead, *Adventures of Ideas*

AP Lambert Wiesing, *Artificial Presence*

"A/V" Gilles Deleuze, "The Actual and the Virtual"

BS Immanuel Kant, *Observations on the Feeling of the Beautiful and the Sublime*

C Félix Guattari, *Chaosmosis*

CI Gilles Deleuze, *Cinema 1: The Movement Image*

C2 Gilles Deleuze, *Cinema 2: The Time-Image*

CJ Immanuel Kant, *The Critique of Judgment*

CN Alfred North Whitehead, *The Concept of Nature*

CL Roland Barthes, *Camera Lucida*

"CMF" M. M. Bakhtin, "Supplement: The Problem of Content, Material, and Form in Verbal Art"

DR Gilles Deleuze, *Difference and Repetition*

F Gilles Deleuze, *The Fold*

GI Jean-Luc Nancy, *The Ground of the Image*

LS Gilles Deleuze, *The Logic of Sense*

PP Vilém Flusser, *Towards a Philosophy of Photography*

PR Alfred North Whitehead, *Process and Reality*

"TE" Félix Guattari, "The Three Ecologies"

TP Gilles Deleuze and Félix Guattari, *A Thousand Plateaus*

UTI Vilém Flusser, *Into the Universe of Technical Images*

WC Steven Shaviro, *Without Criteria*

WP Gilles Deleuze and Félix Guattari, *What Is Philosophy?*

a violent embrace

a violent embrace

> We live with a particular image of thought, that is to say, before
> we begin to think, we have a vague idea of what it means to
> think, its means and ends. And then someone comes along
> and proposes another idea, a whole other image. . . . From then
> on, thought is no longer carried on by a voluntary self, but by
> involuntary forces, the "effects" of machines. . . .
>
> Gilles Deleuze, *Desert Islands*

INTRODUCTION

visuality, cultural literacy, and the affective turn

And so it goes. With individual thinkers, as much as with movements, or indeed with moods in thinking itself. While often dismissed as mere fads or trends that one may or may not resist, shifts or "turns" in critical thinking happen with a certain irregularity, marking emergent moods that allow for (or that enforce) a "whole other image" of thought. This book finds its beginnings in the operations of such involuntary forces, in emergent configurations of critical moods marking the first decades of the twenty-first century. As such, it inscribes itself at various intersections of current modes of thought that follow in the wake of the "linguistic turn," with its focus on the representational and significatory functions of art and literature, as well as of the "cultural turn" in its near-exclusive attention to the constitutive role of cultural processes and systems of signification in the production of the meanings of social realities, in the construction of identities, and in the definition of values and beliefs. My focus, therefore, is on cultural practices as forms of making and doing, as involuntary forces themselves, with their own immediacy, materiality, and vitality.

As the book's title, *A Violent Embrace,* suggests, being carried along by involuntary forces is not necessarily a pleasant or a reassuring experience. It is, however, an interesting one. Interest, from the Latin verb *inter-esse,* meaning literally "to be in-between," is a kind of love. Love, in relation to works of art—and between other entities, animate and inanimate—is about being in-between. It has to do with a willingness—even if, paradoxically, an involuntary form of willingness—to be taken out of what one considers to be one's self, to encounter that which is other. To invest one's interest in a work of art is to open oneself up to its potentially deregulating power. Embracing a work of art is being embraced by it. It is an engagement of both action and passion, at once active and passive, and does not so much dissolve the distinction between self and other, between subject and object, as it marks the moment of an affective encounter: the observing subject being affected by the perceived object as much as the object is affected, informed by the subjective perception. My passionate investment, my interest, in this book is the aesthetic encounter in itself as a form of making and doing, qua activity. Perhaps incongruously, its main concern is therefore with what is ostensibly untouchable, yet embodied: the embodying embrace of various forms of primarily visual art. Since such "embraces" are dynamic, contingent, and mostly unpredictable affairs that are, moreover, ambivalent in their effects, the project of the book is by necessity largely theoretical and/or philosophical in nature.

Central in the chapters that follow is the operation (functioning, working, performance, action) of visual art beyond the traditional terms of semiotics and hermeneutics. Instead of asking questions about the symbolic meaning or the underlying "truth" of a work of art, I am primarily concerned with the actual "work" that a work of art, intentionally or not, voluntarily or not, does in the world in which I encounter it. Why and how does an abstract painting move me to tears? Or, on a less personal level, why do some randomly reproduced cartoons of the prophet Muhammad generate worldwide political outrage? What, in other words, is the compelling force of visual images, even—or especially—if they are nonfigurative, repulsive, or downright "ugly"?

Rather than describing, analyzing, and interpreting individual artworks, my approach to art in this book is to (re)turn to the question of aesthetics as, first, a question of feeling. We see images rather than read them. Aesthesis, in the original sense of feeling, sensation, or perception, therefore marks an affective experience. It follows that the aesthetic encounter constitutes an event that only obtains on the level of actualization. Such moments of affective actualization, it will be clear, do not occur twice, cannot be repeated, and are hard if not impossible to capture in language. In order nonetheless to try and find a way to think and write about art in a nonrepresentational, postformalist, and postdeconstructive manner, I have worked into some of the chapters that follow a kind of "retelling" of a specific artistic event. These "retellings" do not serve to explain what a certain work of art means or how and why it is significant. The main purpose is to place such events in the context of recent interventions in post-Deleuzian aesthetic theory and to offer a glimpse at the aesthetic encounter as a potentially disruptive, if not violent, force field with material, political, and practical consequences.

Assuming the primacy of affect in the experience and in the "event" of art (while taking into account that whatever is defined as "art" is subject to both historical and cross-cultural variation), the guiding question in each of the chapters is the way art affects us, not only emotionally and/or cognitively, but also, if not primarily, in our material, embodied being. Before I say more about the chosen approach to art in this book, let me dwell for a moment on the "turn to affect" more generally and on the "machines" that have carried me toward this "image of thought" in trying to think about the aesthetic, one of which is firmly located in my teaching practice in cultural studies.

In these so-called posttheoretical times, the turn away from "high theory" often implies a return to notions of experiment and experience, as well as a renewed emphasis on motion and becoming, on actualization and expression, and a con-current focus on process, sensation, and indeed on affect. Welcomed by some as a "surge of interest in affect, feeling, wonder, and enchantment,"[1] and dismissed by others as a premature abandonment of the attempt to develop "generally ap-plicable" models of thought in favor of the "unexpected, the singular, or indeed the quirky,"[2] it seems clear that the "fast-changing conditions" of our times, the "transformations, metamorphoses, mutations and processes of change" that Rosi Braidotti presciently—or perhaps not so presciently—identified in 2002 as the "one constant" at the "dawn of the third millennium,"[3] have not left the fields of art criticism and theory, nor that of cultural studies more generally, unaffected.

The invocation of affect, or the "affective turn," has occasionally been hailed, as Clare Hemmings skeptically remarks, as the "privileged 'way out' of the per-ceived impasse in cultural studies."[4] As such it has, quite puzzlingly, not only led to a certain revaluation of, if not at times a retrenchment into, disciplinary domains, but also to an all-too-eager rejection of the transdisciplinary projects of poststructuralism and deconstruction, as well as of attendant minority stud-ies, such as feminist, critical race, and queer theory. But the new millennium has also called into being the relatively new, fundamentally interdisciplinary, and as yet emergent field of visual studies, alternately called image studies, or simply visual culture. If visual culture can be described as a "postdisciplinary" field of study organized around the problem of visuality in its many manifestations, guises, and social effects,[5] the simultaneous coming into prominence of the problem of affect—post deconstruction—may not be so much a coincidence as an overdetermined inescapability: the effect of "machines" generating a "whole other image of thought." My purpose in this introduction is therefore not only to explore the significance of currently circulating notions of affect for the study of visual culture, but also the joint emergence of these two buzzwords in the wider realm of critical theorizing across the humanities and social sciences.

But let me be clear about my investment in this debate. If the affective turn can be maintained also to permeate the field of visual culture, the question remains whether a postideological perspective, an approach of visuality beyond representation—which is to say an affirmative rather than a merely negative mode of critique—may prove helpful in a liberatory critical practice of visual *culture,* especially if such a posttheoretical critique is undertaken from a politically engaged "minority" position. While I am weary of relatively uninformed embraces of the affective turn, particularly if, as Hemmings makes poignantly clear, such a redirection of critical focus is accompanied by a knee-jerk rejection of what some players in the field consider traditional or even old-fashioned poststructuralist critical analyses,[6] my observations will nonetheless serve to suggest why the turn to affect may not only prove helpful, but might be key to effective postideological critiques of visual cultural production, especially in its increasingly multimedia or cross-media manifestations.

The reason I became interested in exploring these issues is in effect twofold. First, a few years ago, I found my research concerns expand from the function of fantasy and, in its cultural expression, of artistic production, in the ways we learn to do and be our bodies, that is to say, in processes of corporeality to include the interrelations between aesthetics and ethics. This forced me to realize that I was no longer exactly thinking within the theoretical frameworks that for several years had constituted the basis of my teaching practice.[7] If my formerly thoroughly poststructuralist and deconstructive framework for cultural analysis no longer satisfied my scholarly needs, how could I justify my reliance upon such frameworks in trying to help my students to become the critical readers of their cultural contexts I hoped they would? Clearly, I had to reconsider the use and recommendation of theoretical tools that did not fulfill their purpose, both inside and outside the classroom. Second, an experience that even more directly relates to my life as a professor at a large, urban, public university, was a growing dissatisfaction on my own and on my students' part with the critical explanations and analytical tools offered by available textbooks on the newly emerging visual culture market. Both the increasing discrepancy between my changing scholarly perspective and the equally shifting intellectual demands of undergraduate students urged me to reflect upon the affective turn and to take in both its critical and pedagogical implications. To clarify the latter, let me single out a recent textbook often used in undergraduate cultural, media, and visual studies classes, *Practices of Looking: An Introduction to Visual Culture,* jointly authored by Marita Sturken and Lisa Cartwright, first published by Oxford University Press in 2001 and currently in its second edition.[8]

According to the publishers' blurb, *Practices of Looking* comprises a "comprehensive and engaging introduction to visual culture," providing an "overview of a range of theories about how we understand visual media and how we use images to express ourselves, to communicate, to experience pleasure, and to learn." Up to date in their selection of visual culture, including paintings, prints, photographs, film, television, video, advertisements, news images, the Internet, digital images, and science images, Sturken and Cartwright do an admirable job exploring how images gain meaning in different cultural arenas, how they travel cross-nationally and cross-culturally, and in assessing how visual culture forms an integral and important aspect of our lives, and they analyze specific images in relation to such issues as desire, power, the gaze, bodies, sexuality, ethnicity. They furthermore discuss visual culture in the context of different methodologies, including semiotics, Marxism, psychoanalysis, feminism, and postcolonial theory. In all fairness, the book is an excellent introduction for students coming to the study of visual culture for the first time, offering concise and accessible explanations of the fundamentals of the selected theories while presenting ample visual examples of how they function. It is a text I have gratefully adopted for cultural studies, gender and sexuality, and visual culture courses, and will continue to do so. Whence, then, the earlier noted dissatisfaction on both my own and my students' part?

Although my own problems with this book are of a slightly different nature than the problems my students have, both are rooted in the same soil, which is the exclusively poststructuralist framework in which the authors place their critical discussions and the ambivalence arising from their nonetheless strenuous attempts to take into account the incisive critiques to which theories of sociocultural and discursive construction have in recent years been subjected. Within the realm of critical theorizing per se, such critiques are neither particularly new nor controversial, as is adequately illustrated by, for example, the more than thirty years of discussion of Laura Mulvey's seminal essay "Visual Pleasure and Narrative Cinema."[9] Almost immediately after its publication in 1975, feminist and other minority critics began taking Mulvey to task for presenting the ideological operations of mainstream Hollywood cinema as inescapable, nonnegotiable, and determinative, rendering the female film spectator utterly powerless to resist the medium's oppressive operations. In addition to the perceived disempowering implications of some "hard-core" poststructuralist theorizing, more recent critiques—for instance those deriving from so-called new materialist approaches—have focused on such models' discursivization of everything to the neglect of the materiality of social structures, of human bodies or "the flesh," and of other less easily deconstructible aspects of/in the world.

Sturken and Cartwright are clearly cognizant of such critiques. In the introduction to the second edition of *Practices of Looking,* they write: "By the beginning of the 1990s, scholars working on the theory of visual culture had become aware that critical theory was in crisis . . . because the writing associated with it was not providing the kind of explanatory power or impetus to social change desired by many of its authors."[10] Hence the need for a "plurality of theories," for an eclectic and wide-ranging critical toolbox to make sense of the ways "we make and use things in the realm of the visual in our everyday lives."[11] Still, perhaps because in some of even the most intellectually enlightened parts of the world the basics of poststructuralist theory have hardly entered the undergraduate classroom, and because the main purpose of their book is to move beyond still largely prevailing commonsense—read liberal humanist—notions of meaning and being, the authors' perceptible ambivalence about the confining and politically disempowering implications of, for example, Lacanian and Althusserian thought, is neither outspoken nor explicitly addressed. What is more, in order to counter the determinist implications of some of the theories that frame their arguments, the authors take recourse to precisely the conceptual framework their book aims to question and supersede, by reintroducing a notion of individual and collective agency firmly based in the liberal humanist concept of the rational and volitional subject. Because of its theoretical inadequacy, it is this "solution" to the problem of the power and effects of images (over and beyond their ideological operations) that forms the main source of my ultimate dissatisfaction with *Practices of Looking* and with similarly oriented critical approaches to visual culture. Although most of my students are probably unable to grasp its theoretical implications, they nonetheless tend to perceive clearly—if not exactly why—that the suggested possibility of agency fails to explain two key issues, issues that may well have contributed to the crisis in critical theory in the first place. First, "agency," in whatever way defined, does not adequately account for their own, often highly divergent engagement with and responses to the bombardment of images that constitutes the context of our everyday lives. Second, the notion of individual and collective agency cannot explicate our inability to effectively resist our subjection to the compelling force of everyday visual culture, despite our awareness of its potentially oppressive and pernicious operations.

In order to salvage the important—and indisputably empowering—lessons of poststructuralism, and to familiarize students new to the field of visual culture with its analytical tools and their critical and political potential while at the same time maintaining the possibility of resistance without reverting to defunct notions of subjective agency, I suggest that certain forms of postideological thought, especially those generating from within the affective turn, may not only prove pedagogically helpful, but also politically indispensable.

For one, although the cinematic model underlying many poststructuralist/

deconstructive models of visual analysis may not have become altogether obsolete, it nonetheless no longer seems adequate to the task of accounting for the functioning and operation of visual culture in the digital age.[12] I am not referring only to the radical difference between "old," noninteractive media, such as cinema and television, and the interactive information and communication technologies that form an intrinsic and pervasive part of our daily lives in a postmechanical society. In a way, the change from visual consumption to media interaction had already been effected by the introduction of the VCR, which gained mass popularity in the late 1970s and early 1980s. This new technology, with its possibilities for freeze-framing, fast-forwarding, slow motion, and endless repetition, allowed for the manipulation of visual/representational time and the material basis of temporal experience. The VCR—largely ignored by the most influential critical theorists/philosophers at the time—dramatically transformed the organization of perception, forging a new relation between the spectator/participant and the cinematic apparatus that had been the center of attention for film scholars in the 1960s and 1970s. The digitization of the image, both in popular cultural domains and in new media art, constitutes yet another radical transformation of structures of perception or, rather, opens up perception in its processual, material dimension. Inaugurated by the manipulative aspects of the VCR, which enabled us to see in the linear, cinematic unfolding of the flow of images things not available to human perception, in the interstices, or what Mark Hansen calls the "between-two of images" of film, it is the uncompromisingly antimimetic nature of digital images, the fact that there is no longer necessarily any referential layer underlying them, that paradoxically calls for a retheorization of perception as a technically enabled rematerialization of the body, an embodied framing of affect.[13]

In his thorough investigation of the interrelations between technology, digitization, and the body—the complexity of which I can by no means do justice to here—Hansen discusses Bill Viola's slow-motion digital video installations, *Anima* (2000), *Dolorosa* (2000), and *Observance* (2002), to argue that the technological possibilities of contemporary digital media do not so much enable us to perceive the "between-two of images" the way VCR options for freeze-framing and slow-motion allow us to do, but rather urge us to "experience the imperceptible in-between of emotional states."[14] (See figures I.1 and I.2.) Hansen submits that by exploiting the technical capacity of shooting film at high speed and, after its conversion to digital video, "project[ing] it seamlessly at normal speed," Viola is "able to supersaturate the image, registering an overabundance of affective information normally unavailable to perception." The image as such thus becomes the support for the "registration of affective microperceptions," entailing an intensification of perception as embodied activity, thereby laying bare the "embodied materiality of subjectivation" itself.[15] What Hansen's analysis makes clear is that

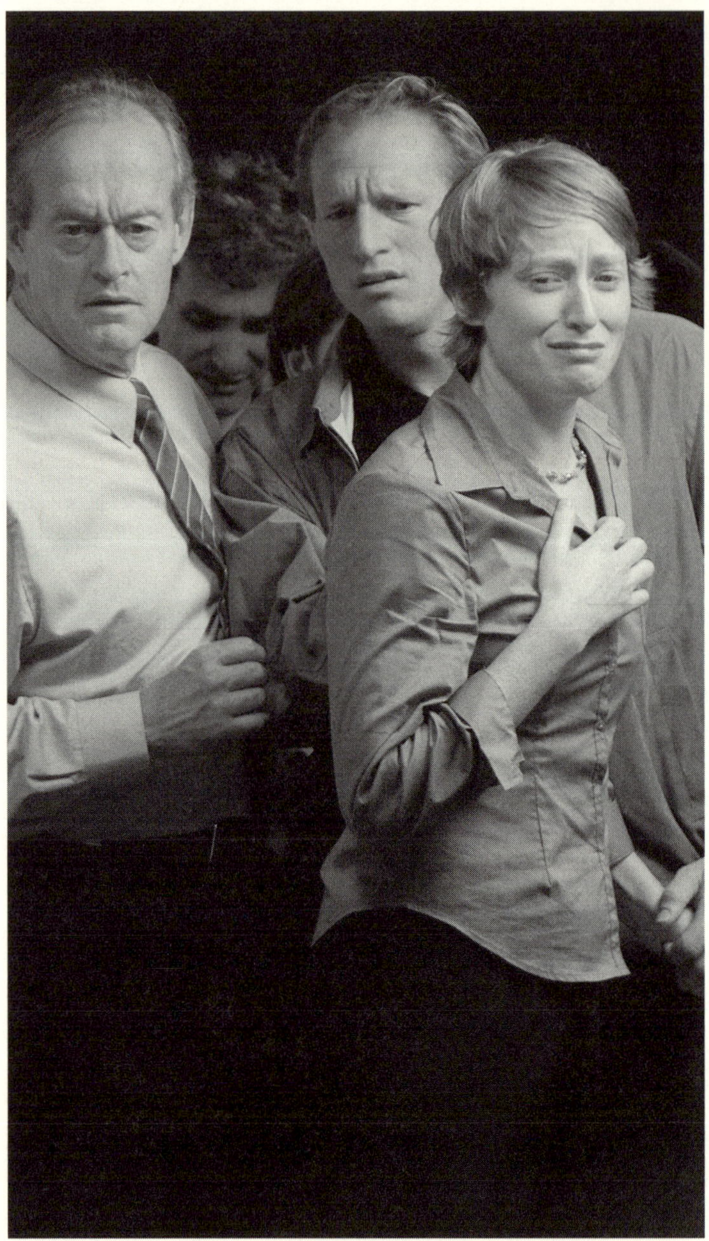

FIG. 1.1 Bill Viola, *Observance*, 2002. Color High-Definition video on plasma display mounted on wall, 120.7 × 72.4 × 10.2 cm. Performers: Alan Abelew, Sheryl Arenson, Frank Bruynbroek, Carol Cetrone, Cathy Chang, Ernie Charles, Alan Clark, JD Cullum, Michael Irby, Tanya Little, Susan Matus, Kate Noonan, Paul O'Connor, Valerie Spencer, Louis Stark, Richard Stobie, Michael Eric Strickland, Ellis Williams. Photo: Kira Perov. © Bill Viola Studio LLC

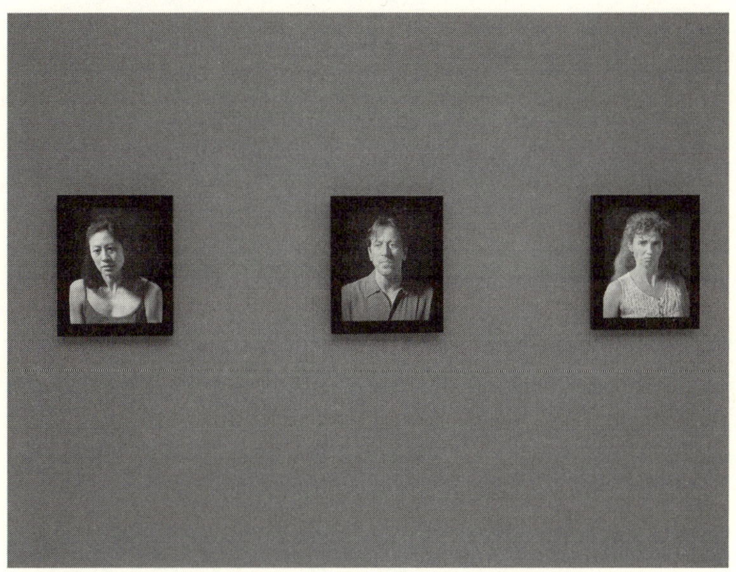

FIG. 1.2 Bill Viola, *Anima,* 2000. Color video triptych on three LCD
flat panels mounted on wall, 41.3 × 190.5 × 5.1 cm (overall dimensions).
Performers: Page Leong, John Fleck, Henriette Brouwers.
Photo: Fred Scruton, courtesy James Cohan Gallery, New York.
© Bill Viola Studio LLC

the digital image, having lost any necessary connection with an independent reality—its "infrastructure" being, in Patricia T. Clough's words, no more than "layers of algorithmic processing of a matrix of numbers"—has become a process, an activity that does not merely invite "the user's interaction," but that rather "requires the human body to frame the ongoing flow of information, shaping its indeterminacy into meaning."[16]

In giving the name affectivity to the intensification of bodily experience, its expansion to the experience of the "imperceptible in-between of emotional states," Hansen follows the lead of one of the most influential theorists of affect, the Canadian philosopher, writer, and political theorist Brian Massumi, whose *Parables for the Virtual: Movement, Affect, and Sensation* (2002) offers an insightful and straightforward account of the need for and possible development of a theory of affect without undoing the deconstructive work effectively carried out by poststructuralism.[17] Since my thought about affect has been strongly influenced by Massumi's Deleuzian approach, I will take a moment to map out some of its central assumptions.

Taking various empirical studies of the emotional effects of media as his starting point, Massumi first establishes that the strength and the duration of an image's effect are "not logically connected to the content in any straightforward way."

Indeed, the measured physiological and subsequent verbal responses of research subjects to selected visual material suggest that the "primacy of the affective is marked by a gap between *content* and *effect*."[18] In other words, there is a certain indeterminacy in the embodied response to the image that distinguishes affect, the level of automatic physiological response, from both conscious perception, language, and emotion. An almost too obvious instance of such indeterminacy is the moment when we find ourselves being pleasurably affected by an image of sadness. While language and social context largely determine the qualities (or content) of a perceived image, the strength or duration of the image, Massumi proposes, with reference to Deleuze, to designate "intensity."[19] While both intensity and qualification are equally immediately embodied, he continues, there is a critical difference in that "intensity is embodied in purely autonomic reactions most directly manifested in the skin," whereas embodied functions such as heartbeat and breathing are "depth reactions" that belong more to the "form/content (qualification) level" of response, marking a "reflux of consciousness into the autonomic depths, coterminous with a rise of the autonomic into consciousness." On this perspective, intensity, being a "non-conscious, never to be conscious autonomic remainder" of primary affect, remains "beside this loop." Language does not necessarily operate in opposition to intensity: if matter-of-fact or commonsensical, it may have a dampening effect, interfering with the image's effect; if, in contrast, language punctuates narrative with qualifications of emotional content, it may enhance intensity, resonating rather than interfering with it.[20]

As a critical element among what Deleuze's counterpart Félix Guattari calls the "heterogeneity of the components leading to the production of subjectivity,"[21] the reorganization of the visual in the age of digitization entails a reorganization of subjectivity itself. Since we do not so much *read* but *see* images, approaches to the image in its relation to language fall short if they merely operate on the semiotic and/or semantic level. The integration of intensity into cultural theory and art criticism would help to (re)gain what such approaches inevitably lose: the "expression *event*—in favor of structure." Massumi explains the "expression event" as the "system of the inexplicable: emergence, into and against regeneration (the reproduction of a structure)," the unassimilable. Actualized in the expressive event, affect or intensity is that which remains outside and eludes theories of signification that "are still wedded to structure even across irreconcilable differences."[22] Conscious perception and emotion put limits on the opening up of embodied affective events, rendering determinate—e.g., in the form of narration—what is and must remain indeterminate, emergent, in the expression event qua event. Affect is thus not the description of a concept, but rather a term that attempts to think, in Braidotti's terms, "through flows and interconnections," to expand a theoretical reason that is "concept-bound and fastened upon essential notions," in favor of representations for "processes, fluid in-between flows of data, experience and information."[23]

By equating intensity with affect, Massumi is capable of establishing a clear distinction between affect, as embodied indeterminacy, as potential and emergent, on one hand, and emotion on the other. Emotion is a "subjective content," qualified intensity captured and fixed in language, appropriated and recognized in signifying terms, and henceforth defined as personal. Intensity, in contrast, may be qualifiable as an emotional state, but it is not to be associated with linear processes. Affect or intensity is a state of suspense, "potentially of disruption," running parallel, but not reducible to sociolinguistic capture, nor to personal psychology. Affects are not presocial. As Braidotti reminds us, "affects are the body's capacity to enter relations—to be affected," and such relations—"the virtual links that a body can form with other bodies"[24]—are not restricted to intersubjective forms of empathy, sympathy, love, or indeed hatred or disgust, but rather cut across the boundaries between species, allowing for multiple, nonunitary, heterogeneous flows of affect in an ongoing process of becoming (other). Emotion and affect, Massumi hence maintains, "follow different logics and pertain to different orders," and what is both theoretically and politically at stake in this distinction is "the new."[25]

There appears to be increasing consensus among media, literary, and art theorists that the cultural condition of postsecular, postideological high capitalism is marked by a "surfeit" of affect. If we are going to make sense of our thoroughly image-saturated and digitally mediated culture, and if the challenge is not only to make sense of a world in which the so-called master narratives are no longer viable but also to enable possibilities for change, then we need a new vocabulary to theorize affect. Not emotion, for theories of emotion tend to return to traditional psychological categories that eventually both personalize and depoliticize the operations of our current information- and image-based culture.[26] Sturken and Cartwright may be perfectly right in problematizing the confining and deterministic implications of certain poststructuralist theories; their attempt to escape from the reproduction of structure and to explain the potentially disruptive, enabling, and innovative effects of images alongside their reactive, reterritorializing operations by reverting to traditional notions of individual and collective agency, however, is not only a theoretical error, but also politically inadequate.

In her critical evaluation of the affective turn cited earlier, Hemmings points to the "myriad ways that affect manifests . . . not as difference, but as a central mechanism of social reproduction in the most glaring ways." She mentions the "delights of consumerism, feelings of belonging attending fundamentalism or fascism" as just a few of the contexts in which affective responses reinforce rather than challenge or dislodge a dominant social order.[27] Whereas Hemmings may justifiably take the advocates of affect theory to task for not spending enough attention to the fact that affect operates in unpredictable ways and that "good" and "bad" affect inevitably function simultaneously, sometimes reciprocally, and interdependently, I would yet suggest that it is precisely on account of its complexity, indeterminacy, and ultimate unassimilability, while yet pertaining to sociality on its multiply entwined levels, that we need to find ways of thinking about its processual operations outside the linearity of conceptual reason.[28] Indeed, the very coexistence of, on one hand, hyper-individualism, personal and corporate greed, diverse forms of religious fundamentalism, a mass media system that continues to produce mind-numbing and degrading reality shows and that provides us with disinformation and feeds us sensationalist junk, the spectacularization of politics, and so on—all playing on and to the "bad" affect that is indisputably rife in an increasingly global informational and communicational culture—*in tandem* with, on the other hand, various grassroots protest movements that make effective use of the Internet and other contemporary technologies, growing ecological concerns, the expansion of social media, and other responsibility- and community-building phenomena engaging "good" affect, in its irreducible complexity and resistance to structural analysis, requires us to think through and account for the operational potential of affect, in both its "good" and its "bad" effects.

Massumi's examples of affective responses do not only suggest what bodies can do, but as Clough astutely points out, they also "show what bodies can be made to do."[29] Responsible and irresponsible behaviors coexist and are partly, if not largely, instigated by new media whose productive and/or destructive potential can neither be predicted nor explained within the terms of structural frameworks that clearly separate emancipatory aspirations from conservative or even reactionary drives, whether of a nationalist, ethnic, or religious nature. As Braidotti forcefully argues, the "point is not to know who we are, but rather what, at last, we want to become, how to represent mutations, changes and transformations, rather than Being in its classical mode."[30] If we are not to slip back into sociological or psychological categories and reify existing structures of signification and modes of being, but instead seek to understand and mobilize individual and collective levels of undecidability, of newly emerging systems of becoming—"good" or "bad"—what is called for instead is, in Massumi's terms, an "asignifying philosophy of affect"[31] that will enable a more complex and more sophisticated critical apparatus to develop and teach a sociocultural literacy. What is needed is a conceptual framework that is adequate to the challenges and possibilities of a sociocultural realm of information and communication that is an increasingly visual, if not multisensual, and shifting hybrid of fluctuation, change, and transformation.

The critical potential of the media today, in the context of global power relations, does not merely lie in the individual subject's volition and cognitive ability to negotiate (whether in agreement or in opposition) the qualitative and/or signifying effects of the image/expression of events in which she is deeply immersed. Obviously, ideology is not a thing of the past, and critical analyses of ideological operations remain crucial. It is just as important, however, to try to understand the ways in which the effects of visual culture obtain on the immediately embodied level of affect: affect or intensity cuts across different structures differently in every actual case, resonating in its specificity with other layers and other orders of the system, enabling moments of emergence, of productive disruption as much as of reactive regression or ideological retrenchment. The political potential of affect lies in its openness, its directness, its operation in an unbounded field of possible actualization. The undecidability of political processes—poignantly manifested in the 2008 U.S. presidential elections—equals the unpredictability of economic developments in high capitalism, as reflected in the recent "credit crunch," the *démasquée* of mortgage bankers, and/or the fall of the Detroit automobile industry. In both realms, it is affect that seems to produce the most powerful effects, over and above the power of politics and economics themselves. Image reception is deeply enfolded in the domain of affect that is virtually everywhere: the ways blocs of affect shift into potential actualization are increasingly utilized by both the reactive and liberatory apparatuses through which they are relayed. If we do not develop a cultural-theoretical vocabulary with which to think about affect, cultural studies will lose the critical momentum generated by the affective turn in its current re-emergence, in both theory and practice, both inside and outside the classroom. It is against this overall political and theoretical background that I turn my attention in this book to visual art as a site—for lack of a better term—where the "new" is most likely to arise and where emergent formations of becoming are primarily (although not exclusively) expressed in their affective operations. In light of the above, one may well ask why I have decided to focus on art in the narrow sense, and not on visual media in their wider implications, to address these issues.

Art and aesthetic experience move us "beyond" what appears to be familiar reality; rather than affirming what we already know, art creates a rupture, forcing us to see and think things differently. The conventional art historical model of description-analysis-interpretation does not satisfactorily account for such rupturing or deterritorializing effects, especially since these are singular, historically and socioculturally specific expressive events, and hence neither universal nor unchanging. Aesthetic force is neither immanent to the perceived object nor to the observing subject, but "happens" only in their encounter, so that Marcel Duchamp's "anti-art" piece *pissoir* (*Urinal* or *Fountain*; see figure I.3), for example,

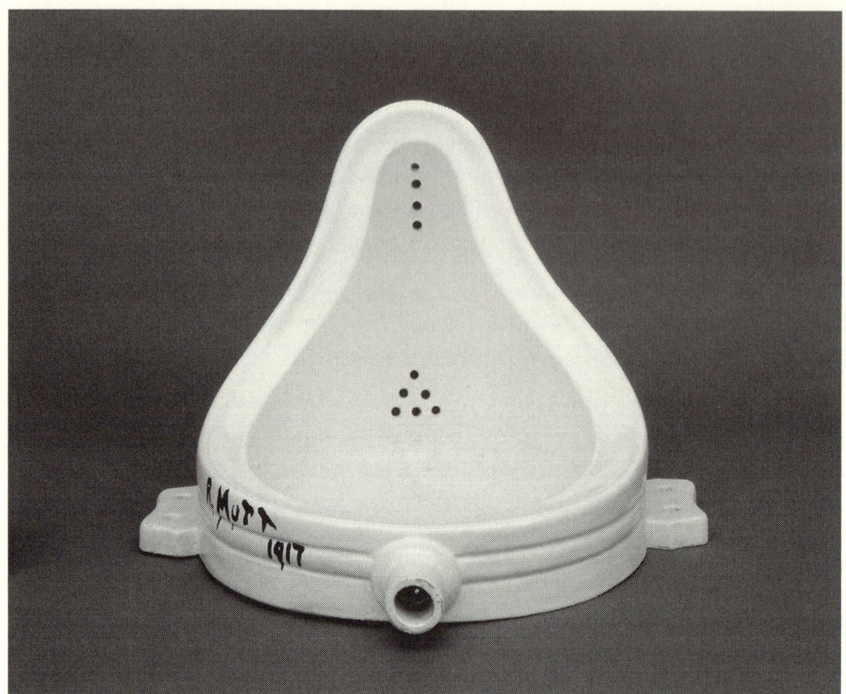

FIG. 1.3 Marcel Duchamp, *Fountain,* 1917, replica 1964. Porcelain, unconfirmed: 360 × 480 × 610 mm. Tate Gallery, London. Purchased with assistance from the Friends of the Tate Gallery 1999. © ARS, NY. Photo: Tate, London / Art Resource, NY

was considered so outrageous that it was hidden from view at the 1917 exhibition of the Society of Independent Artists while it is currently established as a classic work of high modernism, if not as a landmark of twentieth-century art.

To address the unpredictable, often disconcerting, yet always contingent power of art, I do not focus on artworks as mere objects of interpretation, whose meaning can be determined once and for all through careful formal and/or sociohistorical analysis. Instead, I approach the encounter with an artwork as an event that, in its *haecceity* or "thisness," engages us on the level of affect as much as it invites us to analyze and interpret its formal and semiotic operations. To repeat, by affect I do not mean emotion or feeling, but the ability to affect and be affected.[32] Affect is not presocial (it can only happen in the world), but it is nonconscious and abstract: the experience of embodied intensity that cannot be fully captured in language, nor fully determined by form nor by the chains of signification. Perhaps the most immediately "prehensible" and never fully *com*prehensible example of such aesthetic intensity would be the pleasure we derive from music, which has less to do with the communication of meaning than with the way a piece of music "moves" us. Visual cultural expression, whether of a popular or more narrowly defined artistic nature, similarly does its actual "work" as a material, embodied (if not embodying) event by engaging us on the level of affect. Positing the operation of affective forces as primary to the artistic encounter, the examination of particular works of art in several of the chapters that follow enable me to develop a notion of aesthetic experience as at once experiential and material, an event with both potentially enabling and innovative effects, as well as reactive consequences.

In its *differentia specifica,* art—again, taking into account that what counts as "art" is subject to historical and cross-cultural definition—functions as a system of the inexplicable, as a site where the relationship between signifier and signified collapses. Art yet maintains its connections to the world in that it only "happens" in the actualization of the (aesthetic) event. Insisting on the dynamic presentness (as distinct from its *re*presentational dimension) of the artistic event, my project throughout this book is to trace the contours of a radical or neo-aesthetics that runs counter to art historical traditions that emphasize the autonomy of the artistic object, or the genius of the individual artist, or the merely pleasurable or edifying functions of art. On the assumption that there would be no art nor aesthetic inquiry without the possibility of aesthetic experience in its phenomenological sense, that is to say, as an expressive event in which both the subject and the object of perception enter into a force field that is constituted in and by their encounter, I critique both such an object-immanent perspective, as well as hermeneutic approaches to art—that is, the attempt to "read" meaning and being into artistic objects—to posit aesthetic experience as a process of alteration, or a force field, whose consequences are neither pregiven nor unambivalent.

Chapter 1 revisits Kant's "Transcendental Aesthetic" by way of Mikhail Bakhtin's concept of the "aesthetic object" and Steven Shaviro's reconfiguration of aesthetic theory through Alfred North Whitehead's "critique of pure feeling" in order to examine different forms of art as singular modes of relating to the world. To address what different forms of art in their affective operations might share in common and, simultaneously, to explore the specific effects of any artistic event in the moment of its emergence and/or creation, the chapter briefly touches on music, as perhaps the most "disembodied" form or art, and additionally examines the body-related art of modern/art jewelry. While I argue for an understanding of the operations of all cultural expression as an embodied/embedded affective event, my aim in this chapter is to foreground the singularity of any given artistic encounter in its irreducibility to object or form. I develop my approach to art in its historical and sociocultural specificity as a site of experience that exceeds the determination and the materiality of objects while remaining rooted in the world because it only obtains in its affective, material, singular actualization. The Deleuzian notion of "intensity" is introduced to begin to "think" affect as both an experiential force and a material thing that can compel systems of knowledge, history, subjectivation, and circuits of power. The chapter concludes that art, qua event, constitutes a force with a certain autonomy, an activity of partial becoming that transforms, if only momentarily, our sense of our selves and our experience of the world, and thus opens up the possibility of novelty.

I resume my dialogue with Kant in chapter 2, "Violent Becomings: From the *informe* and the Abject to Uncontrollable Beauty." Here I engage Kant's notion of the sublime to trace the idea of the *informe* (formless) as developed by Georges Bataille, back to Hogarth's notion of the "serpentine line," and up to Deleuze and Guattari's concept of the "line of flight." Bataille suggests that "formless" operates within different forms to destabilize the organizing principle of form: the *informe* is defined more by what it does than by what it is. This allows me to distinguish the aesthetic from meaning and morality and to argue in favor of a neo-aesthetic approach that neither coincides with hermeneutics nor with ethics. Taking a particular "reading" of Louise Bourgeois's monumental abstract sculpture as an example of the former, I argue against the common description of the French American artist as the "founder of confessional art," whose work is commonly interpreted as wholly autobiographical and reduced to the traumatic events of her childhood. Instead, I elaborate on the disruptive, if not violent, or violating effects of Bourgeois's art through the operation of the abject in my aesthetic encounters with it. Working from the *informe* through the "serpentine line" to the abject, the chapter additionally explores the political potential of art in its "eventness" and historical specificity—as opposed to the narratives we can also produce about it. I subsequently elaborate on the concept of the "line of flight" to approach the dis- and/or reorganizing force of art in its actualization of connections and multiplicities, evolving into creative metamorphoses and assemblages that open the possibility for the production of new paradigms of subjectivity, of becoming, rather than reinscribing traditional modes of being.

Chapter 3, "Neo-Aesthetics and the Study of the Arts of the Present," takes up the duality at the heart of Kantian aesthetics, as at once the objective and the subjective aspects of sensation, to examine Deleuze's "transcendental empiricist" theory of aesthetics in its significance for the study of the arts of the present. Deleuze's notion of the "encounter" with an artwork, which he defines as a "bloc of sensations," is put to work to accomplish two things: First, to overcome the negativity of poststructuralist modes of ideology critique in favor of a more affirmative, materialist approach to art, an argument that runs from art historian Hal Foster's gloomy appreciation of so-called business art through Andy Warhol and Deleuze's Nietzschean model of an "onto-aesthetic." Second, to propose the classical procedure of *ekphrasis* as a possible model of aesthetic inquiry that allows us to do justice to the aesthetic on its own terms without abandoning or losing sight of the ethical operations of a given artwork. The chapter concludes with a comparative exercise in *ekphrasis,* extending the notion of the aesthetic encounter as a form of partial becoming through a discussion of a several drawings by Kathleen Henderson and a series of Richard Barnes's photographs.

In chapter 4, "The Groundless Realities of Art Photography," I shift my attention to the photograph as a mode of visual culture "after representation" par excellence. The chapter is organized around the work of Dutch photographer Rineke Dijkstra and aims to address the image beyond the parameters of both "simulacrum" (i.e., in a Baudrillardian rather than a Deleuzian sense) and those of the "spectacle," as elaborated by Guy Debord. The emergence of so-called art photography—i.e., the fact that, from the 1980s onwards, photography began moving away from its journalistic/documentary functions and was self-consciously and deliberately made to hang in art galleries and museums—has led to an increase of theoretical interest in photography, which has not, however, resolved its controversial place in the world of art and art criticism: is it art or is it mere documentation? A focus on the photographic image as aesthetic event circumvents this fruitless discussion. The chapter investigates the ambivalence at the heart of the image—as at once representation and operation of art—by a discussion of Dijkstra's group portraits, works that are exemplary of the recent transfiguration of art photography in that they deliberately blur the boundaries between classical traditions of painting and the formerly documentary function of the photographic apparatus. Revisiting both Benjamin's and Barthes' influential writings on photography and the medium's transformation into a theoretical object, the chapter additionally explores the unbinding force of Dijkstra's work through Jean-Luc Nancy's theory of the image as a force field that enables a violent intimacy, the distinct jumping toward the indistinct, defying signification and definition.

My focus on the photographic image extends into chapter 5, "The Ruse of the Ruins, or: Detroit's Nonreal Estate." The equivocation at the heart of the image is here addressed through Czech media theorist Vilém Flusser's notion of the technical image and German philosopher Lambert Wiesing's theory of the image as that which "alone makes the artificial presence of things possible." I interrogate the visual presentation of Detroit as a series of architectural still lifes, of its abandoned buildings and collapsing houses as, quite literally, the hollowed out carcasses of what once constituted the city's reputation as the "Paris of the Midwest." Through a series of recent visualizations of Detroit's ruins—a site somewhere between the beautiful and the sublime—Julia Reyes Taubman's monumental collection of photographs called *Detroit: 138 Square Miles,* I explore the productive power of non-narrative in the polyvalent visual presentation of a city that is both more and less than the sum of its aesthetically compelling visualizations. Arguing against the dismissals of contemporary "ruin porn"—as mere nostalgia for modernity or as a displacement of underlying social issues—the chapter traces Western culture's fascination with ruins to its current postindustrial moment to foreground the pictorial surface of the pictures of Detroit's ruins as a site that brings about consciousness, functioning as an event of partial becoming, which in its turn extends the question of the operational force of the aesthetic as such.

Chapter 6, "Visualizing the Face: *Face Value* and *dévisage*," shifts the attention from the still or photographic image to the moving image of documentary film. Loosely organized around the work of Dutch filmmaker Johan van der Keuken (1938–2001), the chapter returns to the equivocation/ambivalence at the heart of, in this case, the moving image by addressing the question of the face, or of what Deleuze calls "faciality," as it functions in the "affection image" par excellence, the close-up. I trace the differences and commonalities between Levinas's notion of the face as a "source from which all meaning appears"—yet emphatically not the site of meaning itself—and Deleuze's concept of the face in cinema as close-up, as the "expression of affectivity or the emotional quality of a situation." This enables me to discuss the operation of the face/close-up in van der Keuken's film *Face Value* as an exploration, if not an actualization, of "effacement," or *dévisage*, a dissolution of meaning and being as it appears to be written on, yet escapes the signification of, the human body. Rather than representing something else or functioning as a partial object, the face/close-up in cinema, I argue, foregrounds the equivocation of the image by stripping the face of its three ordinary functions—individuation, socialization, communication—to generate a significatory *indifférance*, functioning as a site of zéro degree of signification, which, paradoxically, simultaneously gives it its life, its singularity, as a site of potential becoming.

In the concluding chapter, "Lines of Flight and the Emergence of the New," I bring the various theoretical strands and arguments developed in the preceding chapters together to propose an affirmative and materialist attitude to contemporary art and to posit art as a "project" with multiple levels of implications: scholarly, pedagogical, and sociopolitical. I do so by first elaborating on Deleuze's and Whitehead's respective notions of the "event" from within their shared neovitalist focus. I subsequently trace the implications of their abstract philosophical thoughts on the ethics of becoming for the production of subjectivity in the postindustrial context of "hypermodernity" by way of Félix Guattari's psychoanalytically inspired, ecosophic paradigm of "chaosmosis." My concluding suggestion is that art and aesthetic activity are as essential for change for the new as they are for the invention of sustainable modalities of being on both individual and collective levels, now and in worlds yet to come.

ONE ARTISTIC ACTIVITY

dialogism, *aesthesis,* and corporeality

In one of his early essays, "Supplement: The Problem of Content, Material, and Form in Verbal Art" (1924; hereafter "CMF"), the Russian literary scholar and philosopher M. M. Bakhtin (1895–1975) describes the author-creator of a work of art as a "constitutive moment in artistic form."[1] As such, the personality of the author-creator is "both invisible and inaudible" and is organized and experienced only as activity, as a "seeing, hearing, moving, remembering activity—as an embodying activity, and not as an embodied activity." An author-creator does not exist prior to the work, Bakhtin submits, but acquires his or her "positively subjective creative personality" only in art, in creation ("CMF," 316). Still, for the work of art to actually work, to generate and realize its aesthetic object (which "includes its creator within itself"), there needs to be a reader-recipient to "enter as a creator into what is seen, heard, or pronounced, and in so doing overcome the material, extra-creatively determinate character of the form, its thingness" in order actively to forge an "axiological relationship" with the author-creator—who is present in the work only as "organized activity." The aesthetic object is hence for Bakhtin not a thing, but, in its distinctiveness, rather has the "character of an event," a "realized, distinctive event of the action and interaction of creator and content" in which the reader-recipient feels herself as an "active *subiectum,*" as a "necessary constitutive moment" ("CMF," 317).

Although his main concern in this essay, as in most of his writings, is with verbal art, Bakhtin's philosophical explorations of the aesthetic event, qua event, would appear to be equally relevant to other modes of artistic production, to art generally. Yet precisely because he emphatically claims that artistic creation is not so much an "embodied" as it is an "embodying" event, this does not lead to a notion of aesthetic activity as an undifferentiated process of overall becoming. On the contrary, for Bakhtin, the constitutive, embodying force of artistic form becomes productive only as an "actuality of a special, purely aesthetic order" ("CMF," 315). At once pointing up the subjectivating operations of aesthetic creation and the *differentia specifica* of art as activity, his reflections thus not only allow us to conceive of the aesthetic object as a "completely new ontic formation . . . which arises on the boundaries of a work by overcoming its material—extra-aesthetic—determinateness as a thing" ("CMF," 297), but also invite us to consider the specificity of different kinds of aesthetic events in their differentiated material effects/affects. In this chapter, I wish first to more generally reflect on aesthetic activity, and second, to briefly dwell on two alternative modes of artistic creation, respectively, music, as perhaps the most apparently disembodied form, and in the final section, the intrinsically body-related art of modern jewelry. But let me start with several preliminary observations on artistic creation/activity against the broader framework of philosophical aesthetics.

Bakhtin's dialogical model, with its emphasis on process over structure and on becoming over being at once appears to foreshadow and to acquire new significance in light of the recent turn in critical theory to affect, especially the line of thought that harks back from Deleuze and Guattari to Henri Bergson and Baruch Spinoza.[2] Since my interest here is not to "defend" affect theory per se, but rather to explore ways in which a focus on affect may help us to grasp what Bakhtin calls the "embodying activity" of artistic creation, I wish to place his early twentieth-century concept of the aesthetic object as "not a thing" in relation to contemporary forms of aesthetic theory—in the wake of the "affective turn"—that is to say, in the context of what is variously referred as "the new aestheticism," "the radical aesthetic,"[3] or, quite simply, "neo-aesthetics."[4] I wish to consider the relations between the aesthetic object as a "distinctive event" and growing concerns with art beyond the boundaries of traditional art history, with art—to borrow and slightly pervert Arthur Danto's provocative phrase—"after the end of art."[5]

As suggested in the introduction, by positing a certain specificity for different forms of art, I am not at all interested in defining or demarcating particular realms of contemporary art, for such definitions and demarcations are obviously culturally and historically specific, hence subject to change. My engagement with neo-aesthetic theory arises from my interest in what art does or does not do in the world on the level of subjective experience, in grasping its operations in their specificity, qua art, and thus in approaching particular artworks as force fields distinct from perceptual and sensual phenomena not so defined in a given culture at a certain moment in history. By shifting attention away from the artistic object to the subject of aesthetic experience, I do not, however, mean to set up an alternative essentialized object of inquiry. As Bakhtin's notion of the reader-recipient as an "active *subiectum*," indeed, as a "necessary constitutive moment" in the aesthetic event suggests, the contemplating or observing subject, just as the aesthetic object, similarly only obtains, is only called "forth" or constituted in the activity of artistic co-creation. Hence, just as what may be seen to count as art changes over time and cross-culturally, so can no aesthetic experience ever be repeated in exactly the same way, whether in an individual from one hour to the next, or across and within different sociohistorical contexts. The mere fact, however, that perceptual properties of both objects and subjects are ultimately indeterminable, shifting, as well as insufficient for clearly distinguishing art from non-art, does not mean that aesthetic experiences do not constitute a viable starting point for theoretically exploring them as *events.* After all, without the possibility of aesthetic experience in its phenomenological sense, there would be no art and no aesthetic inquiry.

Admittedly, Bakhtin's seminal concept of "dialogism"[6] in artistic creation sprang from his immersion in neo-Kantianism at the beginning of the twentieth century.[7] It should be clear, however, that the idea of the aesthetic invoked here diverges from the popularized Kantian notion of the aesthetic act as detached contemplation and as a civilizing, humanizing force that enables proper judgments of taste and encourages ethical behavior. Instead, I posit a neo-aesthetic as a specific, transgressive, disorganizing, if not deterritorializing force the ethical implications of which are neither pregiven nor unambivalent. For if we follow the Russian philosopher in conceiving the aesthetic event as an activity, as an act of processual co-creation mutually realized by the author-creator and the reader-recipient, and if, furthermore, artistic creation per se is not so much an embodied as an embodying activity, and, finally, if it is clear that the reader-recipient similarly only comes into corporeal being through her or his participation in this event, by actively partaking in the "organized activity" that constitutes artistic creation, such activity equally entails the possibility, if not the inevitability, of the undoing, of the unbecoming of previously existing embodied selves, and therewith of a becoming anew. In its generality, this conception of the dis/embodying encounter and engagement with the work of art suggests the operation of the prepersonal forces of affect and presubjective emotion[8] to be central to the artistic event and, by extension, to any form of aesthetic encounter.

In his writings of the early 1920s, Bakhtin's objective is to work toward a general systematic aesthetics. And while he does not mention Kant in "Supplement," it seems clear that his criticisms of "representatives of the so-called Formal or Morphological Method" are closely bound up with his engagement with the formalism of Kantian aesthetics as well. In the first section of his *Critique of Judgment* (1799), Kant famously defines aesthetic judgments as "disinterested," in the sense that we judge something to be beautiful irrespective of whether it is "agreeable" to us—which would be a purely sensory judgment—or whether it meets our ethical standards, or conforms to moral law.[9] We can certainly take pleasure in beauty, but this is a consequence of our aesthetic judgment and not its cause. The distinction between the "agreeable" or the "pleasurable," on one hand, and the aesthetic, the beautiful, on the other, leads Kant to posit that the aesthetic judgment must be focused on the formal aspects of an object (shape, design, arrangement), and not on its sensible aspects (color, tone, material, texture), for the latter have a profound connection to the agreeable, and thus to interest. I will have more to say about this and about the additional "moments" (or features) that Kant attributes to aesthetic judgments (i.e., that they are both universal and necessary, and that beautiful objects appear to have been made or designed to be "purposive" without having any practical purpose, to be "final without end") below. Here I wish to foreground the connection between Kant as the founder of formalism in philosophical aesthetics and Bakhtin's critique of the inadequacies of the formalist method that prevailed in literary scholarship and in the so-called *Kunstwissenschaften* in Russia at the time of his writing, the first decades of the twentieth century.

While generally pleased with recent contributions to Russian scholarly literature by "valuable works on the theory of art, especially in the area of poetics" ("CMF," 257), Bakhtin is critical of the "vogue for science" in contemporary art study, which he believes leads to an "extreme lowering of the level of problematics, to the impoverishment of the object under study, and even to the illegitimate replacement of this object—in this case artistic creation—by something entirely different" ("CMF," 258). The misguided reliance upon scientific thinking in the domain of art study, he continues, is in the final analysis the result of a "common transgression of the study of art in all its branches, committed in the very cradle of this discipline: a negative attitude to general aesthetics, a rejection in principle of the guiding role of general aesthetics" ("CMF," 258–59). In line with Kant's attempts a century earlier to found a general systematic aesthetics, Bakhtin's problematization of the three topics listed in the title of "Supplement"—content, material, form—therefore centers on the "aesthetic object" in general terms, on the aesthetic "in its distinctness of the cognitive and the ethical as well as in its interconnectedness within the unity of culture" ("CMF," 259).

His deep involvement in neo-Kantianism—largely imported from Germany and the most prominent school of philosophy at the time—notwithstanding, Bakhtin "abhorred the dualism in Kant's account of how internal thought relates to external experience," as Katerina Clark and Michael Holquist point out in their authoritative introduction to his work.[10] Consequently, he primarily turns his argument against the Russian formalists' investment in Kant as, first and foremost, the founder of formalism. Bakhtin rejects the program of "materialist aesthetics," which he believes cannot but result in the separation of content from form and lead to an ambitious systematicity that fails to do justice to the specificity of any artwork's unique effects in the real world, as well as entail the spurious isolation of art from life. The error of judgment founding the formalist project, Bakhtin argues, is not only its proponents' failure to engage philosophical aesthetics, their disregard of the need to develop a "general systematic aesthetics," but also, in their near-exclusive preoccupation with the materiality of form, to first separate "real life" material from art, and second, to assume that a "scientific" method means to isolate things. Bakhtin maintains that the autonomy of art is, paradoxically, to borrow the words of Bakhtin scholars Gary Saul Morson and Caryl Emerson, "guaranteed not by its isolation from life but by its precise participation in it."[11] For Bakhtin, there are in fact three possible relations for human beings to have with reality: cognitive action, ethical action, and aesthetic action. That we can analytically distinguish among these relations does not mean, however, that we can factually separate them in "real life." On the contrary, he maintains, since aesthetics is that which connects the realms of cognition (or "knowledge in general") and ethics (which only knows "individual particularized value"), life "becomes real for us in 'aesthetic intuition,' and there is no 'neutral reality' that can be opposed to art."[12]

Bakhtin thus places aesthetic activity squarely within the practice of everyday life, as an embodying activity, an enactment, or an en-(rather than an in-)corporation. Still, the fact that his major purpose in "Supplement" is a negative one, an attempt to expose the flaws of the "materialist aesthetics" of Russian formalism, implies that he first and foremost must show that the aesthetic object, which is an activity directed toward the work (or "content," which at once informs and transforms material) of a given work of art, escapes both its organized materiality and its cognitive determination. In doing so, he repeatedly refers to what he calls the most "objectless" of all forms of art: music.

Music, Bakhtin argues, is "devoid of object-related determinateness and cognitive differentiatedness, yet it has a deep content: its form takes us beyond the bounds of acoustic sounds, and certainly not into an axiological void" ("CMF," 266). Perhaps more "palpably" than any other form of art, music hence testifies to the fact that the aesthetic object, "detached and fictively irreversible," is neither a thing nor an object, but the "event of striving, the axiological tension," which, to repeat his earlier quoted phrase, "arises on the boundaries of a work of art by way of overcoming its material—extra-aesthetic—determinateness as a thing" ("CMF," 307). A strictly materialist formalism is an inadequate basis for studying and understanding precisely that which gives artistic creativity its "aesthetic distinctiveness and significance" ("CMF," 263), for what it fails to take into account is the artwork's "axiological constituent," which is the *emotional-volitional tension of form*" ("CMF," 264). Using musical metaphors to characterize the extramaterial aspects of artistic form, Bakhtin thus recasts the terms of formalist aesthetics per se:

> This emotional-volitional relationship [of the author and the contemplator *to* something apart from the material] that is expressed by form (by rhythm, harmony, symmetry, and other formal moments) is too intense, too *active* in character to be understood simply as a relationship to the material. ("CMF," 264)

Bakhtin retains Kant's first and third "moments" of the aesthetic judgment, that it is "disinterested" and thus distinct from the merely sensual pleasure and/ or practical use we may derive from a work of art, by suggesting that an artwork, "understood as *organized material,* as a thing, can have significance only as a physical stimulus of physiological and psychological states or it must assume some utilitarian, practical function" ("CMF," 264). His insistence on the intense, the active, and the emotional operations of artistic *form* nonetheless allow him first, to overcome the dualism of Kant's thought, and second, to situate the dialogic relationship that characterizes aesthetic contemplation squarely in the realm of human experience as a whole, or, to put it even more strongly, to define aesthetic experience as foundational to all human activity. But the distinctiveness of the artwork or, more precisely, the "aesthetic object in its purely artistic distinctiveness" as it is actualized in the creative event, as organized activity, cannot obtain outside the specifically and "purely" aesthetic encounter that constitutes the axiological relationship of the author and contemplator to the work.

In the participative event that is aesthetic activity, the aesthetic object of a given work of art is, for Bakhtin, thus realized only in the actuality of its co-creation, which generates a "completely new ontic formation," a "distinctive aesthetic existent." In his later work, he came to locate this "distinctive aesthetic existent" almost exclusively in the extramaterial operation of language, of the word in its dialogic operations, more particularly, in novelistic discourse, which orchestrates worlds and provides "specific complexes of values, definitions of situation, *potentials* (not merely structures) for kinds of action."[13] The fundamentally antidualist approach to the relation between art and life, meaning and being, that characterizes all of his work, however, requires Bakhtin both to continue to insist on the "unique, necessary, and irreplaceable place" art occupies *within* life and, to cite Morson and Emerson again, to demand of art the "same qualities that he demands of a person living a real ethical life: particularization, commitment, and 'no alibi for being.'" This, as suggested earlier, does not entail a collapse of the distinction between art and life, but rather requires us to identify "the right sort of specificity," which is "obtained not by abstracting a phenomenon or linking it up within a system, but by making it answer for its unique effects in the real world."[14]

In its insistence on the "eventness" of aesthetic activity, on its embodying nature, as well as on its dialogic, enacting, or constitutive potential, Bakhtin's "architectonic aesthetics" (the term "architectonics" refers to the science of relations, which, unlike a system, always requires the presence of human beings) is arguably more anti- than post-Kantian, especially in view of its essentially antidualist and anti-universalist sway. But there is yet another sense in which Bakhtin breaks with Kant and the post-Kantians, and that is, despite his concern with "general aesthetics," in his ultimate rejection of any concept of universal principles, transcendental laws, or systematicity, whether in relation to actual, empirical reality, time and space, ethics, or, indeed, art.

In his early writings, Bakhtin still maintains that works of art offer an aesthetic whole, that they are the result of an act of "finalization" on the part of the artist/creator with which/whom the reader/recipient enters into an active relationship of co-creation. In the course of his career, however, he becomes increasingly wary of any and all finalizing discourses, and especially of the "monologic" conception of truth that, he argues, has characterized modern thought for hundreds of years and which he sees reflected not only in great thinkers like Kant and Hegel, but also in literature (before Dostoyevsky). Bakhtin's concern for openness, for the possibility of innovation, for the genuinely new, and for potentiality, freedom, and creativity leads him to advance the term "unfinalizability" as an "all-purpose carrier of his conviction that the world is not only a messy place, but is also an open space."[15] Such openness is not, in Bakhtin's view, a desirability or a utopian dream, but in fact an ethical and a phenomenal necessity—that is, in the sense that any living organism in the world must constantly respond to her environment and that she is accountable for her responses in their distinctiveness and particularity. This is what Bakhtin means with his statement that there is "no alibi for being." In their discussion of his notion of "answerability," Clark and Holquist define Bakhtin's view as "both Neo-Kantian and Darwinian":

> The Kantian assumption of a gap between mind and world is understood by Bakhtin as a necessary interdependence between the two, making all discussion of a transcendental ego superfluous or at least inadequate. Such an interdependence is Darwinian in the specific sense that the one cannot exist without modification

by the other, and thus the privilege of making decisions resides exclusively in neither.[16]

The ongoing process of mutual modification of mind and world—and of everything that is in it—is thus a phenomenal necessity that renders both self and world unfinalizable, messy, and open, which in turn allows for the new, the surprising, the unexpected, and also for creative activity. In line with his abhorrence of (Kantian) duality and his rejection of "systematizers" generally, Bakhtin's position in relation to the ratio of unfinalizability to finalization at some point definitively shifts to the former: both in life and in art, unfinalizability becomes the supreme value, the temporary need for finalization giving way to the ethical necessity of unfinalizability. Since Bakhtin here truly departs from while yet remaining indebted to Kant, and therewith gives a twist to the modern theory of aesthetics in a way that prefigures what I have called the project of contemporary neo-aesthetics, his notion of unfinalizability opens up the connections between his post-Kantian aesthetics and current theories of affect.

A central concept in Bakhtin's thinking, unfinalizability is a positive term with which to argue against any approach of cultural process that assumes an underlying set of laws or systems from which an actual event merely emerges as a particular instantiation of some pre-existing structure. What such approaches miss, or preclude, is the essential fact of the "eventness" of any form of cultural process and production. Both formalist and structuralist models hence do not merely present a reductive view on cultural phenomena, they also render human creativity fundamentally impossible. Unfinalizability, real creativity, Bakhtin infers from this, cannot be located in a system of laws, but neither can it be assumed to exist in randomness, in a "realm of passive, chance phenomena." That creativity is real, that it is always and everywhere, leads him to the assumption that creativity is, in the words of Morson and Emerson, "immanent in constant, ongoing processes," and furthermore that such processes are open to the future, not because they are outside the law or random irruptions, but because "they are and have been the product of accumulated tiny alterations constituting the daily 'event of being.'"[17]

In his insistence on the indissolubility of art and life, the dialogic character of the relation between mind and world, and the unfinalizability of the creative event in its realness and its eventness, Bakhtin comes close to defining life itself in aesthetic terms. Writing in roughly the same period, yet approaching Kant from a very different perspective, the English mathematician-philosopher Alfred North Whitehead (1861–1947) arrives at a similar position. Whitehead takes Bakhtin's post-Kantian critique a step further by, in Steven Shaviro's gloss, defining aesthetics as both the "immanent criterion for order" and as the mark of "our *concern* for the world, and for entities in the world," thereby placing aesthetics "at the center of philosophical inquiry" per se. To pursue the connections between Bakhtin's "architectonic aesthetics" and Whitehead's response to Kant, I turn to Shaviro's book *Without Criteria: Kant, Whitehead, Deleuze, and Aesthetics,* which, in the overall context of a radical and experimental attempt to rethink postmodern aesthetic theory, presents, particularly relevant to my purposes here, a rereading of Whitehead's "critique of pure feeling" in conjunction with Kant and Deleuze.[18]

I will have occasion to turn to Whitehead directly in later chapters. Here I wish to focus largely on *Without Criteria* (hereafter wc), for what interests me about Shaviro's take on Whitehead is the way he develops the latter's theory of feeling into an affect-laden notion of subjectivity in which *aesthesis* (or sensual perception) plays a constitutive role within a nonphenomenological model of becoming that appears remarkably commensurate with Bakhtin's dialogical prosaics.[19]

Becoming, Shaviro submits, is "not continuous, because each occasion, each act of becoming, is unique," and any appearance of duration, of endurance or continuity, needs to be actively produced, over and over again (wc, 19). Extending Bakhtin's ideas about creative activity as an event of co-creation to the realm of experience and the world as a whole, Shaviro follows Whitehead in positing a notion of the self that is not so much a pre-existing entity that "phenomenologically 'intends' the world," but rather, in direct opposition with post-Kantian thought, something that emerges from its encounters with the world: each subjective, embodied, and perceptual encounter—whether with actual, physical objects, or with ideas or "mental acts"—produces the subject "anew," as so many new selves, as "fresh event[s]" (wc, 21). In Bakhtinian terms, neither the world nor the self is ever finalized, let alone finalizable, for the latter comes into being in the "very course of its encounter with the world" (wc, 21), which, in its turn, is in flux and multiply informed by such encounters.

Bakhtin's rejection of any "monologic" conception of truth finds a parallel in Whitehead's (and Kant's) contention that there is no truth somehow already in the world, waiting to be discovered. There is no knowledge, of self or world, outside subjective experience and such experience is always partial, necessarily limited. "The given," Shaviro writes, "always exceeds our representation of it" (wc, 49). For Kant, our perceptual or sensible reality is the reality of appearances; we do not perceive the reality of "things in themselves," because to perceive objects/ entities in time and space is a function of our minds, not something unchangeable or absolute in the world. It is the faculty of reason that enables us to invest structure into the randomness and order the chaos of our sensible experience. Kantian cognition is thus a dual process involving both intuition and understanding. Extending this founding assumption in his work on aesthetics, Kant argues that it is the function of judgment to recognize beauty and to grasp our aesthetic experiences as part of an ordered, purposive natural world. Bakhtin follows Kant in the assumption that human beings come into existence in their everyday encounters with one another and with the world, but he rejects his dualist account of the relation between internal thought and external experience. Similarly, Whitehead accepts Kant's "Transcendental Aesthetics," according to which sensibility and receptivity are prior to understanding in our experience of the world, but he dismisses his "Transcendental Logic," according to which "ordered experience is the result of schematization of modes of *thought,* concerning causation, substance, quality, quantity."[20]

Kant's mistake, according to Whitehead, is that he ultimately subordinates sensibility and receptivity, the faculty of intuition, and thus the a priori possibility of being affected by that which is given—and all we are given is appearances in space and time—to the imperative of understanding by the imposition of concepts, or Categories, in his formulation of cognition. He thereby, Shaviro writes, "unduly privileges those particular sorts of abstraction that are peculiar to human minds and other 'high-grade' organisms," reserving experience for "rationalist beings alone" (*wc,* 50). By assuming that our intuitions are passive and that appearances are just the raw data of experience that must be processed in the understanding by the imposition of concepts, Kant, Shaviro continues to point out, "in effect reaffirms the *cogito:* the Cartesian subject that is separated from, unconditioned by, and implicitly superior to the world that it only observes from a distance" (*wc,* 50). This reaffirmation of the *cogito* not only reinscribes the traditional opposition between (inert, passive, shapeless) matter and the (active, formative, constructive) mind, and thus "ignores all the *intermediaries* that are at work in any actual process of formation and construction" (*wc,* 53); it also essentially obviates what is crucial to Kant's aesthetics itself: the supposition of the a priori forms of intuition of space and time, of a prior sensibility and receptivity that allow us to be affected by the appearances of things and to be affected by such appearances in a particular way.

Whitehead counters Kant's dualist/rationalist argument by introducing what Shaviro considers to be one of his "most important notions," that is to say, the idea of "'subjective' form." Every "prehension," every grasping or sensing of one entity by another, includes what in traditional epistemological terms would be called a subject and an object,[21] but, more importantly, includes a third aspect, namely the particular way in which a *datum* is prehended, the *quale* of the *sensa;* this is what Whitehead calls "subjective form." Taking into account that prehension is not necessarily conscious and that the subject does not exist before the encounter with the object in which it is produced, it is this third aspect, the "affective tone determining the effectiveness of that prehension in that occasion of experience,"[22] Shaviro maintains, that is the "really crucial one," since it entails that in the determination of an object, there is always "some margin of indeterminacy," depending on how the subject *feels* the (objective) datum (*wc*, 55). Such indeterminacy is the equivalent of what for Bakhtin is, in the artistic encounter, the aesthetic object, that which escapes the object's organized materiality and its cognitive determination as a consequence of the fact that our experience of it is first of all affective in nature. Objects (whether actual material entities or mental acts) affect us, prior to and irrespective of our understanding of them. In the immediacy of our sense perception, our experience acquires a significance that refutes the binary opposition between mind and matter, for the "affective tone" that, in Shaviro's words, "suffuses every experience of perception," both "determines and exceeds cognition." And since perception, he proceeds, is "first of all a matter of being affected bodily," every perception or prehension "provokes the body" into being in a particular way: "Contact with the outside world strengthens or weakens the body, stimulates it or inhibits it, furthers or impairs its various functions." This is "already the 'subjective form' of the prehension," Shaviro writes, for it is the way phenomena are felt, the way the "feeling entity" interacts with other entities—which is the same as saying that being affected or changed in/by the prehension is the "very content of what it feels" (*wc*, 57, 59). Hence Bakhtin's otherwise quite startling assertion that the "organized activity" of an artwork constitutes the (invisible, inaudible) creator as an "embodying, and not as an embodied activity."[23]

Shaviro's reading of Whitehead's philosophy, it will be clear, in the first place seeks to displace the *cogito* from its privileged position by replacing reason with affect in its primacy and productivity, and to expose the reductive implications of any cognitive theory of mind by reading them against Whitehead's "theory of emotions." My reason for discussing the latter's "critique of pure feeling" derivatively, by way of Shaviro, however, is not only that his reading of Whitehead appears to offer an overall philosophical foundation to Bakhtin's contemporaneous yet more narrowly focused "architectonic aesthetics." Shaviro's project in *Without Criteria,* at least the section I have hitherto focused on, also allows me to take Bakhtin's notion of artistic creation as both activity and as embodying event from its primarily antiformalist, originating moment into the current one, that is, into the context of the emergent formation of a neo-aesthetics in the wake of the affective turn. This, finally, enables me to substantiate my initial claims with regard to the *differentia specifica* of art, as activity and as aesthetic event, and briefly to reflect, in the concluding paragraphs of this chapter, on the affective, embodying operations of an art form that is not generally recognized as such, and that in its "ontological ambivalence" thus constitutes a productive site to explore the aesthetic as a "distinctive event" while still being firmly located in the practice of life, which, to recall Bakhtin, only becomes real for us in "aesthetic intuition."

For Kant, as we have seen, the world and everything within it exists for us in our sensible, perceptual experience of it; there is no possibility for us to know the world *sub specie aeternitatis.* Yet in defining the process of cognition as both intuition and understanding, Kant brings our (hence necessarily contingent, messy, and open) experience of the world—and ourselves—under the ordering principle of reason. Whitehead, in contrast, positing feeling rather than cognition as the basis of all experience, assumes our experience to be ordered and organized from within, from within subjective feeling. He thus postulates, Shaviro writes, an "immanent criterion for order" as something that can "only be an aesthetic one" (*wc*, 66). Since there is nothing outside our subjective experience, Whitehead identifies aesthetics as, to repeat Shaviro's formulation, the "mark of . . . our *concern* for the world." On the face of it, such an immanent ordering function would seem to render change, newness, disorder, and novelty impossible, and thereby negate what Bakhtin in the course of his writing came to regard as the supreme value: unfinalizability in art as in life, which, he argues, is not only an ethical necessity, but a phenomenal one as well. Such appearances notwithstanding, Whitehead's notion of prehension nonetheless places newness, novelty, change, at the center of our being in the world, because the critical factor of "subjective form" in every prehension entails that the immanent (aesthetic) order of our experience is always marked by a certain indeterminacy, in the sense that the way we perceive or feel a given object is likely to be different from the way it has and will be perceived by other subjects and, moreover, from the way we feel/perceive it from one encounter to the next. In other words, we are never affected in exactly the same way twice by any "objective datum," and since our selves are continually produced anew in a discontinuous process of aesthetic encounters, novelty is an intrinsic aspect of becoming, of affecting and of being affected. The important thing for Whitehead is "not *what* something is, but *how* it is—or, more precisely, how it affects, and how it is affected by, other things." This may well render novelty, as Shaviro concedes, a "function of *manner,* rather than of essence" (*wc*, 56), but it simultaneously makes it into a necessary, inalienable aspect of becoming, because each occasion, each act of becoming (within the series of occasions that jointly make up the event), is "unique" and thus entails the "production of novelty" (*wc*, 20).

If, as Shaviro argues, an "act of feeling is an encounter—a contingent event, an opening to the outside—rather than an intrinsic, predetermined relationship," and if feeling "changes whatever it encounters" (*wc*, 63), it follows that all entities in the affective event are subject to change, opening onto novelty and to the future. To the extent that any entity exists in its relations to other entities and that it is affected by these relations, an existence of its own may thus be attributed to that which Whitehead calls an "objective datum," but such existence is never fully determined: both present and past relations have and continue to inform it, to affect it, and to be affected by it. To re-evoke Bakhtin's terms, creativity, the creation of the new, is immanent in constantly ongoing, yet discontinuous and transformative processes, and thus not a random interruption but, on the contrary, the constitutive result of the accumulated variations that make up the daily "event of being."

Since subject and object are relational and thus relative terms, the critical function of "subjective form" in every act of prehension means that the "objective datum" is affected itself, informed by the encounter, by the act off feeling that calls it into being in the first place—and never once and for all, never in the same way twice. What is more, even if, for Whitehead, the most important thing is to show that the basis of all sensible experience (and not just in the creation and reception of works of art) is aesthetic, there is a differentiation, even a hierarchy in the modes of feeling, in the degree of intensity that marks the aesthetic fact in its uniqueness, qua experience. Such relativity, rather than leading to an overall indifference, reducing, say, a Rodin sculpture to the rock I bump my toe against (although the latter will clearly produce an intensity of feeling), instead allows us to postulate a specific place for art as a particular zone of intensity in which a given object, already informed by previous relations, by other acts of feeling, past and present, does not so much enter into a relation with my pre-existent subjectivity, but calls me into being as what Bakhtin calls an "active *subiectum,*" as a contemplating subject, a subject that, as Shaviro puts it, "subsists only to the extent that it resonates with the feelings inspired by that object" (*wc,* 13). Such feelings, upon which our existence as subjects depends, are thus both pre- or nonpersonal and pre- or nonsubjective.

To maintain the possibility of a *differentia specifica* of art and, with Bakhtin, to insist on the "unique, necessary, and irreplaceable place" art occupies *within* life, we do not need a definition that helps us to separate art off from non-art on the basis of its intrinsic qualities, of its formal and material aspects, its thingness: the operation of any object as "art" is fully contingent upon the degree of the aesthetic intensity, on the way it affects us, and on the uniqueness of the contemplative event. Decisions about the "value" of artworks, about their function in the activity of aesthetic creation, furthermore, are never final, or finalizable, because there is always a certain indeterminacy about such decisions, depending on the "subjective form," on the way the object is perceived or felt by the observer. Whereas art acquires its necessary place in life from its transformational potential, from the ways the encounter with an artwork is something that actively happens to us, an event that constitutes us anew as subjects, an ambivalent, dynamic event that enables novelty per se, such decisions—or aesthetic "judgments"—on the contrary, are not, nor are they universal. As "happenings" in the world, artistic encounters, or occasions, are at once specific, unique, and purposive only to the effect that they are capable of making things happen—of what Bakhtin calls the production of a "distinctive aesthetic existent," a "completely new ontic formation."

Whitehead's notion of "subjective form," his emphasis on the *how* as distinct from the *what* of prehension, the affective tone that suffuses any and all sense-perception, additionally allows us to grant, evoking Bakhtin, "the right sort of specificity" to a particular artwork in its "unique effects in the real world," in its *haecceity* or "thisness." Such effects, it should be clear, cannot be limited to the artwork's formal aspects, or even to what Bakhtin awkwardly defines as the "emotional-volitional relationship that is expressed by form," to the exclusion of its materiality, its "thingness." Since our experience of the world and the entities of the world primarily affect us, are felt by us, in our bodies, on a corporeal level, that is to say, in our fully animate being, these effects do not merely engage the traditionally (at least in art criticism) privileged modes of sense-perception of seeing and hearing, the detached, distanced contemplation that Kant considered essential for aesthetic judgment. On the contrary, they also centrally involve all other forms of embodied (or embodying) perception, such as the senses of smell, touch, and taste. This entails that in addition to formal aspects, such as shape, design, and arrangement, as well as rhythm, harmony, and symmetry, the material aspects of tone, color, and material texture, those qualities Kant relegates to the interested domain of the "agreeable" and the "pleasurable," are intrinsic and equally active and intense *qualia* of the experience of, and constituted in, artistic creation and contemplation.[74]

That the material, tactile, olfactory, and gustatory aspects of art have generally been neglected and subordinated to sight and hearing is not only the result of the legacy of Aristotle's classical hierarchy of the senses, but it also derives from the conventional distinction, in line with this classical model, of the division of the field of creative practice into that of arts and crafts. This distinction and the different evaluative connotations these terms evoke traditionally find their basis in the differences between both certain practices and certain products. Painting, sculpture, and printmaking, for example, are regarded as practically "useless" activities springing from the imagination and/or from the genius of the individual artist. Ceramics, fiber/textile, and wood- and metalwork, in contrast, are practices associated with technical ability, which result in skillfully produced objects that are largely appreciated in terms of their practical usefulness.

This distinction in evaluation was first formally called into question at the turn of the twentieth century when the Arts and Crafts movement in Britain and elsewhere, in the wake of the Industrial Revolution, sought to elevate the status of craftsmanship and the "decorative" arts and to expand the application of the *aesthetic criterion* hitherto reserved for the "fine" arts to include the "vernacular" forms of the creative practices of craft and design. Writing against this background, and against that of an emerging avant-garde modernist movement that would equally, and perhaps even more fundamentally, call into question all classical distinctions and appreciations of art forms and genres, Bakhtin and Whitehead, each in his own way, and to divergent purposes, appear to respond—whether deliberately or not—to these developments by effectively foregrounding precisely those aspects of aesthetic activity that obtain in the sensual and perceptual body in its entirety, that is, on the prepersonal and presubjective level of affect, and thus provide a philosophical framework in which to place contemporary developments in the world of art and craft at large.

Art as organized and experienced activity, in its eventness, as something active and intense, something that *happens,* does not only mobilize the "higher" senses of sight and hearing, but necessarily includes, if it does not in effect "trigger," the "lower" senses of smell, touch, and taste as well. This phenomenal inevitability is theoretically borne out by Bakhtin's notion of artistic creation, *in tandem* with Whitehead's "theory of pure feeling" and its focus on affect and singularity, of aesthetic activity as not so much an embodied as an "embodying event." The central concern with "the new," which the two thinkers share in common,[25] furthermore unmistakably identifies the *poietic* function of art—that is to say, *poiesis* in the Heideggerian sense of a "bringing-forth," or a threshold occasion, a moment when something shifts from where, what, and how it was, to become another—in the reality of the aesthetic fact.

Transformation, change, novelty, all require the contingent, messy, and open experience of the world—and of ourselves, an equally messy process in which art, when it is truly creative, plays a constitutive, if indeterminate and ultimately indeterminable, role. While claiming such a *poietic* function, and thus also a certain autonomy for art overall, I recognize, pace Bakhtin, that there is no point in "abstracting a phenomenon or linking it up with a system," and that in order to account for its unique and singular effects in the world, we need to approach every aesthetic fact with the "right sort of specificity." Let me therefore, in provisional conclusion and before I narrow my focus in subsequent chapters to various forms of visual art, say a few words about a kind of "threshold" art form in and of itself, a form that necessarily enchains the body and all its senses in its operations: that which is alternately designated "modern," or "art jewelry."

The awkward phrase "modern/art jewelry" serves to distinguish its practice and products from the more commercial and mass-produced objects of fashion jewelry. (See figures 1.1 through 1.4, as well as plates 1 and 2.) It is nonetheless difficult to differentiate, at least in traditional art historical terms, works of "modern jewelry" as particular kinds of *art*works from the products of its "monologic" counterpart, which, as precious objects, largely serve decorative, ornamental func-

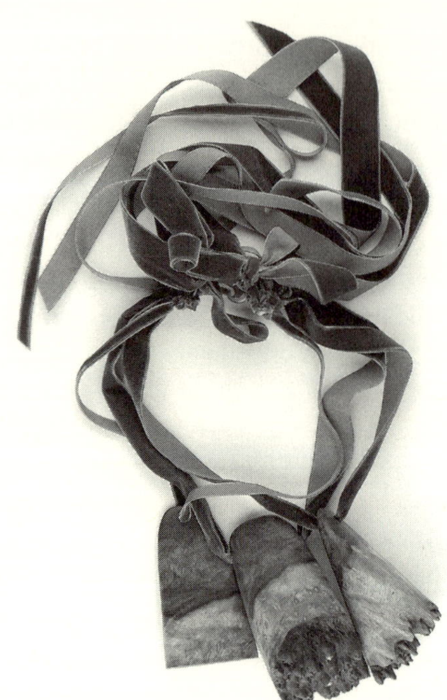

FIG. 1.1 Seth Papac, *Iris Jewelry Portrait,* necklace, 2009. Diamonds, burl wood, silver, velvet ribbon, 28 × 15 × 10 cm. © Seth Papac

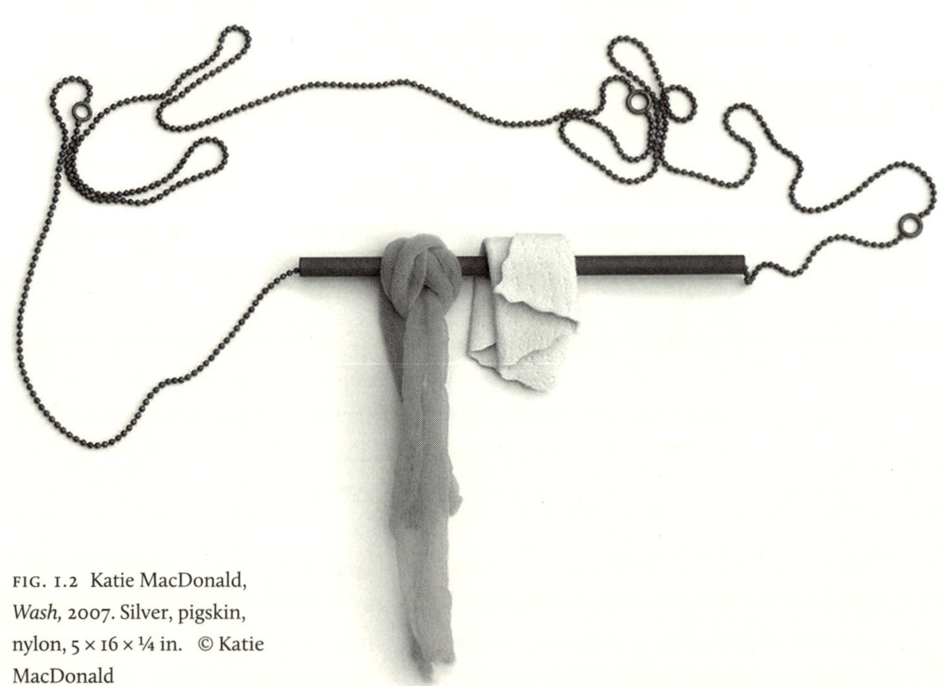

FIG. 1.2 Katie MacDonald, *Wash,* 2007. Silver, pigskin, nylon, 5 × 16 × ¼ in. © Katie MacDonald

tions. While undeniably the result of processes of making and doing, objects of the latter kind, so-called fashion or costume jewelry, do not constitute processes of making and doing in the sense Bakhtin allows us to perceive in the aesthetic event proper; they do not, in other words, serve *poietic* functions themselves. Because of its undeniable connections and its shared traditions (in terms of some materials and techniques) with fashion jewelry, modern/art jewelry is not often credited with the power to generate what Bakhtin calls a "completely new ontic formation," to enable a form of perceptual experience that leads to a "distinctive aesthetic existent." Moreover, as one among a number of art forms inelegantly qualified as "body-related," contemporary art jewelry has traditionally, and at least until the 1970s—not least because of the legacy of Kantian aesthetics—been relegated to the lower regions of artistic hierarchies. Defying the possibility of merely "disinterested" contemplation, and emphatically forging connections with the materiality of the flesh rather than offering themselves exclusively to the eyes or to the disembodied operations of the rational mind, body-related artworks, even if they do not necessarily privilege matter over mind, inescapably inscribe the body of the spectator-recipient into the force field that makes up the aesthetic encounter: the event that is at once intense activity, affective experience, and a process of co-creative reorganization on the level of the body in its actualization, of a de- and reconfiguring corporeality.

Yet whereas some forms of performance art may have, since the 1970s, gained critical respectability (perhaps primarily because of their daring, radical, and, sometimes scandalous qualities), such benevolence has thus far not been generously bestowed on modern/art jewelry, precisely because of its unabashed and inescapable materiality and tactility.[26] In light of what I have been suggesting throughout my discussion of Bakhtin's and Whitehead's respective post- or anti-Kantian critiques, this does not in any way diminish such works' potential operation as art, that is, as temporarily and relatively congealed complexes that generate an "aesthetic object in its purely artistic distinctiveness," or as potentials for specific kinds of conscious and unconscious action. I would go so far as to say that it is its essential "objectness," its ineluctable "thingness," that does not so much obviate the operations of modern/art jewelry as aesthetic event as it points up the crucial function of touch, smell, and taste, in addition to sight and hearing, in our actual experience of art form as activity. Certain forms of body-related art, but especially those art forms in which tactility plays a central, literal role, also underline the requirement, in aesthetic reflection, to identify "the right sort of specificity" that will enable us to make an individual artwork "answer for its unique effects in the real world."[27]

Since modern/art jewelry is directly related to the body rather than to the contemplative mind, in the sense that these works are literally to be worn, affectively present (though not necessarily "knowable") as things-in-themselves, to be touched, handled, and assembled into the clothes, bodies, and flesh of their wearers, instead of being treated with the lofty detachment of the contemplating gaze, modern/art jewelry has, in the post-Kantian context of most traditional art history and criticism, been both feminized with respect to its practice and products and has been marginalized as a form of craft in relation to modes of "high" art, such as painting and sculpture. Placed in the context of an emergent neo-aesthetics, possibilities for which it has been my aim to begin to outline in this chapter, it is because of its distinction from other modes of art, more precisely in its essentially tactile specificity, that modern/art jewelry allows us to acknowledge the centrality of animated/animating feeling, of the forces of embodied affect. Such forces function over and above those of understanding and cognition, that is to say, they obtain in the *poietic,* transformative operations of art in its *differentia specifica*, in that they enable a form of experience that resists the pull of objective determination and material finalization.

Seth Papac's *Iris Jewelry Portrait,* for example, combines a traditional precious metal—silver—with diamonds, burl wood, and a velvet ribbon (see figure 1.1). Forming a loose and changing configuration in warm colors of browns and yellows, the piece plies and folds itself in relation to its context: showcase, human body, wall pin. The diamonds more or less disappear into the burl wood, defying both the symbolic meaning of this most precious of gems and its traditional appearance as the centerpiece of a ring, tiara, or necklace. The diamond's legendary purity is furthermore contained in, and thus overshadowed by the burl, partly polished, partly showing itself in its gross excrescences, like a cancerous growth or an extracted tooth. Burl is a peculiar and highly figured wood, prized for its beauty by many, but the whimsical shape of the unpolished wood underlines the fact that it results from a tree undergoing some form of stress and may be caused by an injury, virus or fungus. Beautiful in terms of arrangement, colors, and composition, the piece's contradictions emerge in its variegated tactility, in the clash between the perishability of the ordinary ribbon, the soft silver, the porous wood, and the rock-hard diamonds. This piece of jewelry is, by definition, in process; it embodies growth, endurance, and evanescence at once. Wearing a piece like this, especially since its title suggests that this is a portrait of a human being who temporarily resides on my body, as part of my body, makes me complexly aware of my experience of embodiedness in its materiality, its inescapability, as well as its finiteness, my mortality, the perishability of the flesh.

Or Iris Eichenberg's strange piece called *Broek*, made of different shades of knitted pink wool and shaping itself into some kind of abstracted conglomerate of truncated human legs, a female breast, a garment (see plate 2). What does this object have to do with ornamentation, how does it relate to jewelry, when all

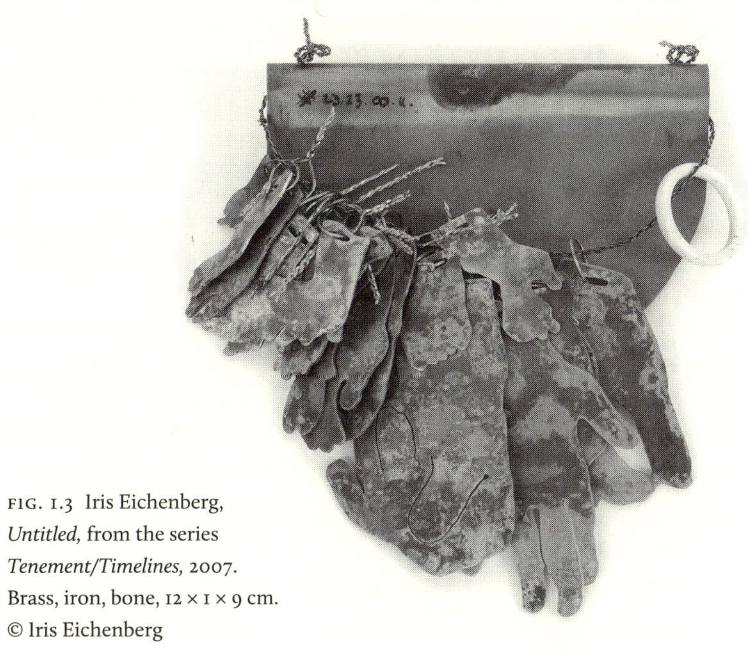

FIG. 1.3 Iris Eichenberg,
Untitled, from the series
Tenement/Timelines, 2007.
Brass, iron, bone, 12 × 1 × 9 cm.
© Iris Eichenberg

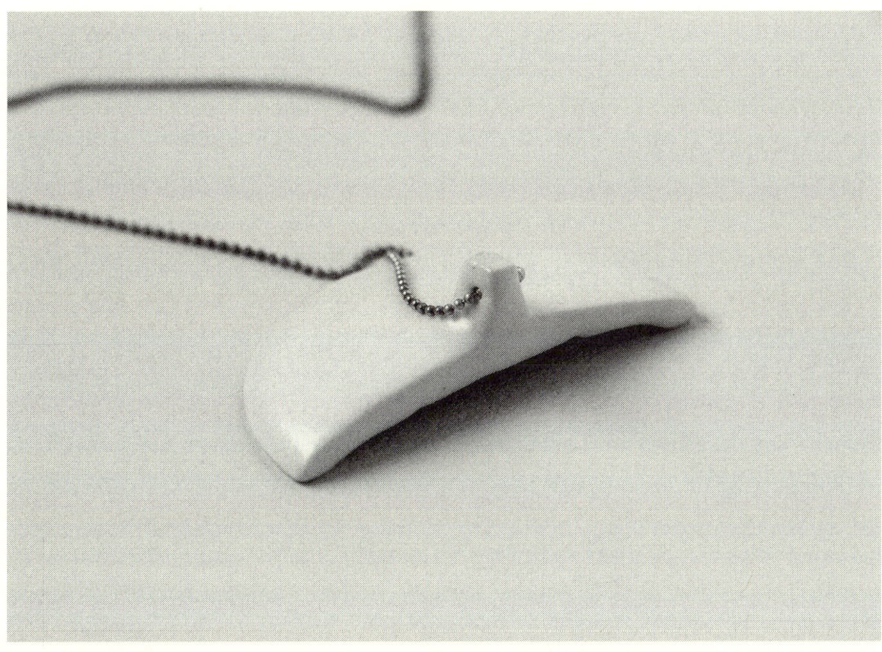

FIG. 1.4 Katie MacDonald, *Half-Stop,* 2007. Porcelain, pigskin, 1½ × 26 × ½ in.
© Katie MacDonald

it suggests is the intensity of a body making something (the traditional craft of knitting) in its most utilitarian sense, suggesting a connection between the animal (a sheep's skin transformed into thread) and pink human flesh—but not in its juicy, blood-filled, throbbing materiality, but rather in its homey coverings, the knitted sock, the warmth of a covering without content? Yet the piece cannot but escape its feel, its suggestion of warmth, of protection, of domesticity, despite its simultaneous lugubrious presentation of tactile and partially visible corporeality.

As a minoritarian mode of artistic expression par excellence, modern/art jewelry provides us with the "exceptional circumstances" under which we can become quite viscerally aware (on the level of our bodily mass) of the processual character of our selves, and of the constitutive function of affect in the process of our continued coming-into-being. By entering into its force field, by attaching myself corporeally (a self that will not outlive this particular moment of its actualization) to an individual work of art jewelry, I find myself solicited into a process of becoming in a Bakhtinian/Whiteheadian sense, that is to say, I experience the unfinalizability of a self, which, to use Shaviro's phrase, is "animated by the feelings that comprise it" (*WC,* 12), and which must thus be constantly renewed, triggered, or brought forth.

The *poietic* (transformative, transgressive, disorganizing, if not deterritorializing) force of the aesthetic in its operational mode surfaces occasionally in the uncanny material aspects of these works. For instance, when, in Katie MacDonald's *Wash* (figure 1.2), the process of making and the choice of materials suggest a familiarity that stands in sharp contrast to the transgression of bodily boundaries the work in its actualizing presence, in its "thisness" or *haecceity,* effects (see also plates 3 and 4).

At the same time, as data, or givens, these objects are constantly in flux, both in their "thingness"—there are, for example, no limitations with respect to the choice of materials for individual works (which hence range from traditional ones such as gold, silver, and other metals, to nylon, pigskin, brass, iron, bone, porcelain, wool, felt, cotton, silk, and wood, some of which emphatically inscribe their own material evanescence, their factual perishability)—and as far as their spatiotemporal operations are concerned, since they move from the hands of the maker, via stores, fairs, and galleries, to the variety of clothes, bodies, and flesh of their equally various owners with whom/which they become momentarily assembled, and from whom/which they inevitably also detach themselves. Unlike my experience of looking at a painting or sculpture in a museum, with the usually explicit instruction "do not touch," the activity of wearing a work of modern/art jewelry urges me to forge singular, sometimes fleeting im/material corporeal connections with its energetic force, its intensity, so that I temporarily emerge as a "fresh event," a new self in and as a never-to-be-fully stabilized or finalized plane of consistency—*and it makes me aware of this.*

It is because of the latter aspect that art jewelry not only quite literally affects me in my actual embodied encounter with it but also provides me with the unusual circumstances that make me inevitably and consciously aware of its *poietic,* transformative force, that the experiential events staged by this "minor" mode of art offer a way of approach of the aesthetic on its own terms. It allows us to begin to see what neo-aesthetic inquiry into art, in its simultaneous indeterminacy and phenomenological actuality, may entail. In the next chapter, I will stage additional artistic encounters, not with a minoritarian art form like modern jewelry, but with the majoritarian practices of sculpture and painting to further explore some of the larger theoretical questions raised by contemporary aesthetics, which will be discussed in connection with, and in distinction from the conventionally related projects of ethics and hermeneutics.

Beauty is not like a superlative of what we imagine, a sort of abstract type we have before our eyes, but on the contrary, a new, unimaginable type that reality affords us.

Marcel Proust, *Contre Sainte-Beuve*

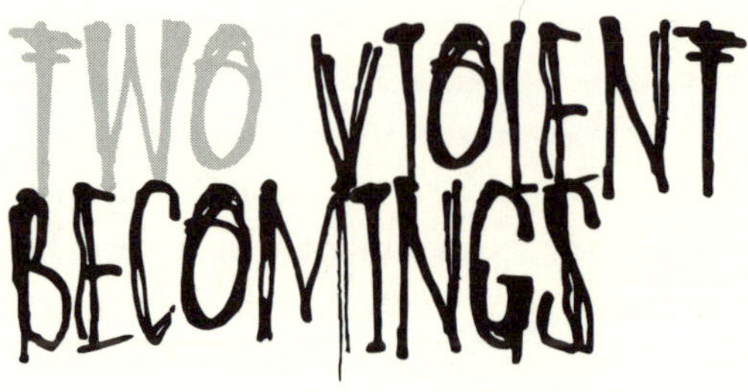

Two Violent Becomings

from the *informe* and the abject to uncontrollable beauty

On September 16, 2001, five days after the terrorist attacks on the World Trade Center, the controversial German composer Karlheinz Stockhausen (1928–2007) gained unprecedented fame, or notoriety, far beyond the relatively narrow circles of avant-garde music lovers, by describing the events of 9/11 as the "greatest work of art of all time."[1] Widely dismissed as highly "distasteful, tactless comments," his statements provoked such a moral outcry that the composer felt forced to apologize formally a few days later. That he publicly asked the "forgiveness of anyone who felt hurt by what he said"[2] did not, however, prevent a series of concerts featuring his work scheduled for the week following 9/11 to be canceled.

Stockhausen's provocative and admittedly insensitive words subsequently became the starting point for extensive debates on a wide range of ostensibly unrelated topics, including the nature of terrorism and contemporary warfare,[3] the power of the media, the "current information war," the "process by which art develops,"[4] as well on the nature, power, and limitations, especially the ethical limitations, of "the aesthetic" as such, both in theory and practice. The latter debates more or less coincided, if they did not also spur on, a renewed interest in ethics in the world of critical theorizing ("post-theory" that is) in which ethics had re-emerged not so much as a "master discourse" to be debunked—as it had been in the overall rejection of liberal humanism by all varieties of 1980s and

1990s poststructuralist and deconstructive theorists—nor as a "kind of moral orthopedics," but instead, and precisely in the wake of the poststructuralist decentering of the subject, to be recentered, and "reconfigured, reformulated, and repositioned," as a "praxis, but also a principle . . . a process of formulation and self-questioning that continually re-articulates boundaries, norms, selves, and 'others.'"[5]

Curiously enough (or perhaps not so curious at all), the "ethical turn" in the world of especially literary critical theorizing in the early years of the twenty-first century appeared to be closely bound up with the renewed interest in theoretical aesthetics developing more or less simultaneously.[6] While obviously a long-standing tradition harking back to at least the eighteenth century, this coincidence nonetheless poses a problem because the association of aesthetics with ethics has frequently led to an unwarrantable collapse of the one into the supposedly larger project of the other (however reconfigured or reformulated). It is against the background of this recurring collapse that I would like to take up the challenge posed by Stockhausen's provocative comments and attempt in the present chapter to further substantiate my claims to a *differentia specifica* of art and, thus, of aesthetics as something fundamentally distinct from ethics. This will be done by thinking through a notion of the aesthetic that runs from Kant's critical aestheticism through "the abject" as a specific mode of aesthetic operation, in conjunction with Bataille's related notion of the "*informe,*" to Deleuze and Guattari's idea of the "line of flight." I will then extend my reflections on Bakhtin's "dialogical prosaics" in tandem with Whitehead's "theory of pure feeling" to posit an overall "aesthetics of existence" in which art nonetheless maintains its specificity as a site of "uncontrollable beauty."[7] By that I mean beauty, not—as Kant suggests—in its radical difference from the sublime, as mere "*restful* contemplation,"[8] but rather as an equally potentially transformational, disorganizing, if not deterritorializing force, whose effects are not necessarily pleasant or reassuring[9] and whose ethical implications are neither pregiven nor unambivalent. To do this, I must begin, again, with Kant.

The connection between beauty and morality is a theme that permeates Kant's *Critique of Judgment* (hereafter *CJ*). It is most prominently implied by two of the four "moments" he attributes to the aesthetic judgment, which are the disinterestedness of the spectator and the judgment's obligatory nature. As a consequence of his overall supposition that the world is and can only be known to us through the senses, in *aesthesis,* Kant is concerned to show that aesthetic judgments are at once subjective and universal. Aesthetic judgments are subjective in the sense that they are the result of the way in which we are *affected* by an object, and that they do not necessarily involve properties of the object itself. Aesthetic judgments are nonetheless universal and not merely personal or individual because they are disinterested; we do not stand to gain anything from the object beyond the "pure" pleasure we may derive from our encounter with it. Significantly, for Kant, even the ethical interest we may take in an artwork's subject is not part of our aesthetic judgment of it: "Any taste remains barbaric if its liking requires that charms and emotions be mingled in, let alone if it makes these the standard of its approval" (*cj*, 69). Kant nonetheless derives a moral function from the demand for the universality of aesthetic judgments and, furthermore, submits that aesthetic experience serves as moral instruction, in that the "beautiful prepares us for loving something, even nature, without interest" (*cj*, 127).

For Kant, beauty and morality are thus not the same, and their operations do not coincide: "The beautiful pleases immediately (but only in reflective intuition, not, like morality, in its concept)." Yet aesthetic experience appears as a condition, as prior to the possibility for moral judgments since the beautiful "pleases apart from all interest (pleasure in the morally good is no doubt necessarily bound up with an interest, but not with one of the kind that are antecedent to the judgment upon the delight, but with one that judgment itself for the first time calls into existence)." As an exercise in selfless attention—the guiding principle of aesthetic contemplation—the disinterested nature of the aesthetic judgment links beauty to morality because it is the selfless attention being given to "pure beauty" that *invokes* the moral point of view: "Taste enables us, as it were, to make the transition from sensible charm to a habitual moral interest without making too violent a leap; for taste presents the imagination as admitting, even in its freedom, of determination that is purposive for the understanding, and it teaches us to like even objects of sense freely, even apart from sensible charm" (*cj*, 230).

At the same time, however, an active attention to beauty for Kant—and it should be clear that he is "strictly" referring to the beauty of nature—functions as a "symbol of morality," as a token of a moral disposition: "I do maintain that to take a *direct interest* in the beauty of *nature* (not merely to have the taste needed to judge it) is always a mark of a good soul; and that, if this interest is habitual, if it readily associates itself with the *contemplation of nature,* this [fact] indicates at least a mental attunement favorable to moral feeling" (*cj*, 166). The ambivalence emerging here as to the priority of the experience of beauty and morality reflects the ultimate duality of Kant's thought—the dualism, or hylomorphism, so vehemently rejected by Bakhtin and Whitehead[10]—that brings aesthetics, as it was defined in 1735 by the German philosopher Alexander Gottlieb Baumgarten (1714–1762) as "the science of how things are known *via* the senses,"[11] under the aegis of understanding or cognition. Sensation, Kant says, may give rise to pleasure but in order to be able to judge something to be beautiful, our sensation must engage our capacities for reflective contemplation. The outer, external, or bodily sense of *aesthesis,* as distinct from the sense of inner consciousness, would thus appear to lose both its priority (Whitehead) and its distinctiveness (Bakhtin).

Most famously reflected in Ludwig Wittgenstein's (1889–1951) dictum "Aesthetics and Ethics Are One,"[12] it is the still generally accepted link between aesthetic experience and ethics that is Kant's legacy and that which has both figured centrally in, and been most frequently challenged by, neo-aesthetic modes of thought, especially by those that presuppose a central function for affect in our engagement with art. In order to see the operation of the aesthetic in its own right, in terms of affect and singularity and not merely as a transitional force to accomplish something else, it seems, then, that we need to get a grip on or, better still, effectively disentangle the persistently recurring link between ethics and aesthetics. For if we follow Whitehead in his contention that the basis of all experience is "emotional," that the "basic fact is the rise of an affective tone originating from things whose relevance is given," then we need to study the affective operations of art as distinct from reflective contemplation, "before," as it were, they become subject to the sway of concepts, or Kant's Categories. After all, for Whitehead, *aesthesis,* or sense-perceptual experience, is largely unconscious and thus has little to do with understanding and cognition. Indeed, he takes this supposition even further in *Adventures of Ideas* (hereafter *AI*) by additionally pointing out that the "notion of mere knowledge is a high abstraction" and that "conscious discrimination itself is a variable factor only present in the more elaborate examples of occasions of experience" (175–76). Reflective contemplation in a Kantian sense is therefore not an immediate part of the a priori "prehension" of an object, the "special activity" that is provoked within a subject in its encounter with the world and with what is in the world, that is, the constructive activity that calls the subject into existence in the very "occasion of experience" (*AI*, 176).

Furthermore, in order to approach the aesthetic on its own terms, it is not only necessary to differentiate between aesthetics/intuition and ethics/cognition on one hand, but also, on the other, and no less importantly, between aesthetic inquiry and hermeneutics. For aesthetic hermeneutics, especially in the tradition of the German philosopher Hans-Georg Gadamer (1900–2002), is primarily concerned with our *comprehension,* our conscious awareness and understanding, or even with the mastering of our experience of aesthetic pleasure, rather than with *prehension,* with the occasion of aesthetic experience (qua activity) as such. Aesthetic hermeneutics also lands us squarely in the domain of phenomenology with its central concern for individual comprehension and, therewith, under the assumption of a subject that exists prior to and that "intends" the world and its objects, rather than a subject that is constituted in the very encounter with the world.[13]

Both the ethical and hermeneutic traditions of thought in art history and criticism prove hard to shed, or even to sidestep, in the hierarchy of established and generally respected disciplinary approaches. As Gabrielle Starr points out in her essay "Ethics, Meaning, and the Work of Beauty" (2002), many contemporary critics "tend to reenact the welding of categories at the heart of eighteenth-century British aesthetics," extending the "merging of aesthetic inquiry with ethics or hermeneutics" so that the function of the aesthetic itself tends to get eclipsed by its presumed "ontological and disciplinary superiors."[14] Whereas it would make no sense, of course, to deny that the aesthetic has ethical, social, or hermeneutic significance, it still remains critical, as Starr correctly stipulates, to acknowledge that "neither ethics nor hermeneutics can answer aesthetic questions."[15]

Before continuing to trace the more elaborate thread that traditionally connects ethics to aesthetics, let me take a moment to discuss an example in which the limitations of the latter project's traditionally "significant other" (i.e., hermeneutics) become strikingly clear. The example is drawn from a mode of art criticism that has gained a certain popularity under the various rubrics of "visual narrative" or "visual narratology," and which thus finds its origins in a methodology invented to study the operation of narrative texts, even if it tends to be substantially reconceived when applied to nonverbal art.

Narrative, writes Shlomith Rimmon-Kenan, one of the founding voices in narratology, in her essay "Concepts of Narrative" (2006), has become an omnipresent term in current thought and discourse, flying across a variety of media and disciplines—or interdisciplines—within which it has acquired equally varied meanings and implications.[16] Starting from her own early definition as "the narration of a succession of fictional events,"[17] a definition that hinges upon the two minimal requirements of a "double temporality" and the "act of mediation or transmission which . . . is verbal," Rimmon-Kenan makes a distinction between concepts of narrative deriving from narratology and those adopted in relation to psychoanalysis, ideology, and the "notion of 'storied lives.'"[18] While deploring the far too "elastic" nature of the latter three and bemoaning their implied neglect of the "formal properties dear to narratologists,"[19] she is nonetheless willing to accede to a broadening of the concept from within narratology itself, an expanded use of the term based on the Russian formalist distinction between *fabula* and *suzjet.*[20] In the sense of *fabula,* Rimmon-Kenan concedes, narrative "was 'always already' . . . open to shaping in different media," in that both "events are open to representation in different media," and their "scope has been open to interpretation both within narratology and beyond."[21] In contrast, narrative as *suzjet,* she insists, is and must remain both language-bound and restricted, as it was originally understood, to "*artistic* composition," as distinct from other modes of verbal organization.[22]

While acknowledging the potentially enriching effects of a given concept's adoption by and within other disciplines, and applauding the possibilities such conceptual travels offer for rethinking it, Rimmon-Kenan also warns against the dangers of collapsing the *differentia specifica* of narrative in the narrow sense into those of the artistic and non-artistic modes of expression or discursive formations with which it shares what Wittgenstein has called some "family resemblance."[23] Eventually, in the final section of her essay, titled "A Modest Proposal," she suggests reserving the term "narrative" for those discursive formations in which a double temporality and a "transmitting (or mediating) agency" are dominant, and to attribute no more than "narrative elements" to those that do not meet these two requirements.[24]

No such qualms about conceptual purity appear to beset another seminal figure in the field of narratology, the versatile, exuberantly interdisciplinary critical theorist Mieke Bal. In her "reading" of artist and sculptor Louise Bourgeois's multimedia *Spider* and *Cells* series (see figures 2.1 and 2.2)—installations that because of their abstractly architectural qualities would definitely fall outside the realm of narrative art as conceived by Rimmon-Kenan—Bal takes the concept and operation of narrative to be the central and defining aspect of these extremely powerful works.

While deploring what she describes as an "overdose of narrativity" in the "cul-

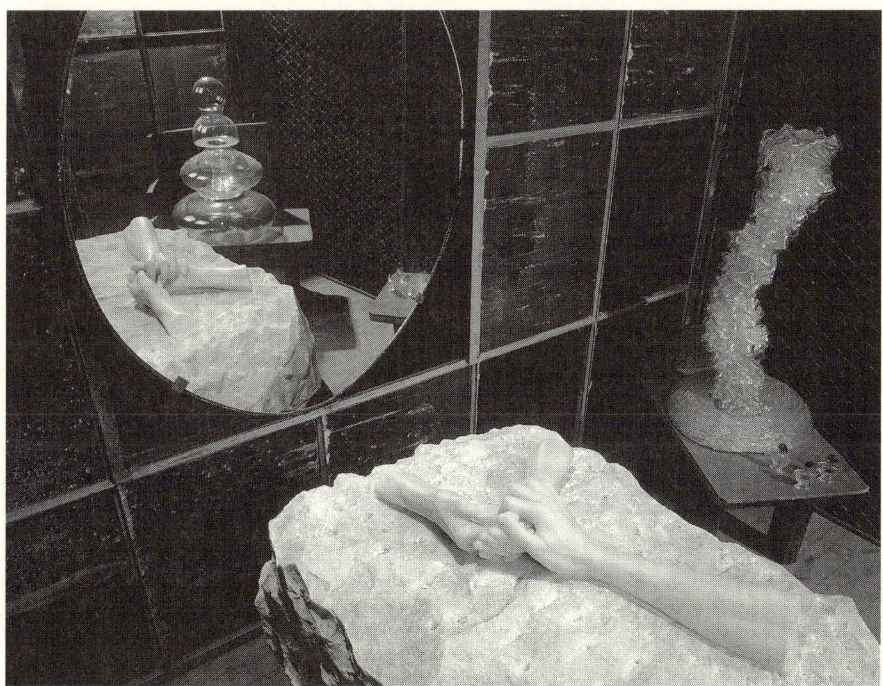

FIG. 2.1 Louise Bourgeois, *Cell (You Better Grow Up)*, 1993 (detail). Steel, glass, marble, ceramic, and wood, 83 × 82 × 83½ in. The Rachofsky Collection. Photo: Peter Bellamy.

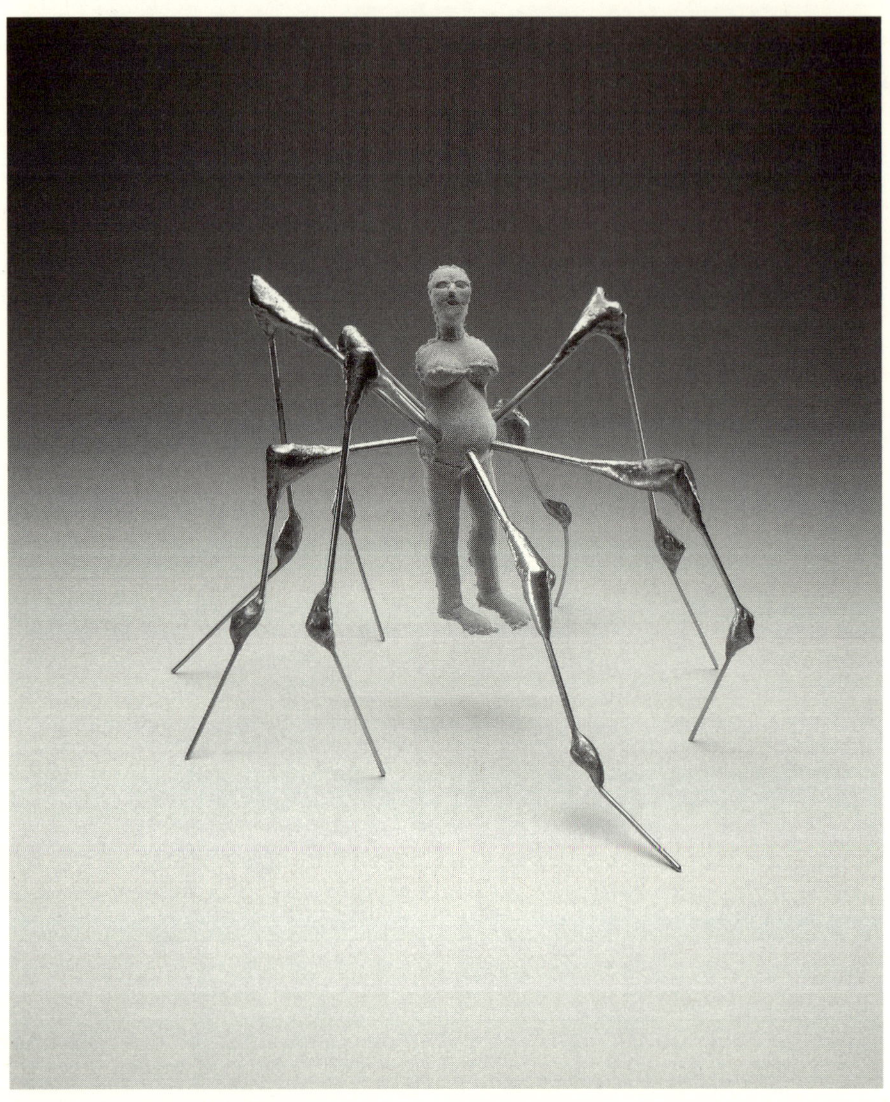

FIG. 2.2 Louise Bourgeois, *Spider,* 2003. Stainless steel and fabric, 9 × 12 × 14 in.
Private Collection. Photo: Christopher Burke. © Louise Bourgeois Trust / Licensed by
VAGA, New York, NY

ture within which art functions today," Bal nonetheless insists that narrative is a "function of Bourgeois's architecture" because the artist "uniquely . . . infuses form, including the form that informs her work's architecturality, with memory."[25] Bal's project in this essay, however, does not just concern the function of narrative in Bourgeois's work; her secondary purpose is—by positing narrative as a "tool," a "mediator," and a "participant"—to evoke Bourgeois as a "philosopher and art critic who offers a theoretical position on the role of narrative in the discourse on art."[26] Clearly not content with merely offering a "modest proposal" about the function of narrative in visual art, Bal's argument meanders through a wide range of theoretical issues, a trajectory in which Bourgeois's work—or, rather, Bal's own instrumental "reading" of it—serves as the site of ultimate proof, that is to say, as the manifestation of the rivalry between the "narrative of viewing" and the "narrative of memory," which the critic suggests to be the indeterminable yet undeniably "sense[d]" bedrock of Bourgeois's work[27] and which, in the final instance, "emerges victorious" against its rival, the force of Bal's own pages-long narrative of description.[28]

To be sure, I do not have any problems with Bal's suggestion that Bourgeois's serial work, evolving over an extended period of time and only to be engaged within an equally extended period of viewing—as the critic quite rightly points out, "viewing is by definition a process"—imposes an awareness of temporality.[29] Nor would I contest her attribution of a certain degree of narrativity—what Rimmon-Kenan calls "narrative elements"—to nonverbal, in this case sculptural, artifacts. After all, as Marie-Laure Ryan reminds us, "from its earliest days on, narratology has been conceived as a project that transcends disciplines and media," a project, moreover, that has French structuralism, more particularly Roland Barthes and Claude Bremond, to thank for the emancipation of narrative from literature and from fiction and for recognizing it as a semiotic phenomenon "present" not only within literature and fiction, but also within "oral conversation, drama, film, painting, dance, and mime."[30] Nor do I find Bal's argument that Bourgeois' work offers a new kind of narrative by "articulat[ing] and activat[ing] temporality" entirely unconvincing.[31] What I do find fault with, however, is first, the suggested *primacy* of narrative in Bourgeois's artwork, to the neglect of its purely visual dimensions (after all, we *see,* rather than *read,* sculpture), and second, that Bal's entire argument is grounded in the idea that every single narrative aspect of Bourgeois's work is ultimately reducible to an undefined concept of "memory." Memories attributed to the artist and memories of the viewer, both evoked by the work and in the descriptive account of the critic's experience of viewing the work *after* the event, are interchangeably presented as the constitutive parts of a "*visual* narrative," defined as a question not so much of "tell[ing]," but of "*build*[ing] a story."[32]

In addition to striking me as a primarily semiotic project rather than as an attempt to ask aesthetic questions, as distinct from ethical or hermeneutic ones, the argument here seems to flounder on Bal's eagerness to read *stories* into, instead of merely acknowledging the narrative aspects of Bourgeois's complex, and as an aesthetic event, unique and singular work. The contradictions of the narratologist's multiple investments in the project of art interpretation come even more poignantly to the fore when she eventually tries to analyze the undeniably representational elements in the artist's "visual narrative" while simultaneously insisting upon the works' unreadability: "Iconographically speaking," Bal maintains, Bourgeois's "work is non- or even antifigurative. At the same time it is far from abstract. Wildly figurative in fact, it nevertheless precludes an analysis that relies on figuration. It is as bodily as it is, and as such it is unreadable"[33]—an assessment with which I heartily agree. The larger part of her essay, however, is precisely an attempt at "reading" these works, more specifically, at bringing close reading practices from literary studies to the study of visual art.[34]

In singling out a narratological approach to suggest the limitations of aesthetic hermeneutics in trying critically to address artworks in their "special, distinctive quality as well as [their] infinite potential," I do not mean to contest the use of the term "narrative" as inappropriately used outside the context of fictional language, for works of visual art obviously may evoke all kinds of stories in a recipient or spectator. The problem arising from Bal's expanded use of narrative or narrativity in her approach to Bourgeois's (and other contemporary artists') work, however, is the interpretive framework's ultimate inadequacy to address the aesthetic dimension, the way the work affects me, how it makes me feel. Put differently, and with reference to Kant, my active experience of these works may well give rise to ideas at the very occasion of my prehension, but such ideas are essentially aesthetic in nature; they are "inner intuitions to which no concept can be completely adequate." As the "counterpart (pendant) of a *rational idea*," to which "no *intuition* (presentation of the imagination) can be adequate," the "aesthetic idea," for Kant, may well be called an "idea," because it "at least strive[s] toward something that lies beyond the bounds of experience." Yet as a "presentation of the imagination," the aesthetic idea "prompts much thought" to which "no determinate thought whatsoever . . . can be adequate, so that no language can express it completely and allow us to grasp it" (*CJ*, 182–83). By insisting on the primacy of narrative in Bourgeois's *Spiders* and *Cells*, Bal loses sight of precisely that which makes these works, in effect, "unreadable," the ineffable aesthetic feelings prompted in and by the occasion of our actual (ap)prehension of them.

If the project of a neo-aesthetics has any viability, that is to say, if there is anything "new" to be thought in the context of the affective turn and, thus, if a so-called new aestheticism is to amount to something more than a reinforcement of several of the main tenets of eighteenth-century theories of art, and therefore be able to answer aesthetic questions rather than ethical and hermeneutical ones, it seems clear that aesthetic inquiry should not be made to produce meanings that are the central concern of other branches of critical thought, but rather should ask what kinds of questions aesthetic inquiry can raise (and perhaps answer) that ethical and hermeneutic inquiries by definition cannot.

Two problems appear to emerge at this point. First, how are we to distinguish between objects and experience in conducting aesthetic inquiry? And second, given that aesthetic experience fundamentally involves affect, sense-perception, and/or intuition, rather than conscious understanding and cognition, how are we to analyze its operations when, as Isobel Armstrong has argued, for affect "we have no (or few) terms of analysis"?[35] As to the first problem, I wish briefly to return to an aspect of Whitehead's re-articulation of the subject-object relation as discussed in the previous chapter. We recall that Whitehead accepts the philosophical account of this relation as the "fundamental structural pattern of experience" but that he departs from the prevailing Cartesian model in which it is cast as the "bare relation of knower to known" (*AI*, 175). Instead, as we have seen, he defines a "prehension" as consisting in the three factors of the encounter, the "occasion of experience" itself, the "datum" that provokes the activity, and the "subjective form, which is the affective tone determining the effectiveness of that prehension in that occasion of experience" (*AI*, 176). This means, as suggested before, that no experience of any object can ever be exactly repeated and that, in line with Kant's critical aestheticism, the aesthetic value of an object cannot be fixed over time and space. This is the case, first of all, because spatiotemporality is neither objective and real, nor a substance, nor an accident, nor a relation. Instead, spatiotemporality is subjective in nature in that it originates from the mind in its attempt to coordinate everything "sensed externally," which is the same as to say, the way we experience the world *aesthetically.* Second, and perhaps more importantly, because even if the object provokes the occasion of its relevance, it is what Whitehead calls the "subjective form" and that which becomes the "occasion of an absolute reality," which "enjoys its decisive moment of absolute self-attainment as emotional unity" (*AI*, 177).

Since experience generally is the occasion, the "moment" at which the subject is born and at which it is born anew in its singularity, over and over again, as so many "fresh events" in an ongoing process of discontinuous transformation, aesthetic experiences not only change in one person from that of another, as much as they change cross-culturally and historically, but they also "bring forth," in a Heideggerian sense, the subject itself as a "threshold occasion" that will never be the same from one occasion to the next. Hence, what we subsequently *make* of a certain aesthetic experience, that is to say, in reflective contemplation *after* the event,[36] is an effect of critical thought, subject to the law of reason rather than the effects of the activity of experience itself. The changeability of the experiential effects of such occasions thus implies that aesthetic experience is by definition transient and elusive, a circumstance that simultaneously differentiates the ways artistic objects work and what they do from what critical discourse tries to capture about them within the determinate system of language or cognitive evaluation.

As to the second problem, the relative lack of terms or tools of analysis when dealing with experiences that are essentially affective in nature, I propose that it may be necessary, at least for the moment, to suspend the critical need for analytical closure and focus instead on the possibilities for actualization that are opened up in/by the aesthetic event, possibilities that emerge precisely because of its transient character. Thinking tools that may nonetheless be helpful in approaching the transformative makings and doings of the aesthetic can be found in, if not quite an alternative, then definitely a complement to the post-Kantian tradition of aesthetic theory, one that runs from the eighteenth-century English painter, satirist, and writer William Hogarth to the twentieth-century French philosophers Gilles Deleuze and Félix Guattari. The connection between these respective thinkers is not only the generally acknowledged "radical" character of their ideas in defiance of dominant post-Kantian modes of aesthetic inquiry, but also, and more relevant to my purposes here, the conceptual echoes between the former's notion of the "serpentine line" in art or aesthetics and the latter's elaborations of the "lines of flight" operative in overall processes of creativity.[37] In order to clarify these conceptual echoes, a brief detour is required through a third critical term, one that has not coincidentally frequently been associated with the work of Louise Bourgeois, and that is the notion of the abject. I paradoxically invoke this term in order to connect Deleuze and Guattari's concept of "becoming" with both Kant's and Whitehead's notions of "beauty" so as to approach the function of art, in its *differentia specifica,* and in the occasion of its actualization, on the level of affect.

In proposing the abject as a critical hinge in trying to think through an operational form of aesthetic inquiry that does not immediately threaten to collapse into ethics or hermeneutics, I do not mean merely to evoke images of objects of disgust. I am thus not using the term in the sense of lacking in dignity or falling short of the standards befitting humans, or the state of being cast out. Instead, I put "the abject" to use in its more abstract sense, as that which falls outside the established order of signification and/or symbolization, as a site where the relationship between signifier and signified collapses, and as a moment that escapes determination and the materiality of objects while yet maintaining its connections to the real world in that it only obtains in the actualization of the aesthetic event.

There are, in effect, two aspects of the notion of the abject as it has gained currency in critical theory and art criticism, following Julia Kristeva's conceptualization of it in *Powers of Horror: An Essay on Abjection* (1982), which are relevant in this context. First, the sense in which the abject dissolves the traditional distinction between subject and object. Kristeva articulates this as follows:

> The abject is not an ob-ject facing me, which I name or imagine. Nor is it an ob-jest, an otherness ceaselessly fleeing in a systematic quest of desire. What is abject is not my correlative, which, providing me with someone or something else as support, would allow me to be more or less detached and autonomous. The abject has only one quality of the object—that of being opposed to it.[38]

Building upon the seminal work *Purity and Danger: An Analysis of Concepts of Pollution and Taboo* (1966) by social anthropologist Mary Douglas,[39] the second aspect that is central to Kristeva's psychoanalytically inspired notion of abjection is its designation of our complex response, a mix of revulsion of and desire for bodily fluids, open wounds, sexual detritus, vomit, slime, spittle, menstrual blood, sperm, putrefaction, and decay. While additionally picked up by Judith Butler in *Bodies That Matter* (1993) to designate the constitutive outside to the domain of the subject, the site where those abjected from society, such as women and homosexuals, are supposed to dwell,[40] it is this second aspect, the idea of the abject as a moment of "horror and wonder," that has since Dada been primarily evoked in relation to art and with respect to successive artistic movements that deliberately set out to transgress against and threaten established standards of propriety. The actual phrase "abject art" has nonetheless only gained particular currency since the Whitney Museum in New York gave these movements their name by staging an exhibition in 1993 titled "Abject Art: Repulsion and Desire in American Art,"[41] which included work by such mainstream artists as Louise Bourgeois, Helen Chadwick, Gilbert and George, Robert Gober, Carolee Schneemann, and Jake and Dinos Chapman (see figures 2.3 and 2.4), while at the time more marginal figures such as Cindy Sherman, Kiki Smith, Ron Mueck, Sarah Lucas, and Sam Taylor-Wood are also generally regarded as key contributors to the abject in art (see figures 2.5 through 2.7).

Using the term "abject" in connection with art inevitably evokes the sense in which it has largely been used in contemporary art criticism, even if the transgressive potential of the work of some of the artists most frequently tagged as "abject art" appears to have substantially worn off since their co-optation by/within the artistic establishment and critical community. As respectable citizens of the dominant art world, the once "minoritarian" visual discourse of some of the artists mentioned above has lost much if not all of its power to shock or to

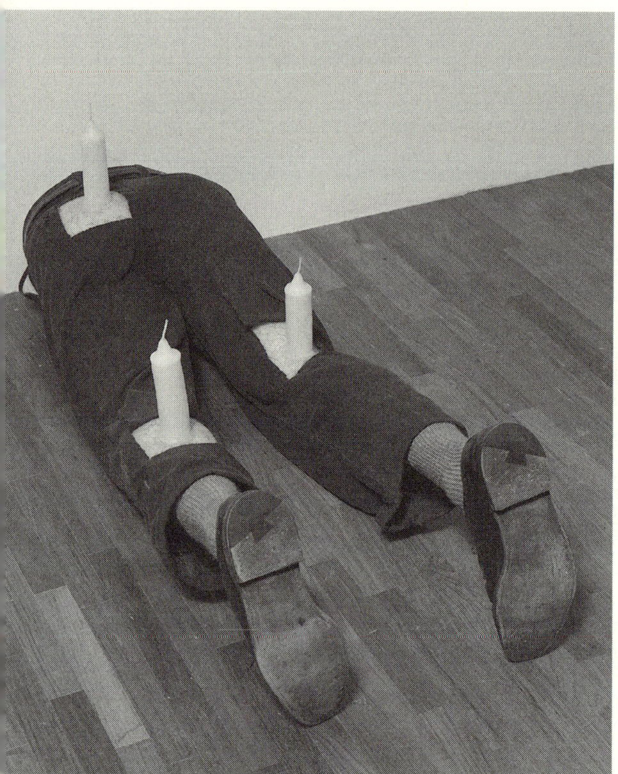

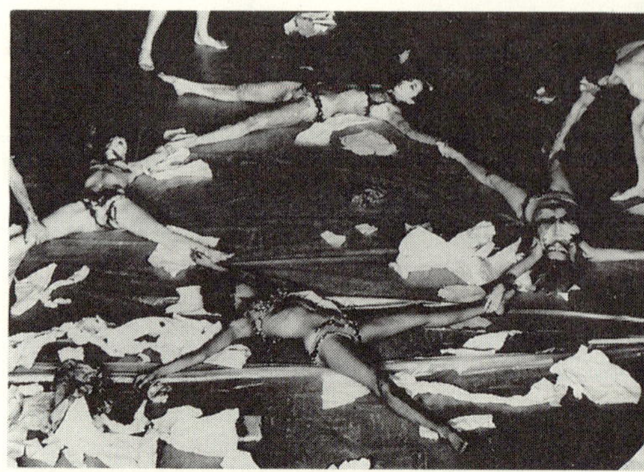

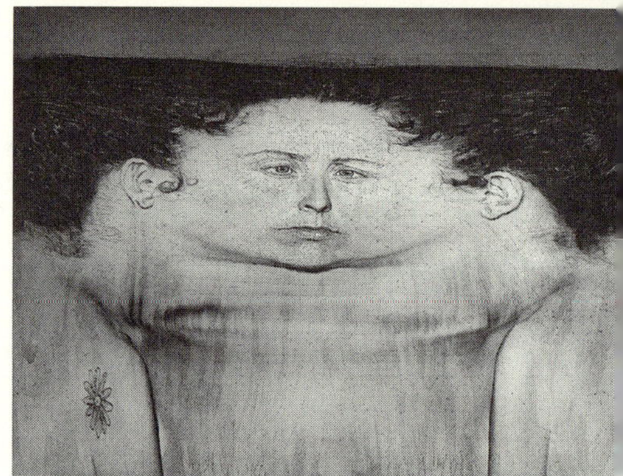

FIG. 2.3 *(left)* Robert Gober, *Untitled,* 1991. Wood, beeswax, leather, fabric, and human hair, 13¼ × 16½ × 45⅛ in. (33.6 × 41.9 × 117.2 cm). The Museum of Modern Art, New York. Gift of Werner and Elaine Dannheisser (173.1996). © Robert Gober, Courtesy of Matthew Marks Gallery. Digital image © The Museum of Modern Art / Licensed by SCALA / Art Resource, NY

FIG. 2.4 *(right top)* Carolee Schneemann, *Meat Joy,* 1964. © Carolee Schneemann. Photo: Tony Ray-Jones, 1964

FIG. 2.5 *(right bottom)* Kiki Smith, *My Blue Lake,* 1995. Photogravure, *à la poupée* inking and lithograph on mold-made En Tout Cas paper, edition 11/41, 43½ × 54¾ in. (110.4 × 139 cm). Albright-Knox Art Gallery, Buffalo, New York. © Kiki Smith and Universal Limited Art Editions, Inc. Photo: Albright-Knox Gallery / Art Resource, NY

produce outrage or disgust. While this does not mean that these works have also lost their deterritorializing force, to use the terms of Deleuze and Guattari, it does mean that the qualification "abject" no longer appears to apply or to suggest anything meaningful about the function of these works in the "concern" they are likely to provoke in the experience of the contemporary spectator.

The reason I introduce the abject in the context of an attempt to think through neo-aesthetic activity is therefore not that I wish to retain the second aspect of Kristeva's influential formulation, that is, its association with revulsion and

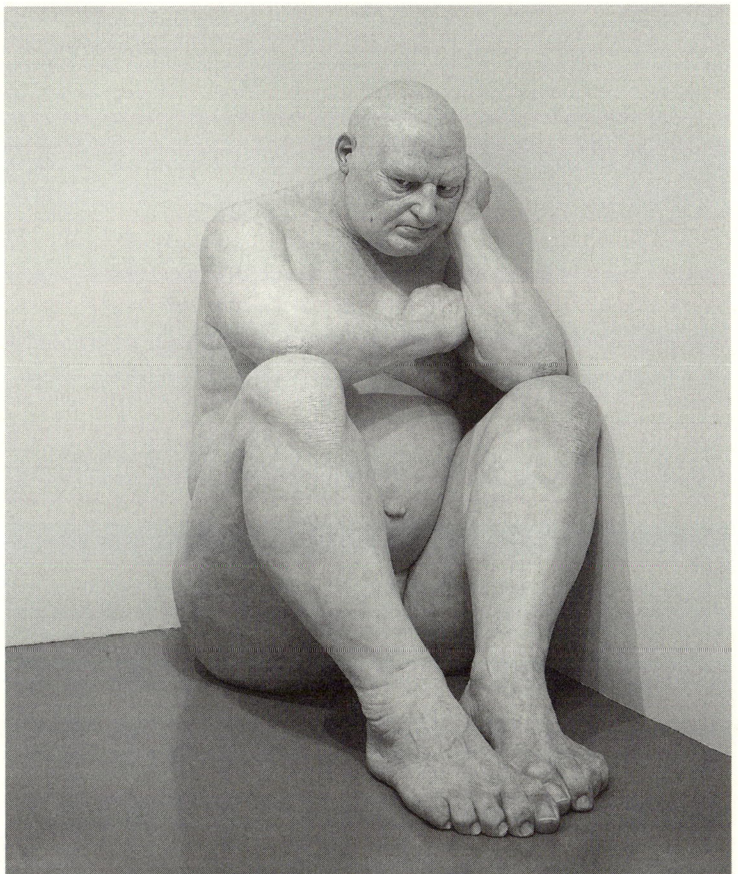

FIG. 2.6 Ron Mueck, *Untitled (Big Man),* 2000. Pigmented polyester resin on fiberglass, 80¼ × 47½ × 80½ in. (203.8 × 120.7 × 204.5 cm). Hirshhorn Museum and Sculpture Garden, Smithsonian Institution, Museum Purchase with Funds Provided by the Joseph H. Hirshhorn Bequest and in Honor of Robert Lehrman, Chairman of the Board of Trustees, 1997–2004, for his extraordinary leadership and unstinting service to the Hirshhorn Museum and Sculpture Garden.   Photo: Lee Stalsworth

disgust, explored within a largely psychoanalytic framework. It is the first, more philosophically framed problematic of the subject-object relation of the Kristevan notion of abjection that interests me, that is to say, a sense of the abject in which it was originally introduced by the French surrealist Georges Bataille (1897–1962), in its connection with and distinction from the latter's concept of "formless," or the *informe,* which he elaborated in the "critical dictionary" published in his periodical *Documents* (1929–1930). In its ostensible simplicity, and because of its current notoriety, it is worth quoting Bataille's entry on the *informe* in full:

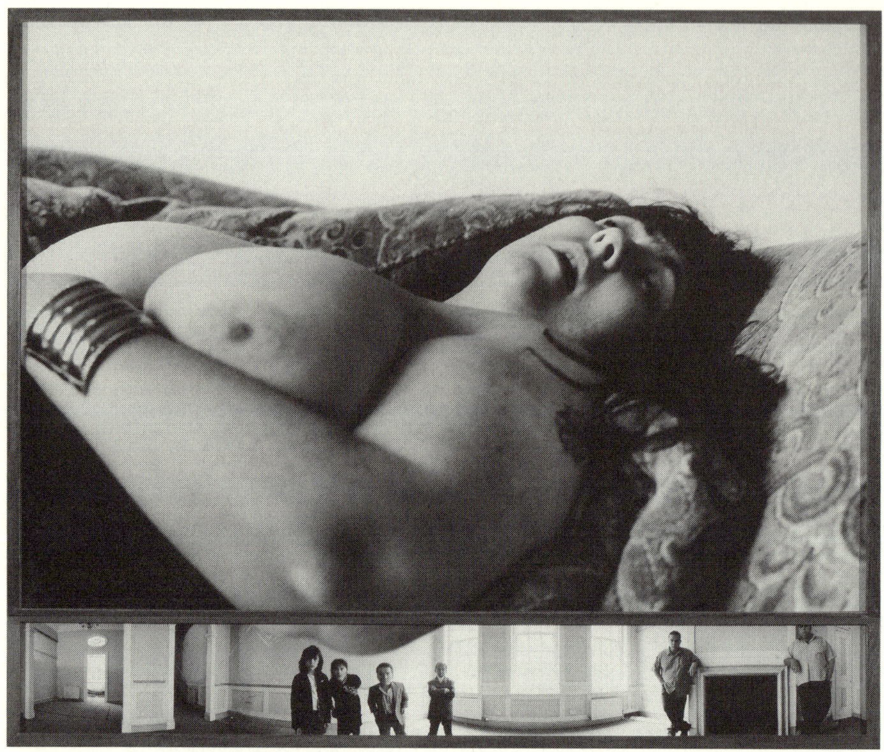

FIG. 2.7 Sam Taylor-Wood, *Soliloquy IV,* 1998. C-type color photograph in artist's
wood frame, 87 × 101 in. (221 × 256.5 cm). Hirshhorn Museum and Sculpture Garden,
Smithsonian Institution, Gift of Heather and Tony Podesta Collection, 2003.
Photo: Lee Stalsworth

A dictionary begins when it no longer gives the meaning of words, but their tasks.
Thus formless is not only an adjective having a given meaning, but a term that
serves to bring things down in the world, generally requiring that each thing have
its form. What it designates has no rights in any sense and gets itself squashed
everywhere, like a spider or an earthworm. In fact, for academic men to be happy,
the universe would have to take shape. All of philosophy has no other goal: it is a
matter of giving a frock coat to what is, a mathematical frock coat. On the other
hand, affirming that the universe resembles nothing and is only formless amounts
to saying that the universe is something like a spider or spit.[42]

While often seen as closely related terms, the differences between the "abject"
and the *informe,* as used with respect to contemporary art practice, are nonetheless considerable. Indeed, as Rosalind Krauss has suggested, in its thematization of the marginalized, the traumatized, and the wounded, much of what is

categorized as "abject art" in fact runs counter to the idea of the *informe* in that it produces a "thematics of essences and substances" that advances a semantic engagement with the work rather than foregrounding its operations as a "process of 'alteration,' in which there are no essentialized or fixed terms, but only energies within a force field, energies that, for example, operate on the very words that mark the poles of that field in such a way as to make them incapable of holding fast the term of any opposition," whether between subject and object, pure and impure, inside and outside, or signifier and signified.[43] That I would still, for the moment and albeit provisionally, like to hold on to the term abject, rather than fully revert to Bataille's notion of the *informe,* has to do with the fact that, first, the qualification still appears to have some purchase in art critical discussions, and second, because, in its boundlessness, in its insistence on breaking down borders, provoking both horror and wonder, the abject resonates remarkably with the Kantian sublime, to which I will turn below.

Thinking of the abject *operationally,* as suggested by Bataille's term the *informe,* and as distinct from the thematization of the marginalized, the traumatized, and the wounded, privileged by the conventional art critical use of the term, the concept of abjection would refer to the splitting apart of meaning from within, to the unassimilable, nonrepresentational, fundamentally processual aspects of the aesthetic event that effectively resist or actually foreclose its recuperation within either the project of ethics or the practice of hermeneutics. Seen in this light, Stockhausen's comments on the collapse of the twin towers, whose endlessly repeated televised relays kept us all glued to the screen in fear and fascination, do not so much suggest a fundamental lack of good taste or insensitivity on the part of the septuagenarian composer, but rather a keen insight into the compelling force of the abject, that is to say, *not* as a quality or an essential aspect of any object, but as a singular response or reaction, as a particular structure of experience in a Whiteheadian sense, where the "occasion" of experience "at once places the object as a component in the experience of the subject, with an affective tone drawn from this object and directed towards it" (*AI,* 176). In a day and age in which little, if anything at all, has retained its power to shock, to destabilize, and, with specific respect to art, to resist co-optation and assimilation into an increasingly market-driven, commercialized art world, it was perhaps the unimaginable mediated reality of 9/11 that was still capable of generating the "abject" feelings of horror-*cum*-wonder, the ambivalence of what Kant calls the *"terrifying sublime."*[44]

By not entirely disconnecting the abject from the *informe,* as Krauss appears to advocate in the essay cited above, it becomes possible first to foreground the fundamental interdependence of the terms in the subject-object relation while not losing sight of the fact that the (abject) object is nonetheless given, something to be received, potentiality to be actualized in the occasion that is the subject/ experience, and that the only reason for its actualization is, in Whitehead's words, our active "concern" for it, concern "divested of any suggestion of knowledge" (*AI*, 176), including the modes of knowing required for ethical judgments. Second, by retaining a notion of the abject in an operational sense, as an entity in a process of alteration in which the critical term is what Whitehead identifies as the "subjective form," that is, the affective tone that permeates our immediate perception (prehension), we can not only recognize the appeal of that which, in a rational sense, would merely provoke our revulsion and disgust (and thus the fact that such effects wear off and are fundamentally contingent), but also that the difference between the attractive and the repulsive, the beautiful and the sublime, is one of degree rather than kind. That is to say, it is a difference not so much in terms of an opposition as one originating in the degree of affective intensity that marks the occasion of highly differentiated aesthetic experiences—experiences that, critically, include a sense of beauty.

To be sure, to bring beauty into a discussion of contemporary aesthetics is a risky, if not regressive, undertaking. As Shaviro aptly points out, "most aesthetic theorists and innovative artists of the twentieth century tend to disparage the very idea of beauty" and to privilege the sublime for its "disruptive, transformative, potentially redemptive" qualities, in comparison to which beauty appears "staid, conservative, and recuperative." Shaviro continues to suggest that there are also considerable political risks involved in returning to or hanging on to the notion of beauty, in that "beauty" today has become, on one hand, a "mere adjunct of advertising and product design," and, on the other, is "exalted as an eternal value, an essential attribute of great art, something that miraculously transcends, and nullifies, all social and political (let alone commercial) considerations" (*WC*, 153, 154). In this section of *Without Criteria*, it is Shaviro's aim to elucidate the ways in which Whitehead's aestheticism, even if the latter does not "himself offer us any concepts of directly political import," is nonetheless "radical enough that it nudges and cajoles us away from the complacencies and satisfactions of commodity culture" (*WC*, 157, 159). My desire to "return" to beauty must be understood in the more narrowly defined terms of my major concern in this chapter, which is the specific, if not privileged, position of art as a transformative force field in the context of a general aesthetics of existence.

In interrogating the relations between beauty on one hand, and the abject, the *informe,* and the *"terrifying sublime"* on the other, I follow Kant and Whitehead in the supposition that in distinguishing among such qualifications, we are not making a distinction between object-immanent qualities but instead between different feelings or affects. As Kant writes in *Observations on the Feeling of the Beautiful and the Sublime* (hereafter *BS*), the "various feelings of enjoyment or of displeasure rest not so much upon the nature of the external things that arouse them as upon each person's own disposition to be moved by these to pleasure or pain" (*BS*, 45). This does not mean that such feelings of "pleasure or pain" are merely personal, solely the effect of individual predilections or taste. To the extent that all our affective reactions to the world are largely unconscious and hence prepersonal, a judgment of taste, in Shaviro's words, "involves an uncoerced *response,* on the part of the subject, to the object that is being judged beautiful" (*WC*, 2). The object that produces the occasion of our experience presents itself, in Whitehead's compelling phrase, as a "lure for feeling" (*Process and Reality* [hereafter *PR*], 25),[45] and it is in the way we uncoercedly respond that the subjective form is actualized. Whitehead infers from this that the "only actuality implicated in the subjective form is the immediate occasion in process of self-formation" (*AI*, 254).

The moment I part ways with both Kant and Whitehead is, it will be clear, in their insistence on a strict separation between beauty and the sublime. If the difference between these two basic forms of aesthetic experience is, in Shaviro's helpful gloss, that the "sublime is about immensity, excess, and disproportion" and "concerned with questioning the limits of representation and form," whereas beauty is "about harmony and proportion" and "entirely contained within, and satisfied with, those limits" (*WC*, 153), it would appear that this difference, in oversimplified terms, revolves around the separation between the formed and the formless or, more precisely, between form and the *informe.* To the extent that the function of all art, at a minimum, is to provide us with unexpected "lures for feeling," to prevent us from succumbing to the ease of nonfeeling, the *informe,* as, to recall Krauss's description, a "process of 'alteration,' in which there are no essentialized or fixed terms, but only energies within a force field," is as critical to the operation of the beautiful as it is to the sublime, so that the differential relationship between them is not so much oppositional as it is complementary. As Bataille's dictionary entry on the *informe* makes sufficiently clear, the differential between these two forms of aesthetic experience plays out in art—as much as it does in the (always contingent) distinction between art and non-art—in the degree of intensity that marks each aesthetic fact in its singularity. This, finally, brings me to the suggested conceptual echoes between Hogarth's "serpentine line" and Deleuze and Guattari's "lines of flight."

Originating in the Renaissance *figura serpentinata,* the "serpentine line" finds its paradigmatic definition and exploration in Hogarth's *The Analysis of Beauty* (1753), "written with the view of fixing the fluctuating ideas of taste," as the work's subtitle reads.[46] Hogarth's theory of aesthetics is, like Kant's and like that of most other eighteenth-century thinkers, primarily concerned with natural beauty, with the harmony and grace of natural form, and with the superior beauty of the form of the human body in particular: "The human frame hath more of its

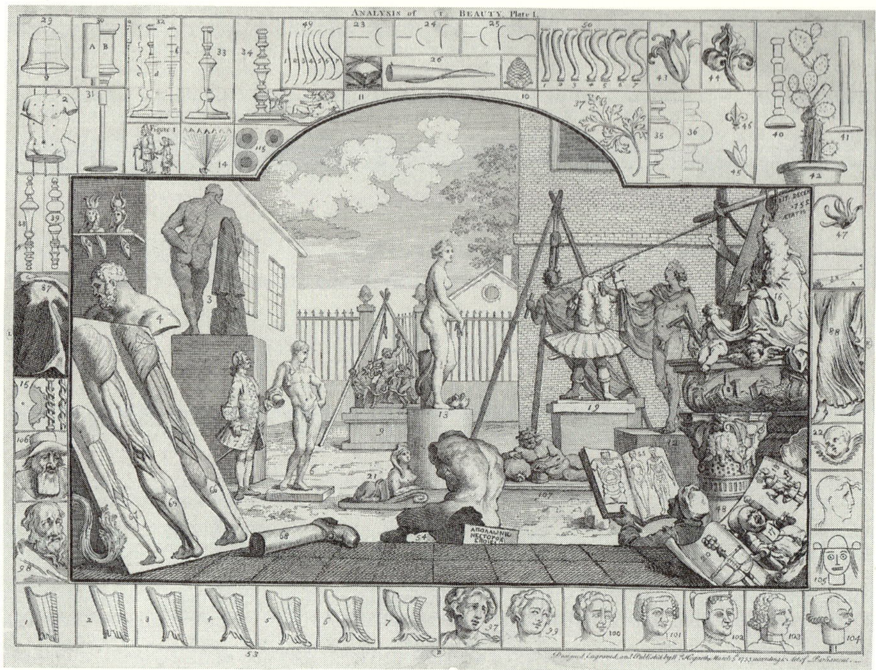

FIG. 2.8 William Hogarth, *Analysis of Beauty, Plate 1*. © The Trustees of the British Museum

parts composed of serpentine-lines than any other object in nature; which is a proof both of its superior beauty to all others, and, at the same time, that its beauty proceeds from those lines." Also defined as the Line of Beauty, the term the "serpentine line" qua form refers to a "two-dimensional waving line that has been twisted so that it spirals into three dimensions" (see figure 2.8).

Despite Hogarth's focus on the classical representation of the graceful human body, the line makes less sense as an actual form than as that which embodies aesthetic desire; it "mimics the processes the mind performs in searching for and in apprehending the beautiful."[47] It is important to bear in mind, though, that some serpentine lines are not beautiful, in the sense that they do not mainly involve "restful contemplation" (Kant). On the contrary, within an object, as the boundary line of an object, or as a virtual boundary line formed by the composition of several objects, serpentine lines generate liveliness or activity and energize the attention of the recipient/spectator, in contrast to straight lines, parallel lines, or right-angled intersecting lines, which convey stasis, finitude, closure. This concept of the serpentine line incorporates and resembles the operation of the Kantian sublime in its encounter with which the "mind feels *agitated*." Such "agitation," says Kant, can be "compared with a vibration, i.e., with a rapid alteration of repulsion from, and attraction to, one and the same object" (*cj*, 115). It also prefigures Whitehead's ostensibly paradoxical—in the sense that it appears to clash with his privileging of the harmonious function of the beautiful over the destructive operation of the sublime—elaboration on the relation between "Harmony and Discord."

"Fortunate experience," Whitehead writes, is the "enjoyment of Harmony," and a "factor in this enjoyment is the intuition that the future . . . is increasing the grounds for Harmony." Destruction is absent from such experience. Yet, he goes on to suggest, "there can be intense experience without Harmony," since the requirement for the new, for novelty, for change to be possible, some form of discord appears to be quintessential: "In Discord there is always a frustration. But even Discord may be preferable to a feeling of a slow relapse into general anaesthesia, or into tameness which is its prelude. Perfection [beauty/form] at a low level ranks below Imperfection [destruction or the sublime/formless] with higher aim" (*AI*, 263–64). Hogarth's Line of Beauty situates such discord and its power to animate, to energize, at the very site where Whitehead conceptualizes "subjective form," as the third, yet critical aspect of the subject-object relation, and thus as a processual phenomenon, rather than as a factor that is immanent either to the object or as a subjective state or condition. By identifying the animating or "agitating" force of the serpentine line *in art* at the very heart of beauty, Hogarth, essentially simply ignoring the dualism of Kantian aesthetics, furthermore anticipates what in the vocabulary of Deleuze and Guattari would become "lines of flight," as characteristic of the "untimely" operations of art and philosophy.[48] I will have more to say about Deleuze's aesthetics in subsequent chapters. I wish to conclude the present one, however, by introducing the idea of "lines of flight" in its specific relation to art further to support my claim to art's *differentia specifica* while still remaining within the framework of the overall aesthetics of experience offered by Whitehead's metaphysics, that is, within his "critique of pure feeling."

Put in oversimplified terms, the notion of "lines of flight," first developed in the second volume of *Capitalism and Schizophrenia: A Thousand Plateaus* (1980/2003; hereafter *TP*)—Deleuze and Guattari's collaborative effort to "construct," in Massumi's phrase, a "smooth space of thought" (*TP*, xiii)—is a specific mode in the overall process of becoming. Approaching things not as substances, as "things in themselves," but as "assemblages" or multiplicities, as well as in terms of unfolding forces, that is, bodies and things in their power to affect and be affected, Deleuze and Guattari invent concepts that foreground the ways things connect rather than how they are. "Reality," for them, is not a given or a mere inversion of the past, but rather the result of tendencies that could evolve in "creative mutations." A line of flight is in this context, then, to borrow Tamsin Lorraine's words, a "path of mutation precipitated through the actualisation of connections among bodies that were previously only implicit (or 'virtual') that releases new powers in the capacities of those bodies to act and respond."[49]

While a "line of flight" is critical for such creative mutations to occur, and whereas they are in fact everywhere—"lines of flight are immanent to the social field" (*TP*, 205)—a line of flight is only one of three kinds of lines that Deleuze and Guattari ascribe to every assemblage in its interaction with the world. There is the "molar" line that sustains the "territorial" connections that define the assemblage, its stability. There is the "molecular" line that is capable of "deterritorializing" or destabilizing the assemblage but the effects of which may be resubjected to stabilization or "reterritorialization." Then there is the line of flight, or the "*cutting edges of deterritorialization,*" that carries away all the assemblage's stabilized, territorial sides, and propels a new, different actualization of connections (*TP*, 88, 89). In distinguishing among these lines, we should bear in mind that—as suggested by the fact that lines of flight are "immanent to the social field," are not substances or fully determinable—the three lines cannot in fact even be neatly separated, for they always coexist and may transform into one another.

Equally importantly, especially in the context of what I have been trying to think through in this chapter, which has been the interrelations and distinctions between aesthetics and ethics on one hand, and those between aesthetics and hermeneutics on the other, is, first, that the line of flight may take up a privileged position in art and philosophy, in that it disconnects singularities or planes of consistency, effecting a process of deterritorialization, the place and nonplace where new mutations may be actualized, where new hybridities, novelty, may be enunciated. This does not mean, however, that its powers are necessarily beneficent or even desirable. Indeed, Deleuze and Guattari emphatically warn us against such an assumption: "The line of flight blasts the two segmentary series apart; but it is capable of the worst, of bouncing off the wall, falling into a black hole, taking the path of greatest regression, and in its vagaries reconstructing the most rigid segments" (*TP*, 205). It is for this reason, because of the unpredictability of its operations in art, in its equal potential for regressive as well as liberatory effects, that the transformative power of the aesthetic as a line of flight, a modality of becoming that breaks through established forms and frames of meaning and being, cannot be equated with the ethical. In effect, the deterritorializing force of the *informe,* as much as that of the line of flight, renders the collapse of the two "projects" not only theoretically unwarrantable, but also fundamentally irresponsible, if not politically dangerous.

Second, the fact that lines of flight, again, particularly in the "privileged" context of artistic activity, may well be seen as a productive force, as the power of becoming anew, precipitating a crossing of boundaries, an escape from figuration, metaphor, and the proper name, does not mean that its operations are meaningful in and of themselves. As we have seen, lines of flight are not given or even entities that are easily separable from the two "segmentary" lines with which they share a "mutual immanence." Deleuze and Guattari write: "It is not easy to sort them out. No one of them is transcendent, each is at work within the others. Immanence everywhere" (*TP*, 205). This means that in an attempt to approach or to trace the function of the aesthetic as a force field, as a provisional coagulation of singular and affective energies, or, in Deleuze's own, much more succinct phrase, as a "bloc of sensations," hermeneutics, being a search for meaning and interpretation, simply falls short. For the lines that compose the artistic assemblage, just as they do any other assemblage, Deleuze and Guattari maintain, essentially "mean nothing":

> It is an affair of cartography. They compose us, as they compose our map. They transform themselves and may even cross over into one another. Rhizome. It is certain that they have nothing to do with language; it is, on the contrary, language that must follow them, it is writing that must take sustenance from them, *between* its own lines. It is certain that they have nothing to do with a signifier, the determination of a subject by the signifier; instead, the signifier arises at the most rigidified level of one of the lines, and the subject is spawned at the lowest level. It is certain they have nothing to do with a structure, which is never occupied by anything more than points and positions . . . and which always forms a closed system, precisely in order to prevent escape. (*TP*, 205)

In order to maintain the possibility of "escape," of the new, of novelty and creativity—which for both Whitehead and Deleuze, Shaviro reminds us, is the "highest criterion for thought" (*WC*, 71)—or, in Heidegger's alternative terms, for the *poietic* function of art to remain viable in an increasingly disagreeable consumerist and politically destructive commodity culture, it is necessary to continue to take the risk of the aesthetic in its indeterminate, if not indeterminable, de- and reterritorializing function, in both its "uncontrollable beauty" and in its essential "untimeliness." Put differently and more poetically, it is necessary to remain open to the "lures for feeling" given in and by art, and to accept the attraction/repulsion force of its violent embrace.

Without denying the ethical, social, or hermeneutic dimensions of aesthetic creation—which would be clearly nonsensical—what needs to be acknowledged is that neither hermeneutics nor ethics can answer aesthetic questions. The encounter with a work of art, as aesthetic experience, consists in the "eventness" of its singularity and in the intensive time of its duration. Irreducible to symbolic meaning, escaping the control of the signifier, and thus neither necessarily pleasant nor reassuring, it is in the *haecceity* of the aesthetic event, qua activity, that we literally find our selves (anew). What this may entail for contemporary art study will be addressed in the next chapter, in which I will pursue my post-Kantian inquiry into aesthetics by continuing my engagement with the work of the decidedly anti-Kantian, schizo-philosophers, Deleuze and Guattari.

THREE NEO-AESTHETICS AND THE STUDY OF THE ARTS OF THE PRESENT

As more than one critic has noted, aesthetics has, since Kant, suffered from what Deleuze calls in *The Logic of Sense* (hereafter *LS*) a "wrenching duality."[1] On one hand, Kant uses the term "aesthetics" to define the objective element of sensation, the theory of sensibility as the form of possible experience, which critically rests on the a priori forms of time and space—this is the "Transcendental Aesthetic" developed in the *Critique of Pure Reason*. On the other hand, Kant deploys the term aesthetics to describe the subjective form of sensation, which, as we have seen in the previous chapter, is the experience of pleasure and/or pain, the conditions of the real, or actual experience, advanced as the theory of beauty (and the sublime) in the *Critique of Judgment*.

Following William James, Deleuze adopts a "radical" or "transcendental" empiricism in his theory of art[2] and insists that we should not impose a priori criteria upon experience but must detect and intuit the conditions of experience from experience itself, and thereby overcome this founding duality of Kantian aesthetics. He claims that "for these two meanings" of aesthetics to be "tied together," the "conditions of experience in general must become conditions of real experience; in this case, the work of art would really appear as experimentation" (*LS*, 260). The groundwork for the more elaborate theory of art he later developed in collaboration with Guattari was laid in Deleuze's fundamental critique of Western metaphysics in what is by some critics considered to be his magnum opus, *Difference and Repetition* (1968; hereafter DR):

> It is strange that aesthetics (as the science of the sensible) could be founded on what can be represented in the sensible. True, the inverse procedure is not much better, consisting of the attempt to withdraw the pure sensible from representation and to determine it as that which remains once the representation is removed (a contradictory flux, for example, or a rhapsody of sensations). Empiricism truly becomes transcendental, and aesthetics an apodictic discipline, only when we apprehend directly in the sensible that which can only be sensed, the very being of the sensible: difference, potential difference and difference in intensity as the reason behind qualitative diversity.[3]

As Daniel A. Smith has phrased it, this proposition entails that the two aspects of aesthetics can be "reunited only at the price of a radical recasting of the transcendental project" so that the conditions of *real* experience become one with the "structure of works of art."[4] My purpose in this chapter is to work through some of the implications of such a "radical recasting" and to explore what a Deleuzian model of art, based on a "transcendental empiricism," may contribute to the development of a neo-aesthetics, an aesthetics that can be claimed as an "apodictic" discipline or, in effect, as a first philosophy, that is, to what extent it might meet the demands of the work done by the works of art today, by the arts of the present, and how we might go about studying such work.

For what does it mean, I ask myself, to study the arts of the present? In what ways or to what extent would this be different from studying the arts of the past? What kind of work does art do in this moment that we call the present, and how can we study such work? Let me begin by clarifying my use of the word "study" in this context, which I do not intend to mean to devote time and attention in order to *acquire knowledge* on or of certain artworks. Rather, I am returning the word to its original basis in the Latin *studium,* meaning "zeal, painstaking application," so as to underline the active, animate, and animating aspects of studying art as activity, to foreground the passion, ardor, appetite, and intensity that come into what Kant (characteristically placidly) calls aesthetic contemplation. In addition to, and perhaps as a result of my desire to foreground the embodied or, to recall Bakhtin, the embodying dimension of aesthetic activity, I take the "study of the arts of the present" necessarily to suggest an approach to artworks that situates itself in the wake of the cultural turn, that is to say, as I put it more precisely in the subtitle of this book, to consider art and aesthetics after representation.[5] This is an immediate consequence of my adoption of a perspective generally inspired by Deleuze and a result of his insistence on the decentering operations of the modern artwork in its "pure presence," and therewith in its "abandonment of representation" (*DR*, 69).

In *Difference and Repetition* (which appeared a year before *The Logic of Sense*), Deleuze brings these two aspects of the study of the modern artwork explicitly together and connects them directly to the "wrenching duality" of post-Kantian aesthetics:

> The elementary concepts of representation are the categories defined as the conditions of possible experience. These, however, are too general or too large for the real. The net is so loose that the largest fish pass through. No wonder, then, that aesthetics should be divided into two irreducible domains: that of the theory of the sensible which captures only the real's conformity with possible experience; and that of the theory of the beautiful, which deals with the reality of the real in so far as it is thought. Everything changes once we determine the conditions of real experience, which are not larger than the conditioned and which differ in kind from the categories: the two senses of the aesthetic become one, to the point where the being of the sensible reveals itself in the work of art, while at the same time the work of art appears as experimentation. (*DR*, 68)

This passage deserves to be quoted in its entirety, first, because Deleuze here effectively extends the Whiteheadian idea of the "reality of the real" as a question of aesthetic experience that nonetheless allows for a differentiation of the artistic encounter in its singularity and specificity, as experimentation, and second, because Deleuze's dismissal of the Kantian categories as the "elementary concepts of representation" points the way to a possible mode of studying art that does not conflate hermeneutic procedures and ethical questions with aesthetic inquiry. Key in this undertaking is the notion of the encounter. An encounter in the Deleuzian sense is, not unlike Whitehead's "prehension," neither restricted to material entities nor defined by what we already know, nor is it determined by the traditional subject-object relation, that is, as an occasion at which one entity runs into or bumps up against another, with both entities existing before the event and remaining intact. An encounter is, Deleuze submits, a "happening" that makes us think. He writes, "Something in the world forces us to think. This something is an object not of recognition but of a fundamental *encounter*. What is encountered may be Socrates, a temple or a demon. It may grasped in a range of affective tones: wonder, love, hatred, suffering. In whichever tone, its primary characteristic is that it can only be sensed" (*DR*, 139). As something that makes or forces us to think, the encounter is something that can only be sensed (or prehended) and is hence aesthetic in nature, that is, prior to thought, and has therefore nothing to do with either (re)cognition or with representation. As defined by Deleuze, an encounter is accordingly not yet caught up in any system of meaning and being, at least in the moment of its occurrence, in its presentness.

Deleuze observes that in recognition, which is immediately related to both representation and to the practice of interpretation, the sensible is not that which can only be sensed, but instead that which "bears directly upon the senses in an object which can be recalled, imagined or conceived," and which engages the exercise of the senses and other faculties in a "common sense," or comprehension. In the encounter, the object is not a "sensible being but the being of the sensible"; it gives rise to "sensibility with regard to a given sense" and is consequently the "imperceptible," the ungraspable, but only so from the perspective of common sense. In the encounter, sensibility reaches its own limits, finds itself before that which cannot be grasped or apprehended by the other faculties, and must thus raise itself to the "level of a transcendental exercise: to the 'nth' power." Since the encounter is a happening both in and of the world, in relation to which common sense functions as a limit to mark off the "specific contribution of sensibility to a joint labour" (*DR*, 139–40)—in that something that can only be sensed is crucial for the possibility of thought—Deleuze's notion of the encounter [*rencontre*] gives us our first glimpse of what a "transcendental empiricist" approach to art permits.

Encounters, Deleuze suggests, are what make work possible, work, that is, that necessarily occurs in solitude: "The only work is moonlighting and is clandestine." Such solitude does not mean that there is nothing there; the workspace/time is densely "populated," not with "dreams, phantasms or plans," but with encounters, which may include people ("sometimes without knowing them"), but also with "movements, ideas, events, entities." Although all these things have proper names, such denominators do not, Deleuze continues, "designate a person or a subject," but rather name an "effect, a zigzag, something which passes or happens between two as though under a potential difference." Being perhaps the "same thing as a becoming, or nuptials,"[6] an encounter thus is a participation, an occasion from which something is taken in order to become something that is neither the property of the one nor of the other, but rather a kind of "double capture," a "double-theft"; it is that which "creates not something mutual, but an asymmetrical block, an a-parallel evolution . . . always 'outside' and 'between'" the forces that create it. Encounters, therefore, do not involve a subject and an object, or even two subjects, and as such do not belong to one or the other, but instead form something "which is between the two, outside the two, and which flows in another direction." As a becoming, the encounter has, as suggested, nothing to do with recognition—which is in fact its opposite; it is not a meeting of two minds, or a question of kindred spirits, but a finding or stealing without any method other than a "long preparation"[7]—what I have called application or zeal, or, indeed, love.

While often evoked in relation to Deleuze's notion of "the fold," especially the folds of friendship as an existential mode of doing philosophy,[8] my interest in the idea of the encounter springs from the fact that as occasions or happenings that force us to think, *rencontres* do not merely involve other human beings but equally include the intensities and multiplicities that constitute the experience of art and literature, of the aesthetic encounter in the narrow sense. In *L'Abécédaire,*[9] Deleuze declares that any form of cultural activity may enable—if it does not form a pre-condition for—the kind of encounter that engages the very possibility of thought and creativity. As the evocation of a "long preparation" indicates, however, such encounters do not necessarily simply "happen." We need to seek them out, we must be on the lookout, with a certain commitment to being open to creatively productive possibility, to new becomings and to new sensations. Nor are these encounters necessarily or merely entertainment: it may be something troubling or amusing that one draws out of an encounter, but any encounter requires that we are being touched, that we are affected. Deleuze therefore encourages us to search for works of art that affect us, that insert us into the fold of the event that operates according to what he calls a "logic of sensation."[10]

For Deleuze, the encounter with an artwork is, in the first place, the precondition for work, for intellectual discovery, the possibility to "get beyond philosophy through philosophy."[11] Yet where philosophy, as a constructivism, consists in the creation of concepts and the laying out of a "plane of immanence" or a "plane of consistency,"[12] art, in contrast, produces percepts and affects. Although he elsewhere maintains that concepts themselves involve the "two dimensions" of percepts and affects,[13] it is in his collaborative work with Guattari, more haphazardly in *A Thousand Plateaus* but more consistently in *What Is Philosophy?* (hereafter *WP*), that Deleuze expressly unfolds his theory of art in terms of sensation, more precisely, of the artwork as a "bloc of sensations," as something functioning in the terms of an assembled logic of sensation.

Bakhtin calls that which escapes both the material form and the symbolic determination of the artwork and that which neither resides in nor springs from the artist/creator, or in/from the reader/spectator, but which is what happens, the event of their "co-creation," the "aesthetic object." In Deleuze, this becomes the something that is preserved in the work of art: "Art preserves, and it is the only thing in the world that is preserved." What is preserved, "and is preserved in itself," however, does not outlast its support or materials: "If art preserves it does not do so like industry, by adding a substance to make the thing last" (*WP*, 163). What is preserved, then, the "thing or the work of art," is a *compound of percepts and affects.* Percepts escape the ones who experience them; they are not perceptions. Affects, similarly, are not feelings or emotions tied to a subject, but the prepersonal forces that make feelings possible in the first place: "Sensations, percepts, and affects are *beings* whose validity lies in themselves and exceeds any lived" (*WP*, 174). "Harnessing forces" that are neither subjective nor objective[14] but that are in the world, that populate the world, that affect us, that make us become, yet that are invisible and inaudible, artworks "wrest the percept from perceptions of objects and from states of a perceiving subject" as much as they "wrest the affect from affections as passage from one state to another" (*WP*, 167). Since their function (or their potentiality) is to "extract a bloc of sensations, a pure being of sensation" from the universe, the work of art is a "being of sensation and nothing else: it exists in itself" (*WP*, 163).

Earlier we have seen Bakhtin struggle with the ostensible contradiction of the nature of the work of art whose aesthetic object does not reside in and cannot be inferred from its material form, while yet exerting its embodying force in the concrete "act of co-creation" that makes up the axiological relationship, the act of striving, qua activity, between the author/creator and the reader/recipient, neither one of whom exists prior to the artistic event. Deleuze and Guattari similarly attempt to get at the *being* of art by stressing the materiality of the artwork, the matter in which it is realized, and the living forces of which it is composed. These forces, the compound of percepts and affects harnessed by/in the work of art, are both nonhuman and prepersonal, and yet material: "We paint, sculpt, compose and write with sensations," but sensation is "not the same thing" as material, in that "sensation is not realized in the material without the material passing completely into the sensation, into the percept or affect. All the material becomes expressive" (*WP*, 166–67). It is as expressive materiality, then, a materiality that passes into sensation, that the artwork can be seen to function as a part of our environment, our lifeworld, and of the ways we orient our embodied selves in the world, within the circulation of the forces of life, of the universe.

In order for material to pass into sensation, to become expressive, and thus to preserve the sensation it embodies—"art preserves, and it is the only thing in the world that is preserved," but it is "only preserved in itself"—the material needs to be worked, to be subjected to a method, to be organized or formed, which takes place on the "plane of composition." When Deleuze and Guattari claim that "composition is the sole definition of art," they do not mean, or at least not only, technical composition or technique, but instead aesthetic composition, "which is the work of sensation." Indeed, "only the latter fully deserves the name *composition,* and a work of art is never produced by or for the sake of technique" (*WP*, 166–67).

The technical plane of composition is "absorbed" by the aesthetic one, and it is "on this condition that matter becomes expressive": either the "compound of sensations is realized in the material, or the material passes into the compound, but always in such a way as to be situated on a specifically aesthetic plane of composition" (*WP*, 196). Just as for Bakhtin the author-creator is present in the artwork only as "organized activity," so does the artist for Deleuze and Guattari wrest percepts and affects from the world of everyday experience in order to use them as compositional elements, to render them expressive, and create sensations *within* the artwork. And only as such do they become available, perceptible to us. New beings of sensation created in the artwork in their turn call us forth in our encounter with it, where every encounter produces us as so many new selves: "Artists are presenters of affects, the inventors and creators of affects. They not only create them in their work, they give them to us and make us become with them, they draw us into the compound" (*WP*, 175). As sensory, aesthetic experience, the encounter with an artwork is activity, an action of becoming, of "ceaselessly becoming-other," in a "matter of expression."[15]

The definition of art as a "bloc of sensation," as a "compound of percepts and affects," enables us, first, to overcome the reductive operations of hermeneutics and/or semantics and to approach artworks in aesthetic terms. Art, when it succeeds, that is to say, when it is genuinely creative and allows for the production of the new, for the possibility of novelty, and for different varieties of becoming-other, does not serve to re-present what is already there, what is already in existence, and thus cannot be a question of representation. As Deleuze puts it in the context of his critique of identity that is the major project of *Difference and Repetition:* "Representation fails to capture the affirmed world of difference. Representation has only a single centre, a unique and receding perspective, and in consequence a false depth. It mediates everything, but mobilises and moves nothing" (*DR*, 55–56).

Second, this radically empiricist approach to art exposes the fallacy of studying art as the work of memory or even as "narratives of memory" (Bal). As presentations, in the matter of expression, of new and different varieties of affect, wresting affects from affections, and thus moving beyond everyday experiences already lived, art rather functions as the opposite of memory, "which summons forth only old perceptions." Deleuze and Guattari write: "It is true that every work of art is a *monument,* but here the monument is not something commemorating a past, it is a bloc of present sensations that owe their preservation only to themselves and that provide the event with the compound that celebrates it. The monument's action is not memory but fabulation" (*WP,* 167–68).[16]

Third and finally, a Deleuzian theory of art, with its central emphasis on composition—"composition is the sole definition of art"—while clearly connected to Whitehead's constructive aestheticism, allows us to preserve the *differentia specifica* of art and to distinguish its function and operations from any other entity in the world that we experience through the senses, as a "bloc of sensations" that exceeds our perceptions and affections, that is, the subjective sensations from which the artwork wrests the nonhuman, nonpersonal compounds of percepts and affects. Whether the sensation realizes itself in matter or, conversely, whether the material passes into sensation itself, the formation of matter on the plane of composition is necessary for matter to become expressive in the artwork.

All this may sound like a kind of neoromantic, all too naive, mystical undertaking, the forces of the universe or the cosmos—or, better, "chaosmos"—being "harnessed" in works of art that themselves are "blocs of sensation," expressive matter. How can we study such works? And what has happened to critique in this life-affirming process of differentiation, of ceaselessly becoming-other? The increasing influence of Deleuzian thought in literary and art criticism, and indeed the affective turn generally, has provoked a range of similar questions, couched in more or less sophisticated dismissive arguments,[17] and, I admit, with a certain legitimacy: the highly allusive style of their writing, the dizzying range of neologisms that populate their works (and that do not stay in place from one work to the next), the radicalness of their ideas, and, perhaps, their close association with "1968" and beyond, do not make for an easy transition between the two schizo-philosophers at the center of the affective turn and the mode of critique that dominated theoretical debates in the era succinctly described as that of the "discursive turn." Yet to accuse Deleuze and Guattari of naiveté is erroneous.[18] What is even more worrying about some of the objections raised against any of the current affirmative philosophies, and the affirmative aesthetics I have so far explored, is that such expostulations tend to revert to precisely the kind of cynicism, even nihilism, that they purport to identify and refute.

A case in point would be several shorter writings by art critic and art historian Hal Foster, whose work on the *avant-garde* in contemporary social and political critique, especially in the context of a radical postmodernism, I have always admired and greatly benefited from.[19] His recent essays nonetheless strike me as both unproductive and, in their overall negative sway, expressing a profound sense of disgruntlement in a voice that sounds almost as "forlorn" as he suggests the "quasi-Adornian" position in contemporary critical theory is.[20] Before going into this in more detail, let me backtrack a little and point out, perhaps in his defense, that Deleuze clearly perceived that the late 1990s, the heyday of postmodernism and a certain "brand"—and I use the word advisedly—of conceptual art, the period in which *L'Abécédaire* was recorded and broadcast, was a period of cultural crisis and impoverishment, a "period of the desert."

What Deleuze deplored and found disturbing, however, was not the cultural "poverty" itself, but rather the "insolence and arrogance of people who occupy the impoverished periods." The "stupider they are," he says, the "happier they are, like saying that literature is now a tiny little private affair." Inveterate and irrepressible affirmative thinker that he is, Deleuze yet goes on to state "that it's not all that serious, since there will always be either a parallel circuit for expression, or a black market of some sort."[21] It is this possibility for something different, however minor, to emerge alongside "mainstream" (commodity) art, for some mode of expression that does not validate an overall cultural despair, that I find sorely lacking, and whose lack I find troubling, in Foster's take on contemporary art and on art criticism. To be sure, I am not singling out Foster as a critic of a Deleuzian-inspired or vitalist aesthetics, even if he does, as we shall see below, appear casually to dismiss an affect-based approach to contemporary art. The point rather is to show the limits of the primarily negative mode of critique enabled and encouraged by poststructuralist and deconstructive modes of thought, the prevalent model of "critical theory" developed in the late twentieth century that was, as Sturken and Cartwright put it, "seen to be in crisis by the end of the century because the writing associated with it was not providing the kind of explanatory power or impetus to social change desired by many of its authors"[22]—Hal Foster included. Let me explain this in more detail.

In October 2008, Foster published an essay in *The London Review of Books* titled "The Medium Is the Market"[23]—a not-too-subtle reference to Marshall McLuhan's insight that a medium affects the society in which it plays a role not by the content delivered over the medium, but by the characteristics of the medium itself.[24] Foster does not quite follow through on the promise of his title, but his discussion of so-called Business Art, sparked by Damien Hirst's auctioning of 223 new works directly at Sotheby's in September 2008, bringing in a staggering total of £111.5 million, adequately suggests his gloomy view on the arts of the present and, more eerily, on their functioning in what art critic Peter Sheldal has called "our plutocratic democracy."

Although, as Foster admits, the "production for the marketplace has been a fundamental condition of art since the Renaissance," the Hirst phenomenon (see figure 3.1 and plate 5), which he defines as "an entire career strung together by shock and scandal and a body of work whose medium is a compound of media and market events,"[25] not only indicates a structural shift in the relations between art, mass culture, and corporate capitalism. It has also, he maintains, profoundly affected contemporary art as such. The rise of the celebrity artist who produces work that plays up to commodity culture and the fashion industry, corporate sponsorship, and an overall lack of critique are among the immediately visible effects of some artists' enthusiastic embrace of the business model and their perfection thereof in multitasking studio factories. Foster numbers Jeff Koons and the Japanese artist Takashi Murakami—not coincidentally, both representative of the open, if not defiant, celebration of kitsch, cuteness, and bad taste in their successful attempts to reach across socioeconomic registers—among Hirst's most prominent peers in Business Art. (As an aside, the largest sum paid for a work by Koons is *Balloon Flower (Magenta)* [figure 3.2], which sold for £12,921,250

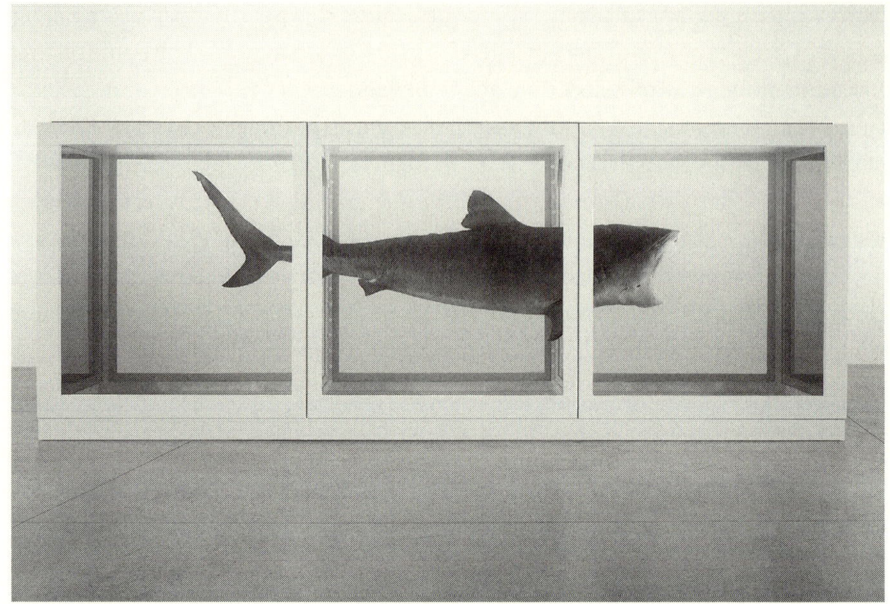

FIG. 3.1 Damien Hirst, *The Physical Impossibility of Death in the Mind of Someone Living,* 1991 (sideview). Glass, painted steel, silicone, monofilament, shark, and formaldehyde solution, 85.43 × 213.39 × 70.87 in. (2170 × 5420 × 1800 mm). © Damien Hirst and Science Ltd. All rights reserved, DACS 2013 / ARS, NY. Photographed by Prudence Cuming Associates Ltd.

($25,765,204) at Christie's London in June 2008. Murakami's "My Lonesome Cowboy" [1998], an anime-inspired sculpture of a masturbating boy, sold for $15.2 million at Sotheby's in May 2008.) All three "business artists" oversee studio factories in which the production of computer-generated designs—to be fabricated by assistants and merely signed by the artist—clothing lines, restaurants, publishing houses, radio shows, packaging, animation, and consultancy services, as well as exhibition development and website production, unproblematically converge into the most spectacular model of artistic practice in what Gilles Lipovetsky has called our "hypermodern times."[26]

Not surprisingly, Foster concludes his essay on a somber note, declaring the "ambiguous achievement" of the trio of Koons, Hirst, and Murakami to be the updating and extension of what Walter Benjamin, in his reflections on the "embittered realisms and bankrupt surrealisms" of the 1920s and 1930s, famously designated the "incorporation of nihilism into the bourgeoisie's apparatus of domination."[27] I am not suggesting that Foster does not have a point: the callousness of an increasingly market-driven contemporary art scene and the lack of sustained critique are undoubtedly worrisome. Bearing in mind, however,

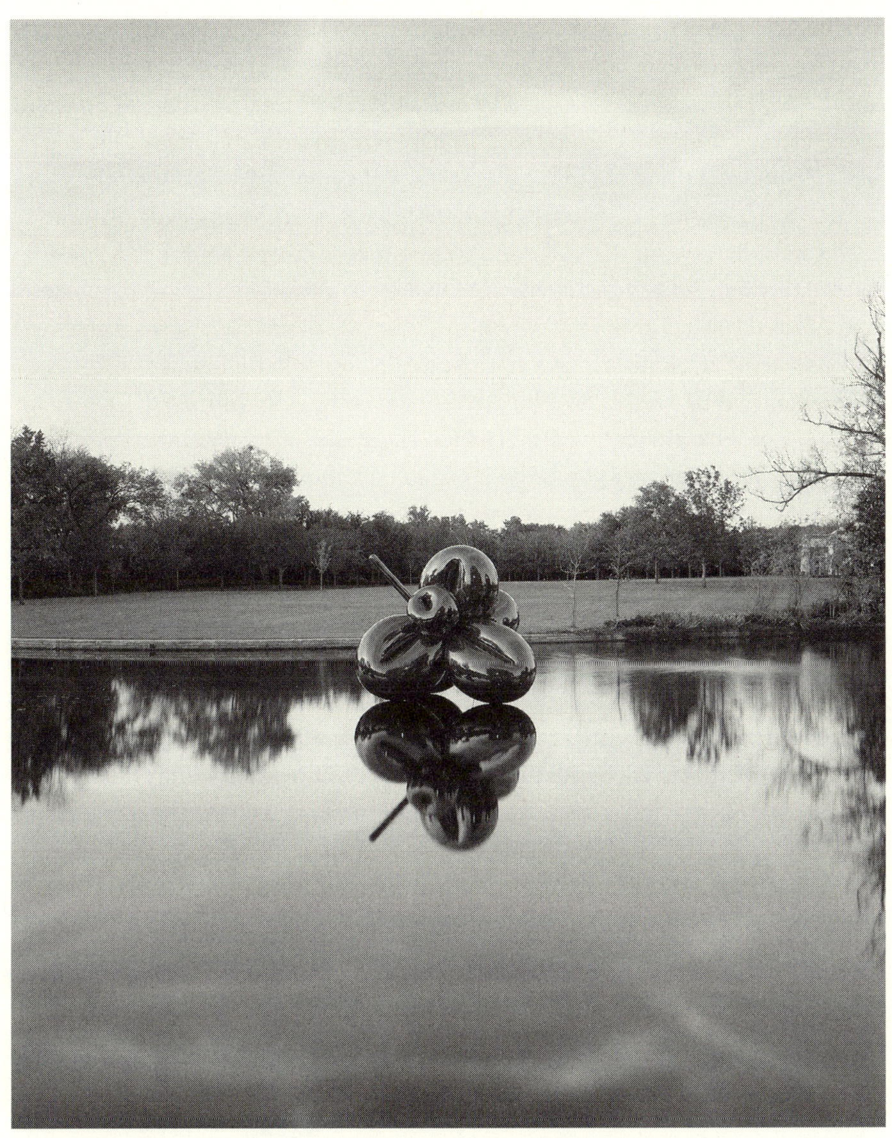

Fig. 3.2 Jeff Koons, *Balloon Flower (Magenta)*, 1995–2000. High-chromium stainless steel with transparent color coating, 133¾ × 112¼ × 102¼ in. (340 × 285 × 260 cm). © Jeff Koons

Deleuze's suggestion that the "cultural poverty" Foster quite rightly identifies in/with contemporary Business Art may not be all too "serious," and definitely not the only thing that is happening, his altogether negative critique does not allow us much room to look for what is happening in what Deleuze calls a "parallel circuit for expression, or a black market of some sort." This is all the more disturbing since the line from Benjamin's relentless socio-aesthetic critique to Foster's implicit declaration of contemporary art's ethical bankruptcy runs, of course, through Andy Warhol, invoked by Foster as the "master" of 1970s Business Art and subject of the art critic's sustained scholarly interest, as well as the only pop artist referenced, however marginally, by Deleuze.

As is commonly known, Warhol, whose studio was not called the Factory for nothing, used silkscreens to mass-produce images the way capitalist corporations mass-produce consumer goods. He assembled a menagerie of "art-workers" to help him create his paintings and star in his films, and he wrote in *The Philosophy of Andy Warhol* that "making money is art and working is art and good business is the best art."[28] Although this would seem to render Warhol an ideal target for Foster's socio-aesthetic critique, the fact that he keeps returning and writing about the pop artist's work suggests otherwise, or at least points to a much more ambivalent position than his essay on Hirst et al. would appear to validate. I will return to this in a moment.

In the more recent essay cited above, Foster continues his gloomy musings on the conditions for the study of the arts of the present, shifting his perspective from contemporary art per se to the "sheer out-of-date-ness of criticism" in an art world that, he submits, evidently "couldn't care less." Foster laments the loss of support for and investment in the project of what he alternatively names "critical theory," "critical art," "critique," and "criticism," a broad dismissal he sees to have pervaded both the academy and the art world at large from the 1980s onwards. Foster's analysis of the situation is sound and worth considering—he mentions as some of the main causes for the "fatigue that many feel with critique today," among other things, the poststructuralist critiques of representation and of the subject, the popular presentation of postmodernism as the "rote expression of neoliberal capitalism," critique's "dependence on demystification," and the reduction of the viewer to passive consumer in critical investigations of cultural power structures.[29] In this sense, he and I are in full agreement: the limitations of an overwhelmingly negative mode of critique do not only emerge in the art world at large, but also in the academic fields in which the linguistic and cultural turns respectively have most dramatically changed the direction and purport of critical/analytical debates. Foster's outright rejection of alternative, "post-critical" approaches to contemporary art and culture, effectively (and admittedly quite amusingly) framed as a string of rhetorical questions—"What are the options on offer? Celebrating beauty? Affirming affect? Hoping for a 'redistribution of the sensible'?"[30]—nonetheless appear to be as crude as the reduction of postmodernism to commodity capitalism. Nor does his conclusion—that the "post-critical condition" has "for the most part . . . abetted a relativism that has little to do with pluralism"—strike me as particularly convincing.[31]

So even if I do share some of Foster's concerns, I cannot ultimately subscribe to his overall analysis of the contemporary art critical climate. First, because a Deleuzian approach to art and aesthetics—unmistakably evoked by the dismissive rhetorical question/phrase "affirming affect?"—does anything but preclude "critique," if what we mean by critique is not so much criticizing existing or prevailing values but to create new or better ones. Deleuze professes that his Nietzschean definition of critical philosophy has "two inseparable moments: the referencing back of all things and any kind of origin to values, but also the referencing back of these values to something which is, as it were, their origin and determines their values." This leads to an affirmative notion of critique that is firmly grounded in the later philosopher's "radical empiricism" and that is neither a random embrace of cosmic forces nor a mere celebration of affect. Whereas for Deleuze critique is just as "opposed to absolute values as it is to relative or utilitarian ones," it simultaneously is, as it is for Nietzsche, "never conceived as a *reaction* but as an *action*." Refuting both "criticising things in the name of established values" and criticizing or respecting values by "deriving them from simple facts, from so-called 'objective facts,'"[32] Deleuzian critique is an activity, and at its most positive (and this is its affirmative aspect) an act of creation.

Second, I find myself reluctant to subscribe to Foster's wholesale condemnation of both contemporary art and art criticism on the basis of the exceptionally spectacular and supra-lucrative careers of the trio of Hirst, Koons, and Murakami, because his analysis practically erases the differences between these latter-day Business Artists and less economically successful contemporary artists populating a "black market of some sort," but also between their "empires" and the much more ambivalent Andy Warhol Enterprises established in 1957. As I have already suggested, Warhol is—in light of the above, perhaps paradoxically—of obvious interest to Foster. In his recent book on Pop art, the critic devotes a chapter to the one-time "master of business art" titled "Andy Warhol, or the Distressed Image."[33] This highly informative book generally engages the postwar shift in artistic practices that collapsed traditional distinctions between "high" and "low" culture, between private and public, and between image and self, or Imago and Subjectivity, which Foster sees most suggestively registered in the work of the five artists he discusses (Richard Hamilton, Roy Lichtenstein, Andy Warhol, Gerhard Richter, and Ed Ruscha), who initiated the "first age of Pop" and whose origins are assumed to lie in the mid- to late 1950s.

In the chapter on Warhol, Foster takes Freud, Lacan, Barthes, and Benjamin as his main theoretical interlocutors to explore Warhol and his serial work in terms of the question of difference and sameness in relation to repetition, a question the ambivalent locus of which he projects onto the notion of "distress."[34] The word "distress" is used both literally, in relation to the "Warholian distressing of the image," as well as metaphorically, in relation to both the postwar subject-in-distress, a subject increasingly mediated by (then) new (now old) technologies, such as photography, television, and cinema, a subject increasingly suspended upon such technologies' imaginary operations, and in relation to the actual feelings of trauma, loss, melancholy, and mourning that Foster perceives to be compulsively repeated and produced in Warhol's life and work.[35] In view of these key concerns (difference and repetition, affective states, new becomings that necessarily entail unbecomings), it is surprising to find that Deleuze is not mentioned once in the almost sixty pages to which the chapter runs. I think this is a pity. A more affirmative perspective (rather than the negative critiques of Freud, Lacan, Barthes, and Benjamin) might have led Foster to a less desolate—if not a less distressed—appreciation of Warhol's work in its expressive materiality, and, furthermore, might have enabled him to much more effectively capture the critical and revolutionary power of the quintessential Pop artist's techniques and repetitions. Let me try to clarify this supposition in more detail.

Previous critics of Warhol, especially those arguing against Arthurs Danto's well-known interpretation of his serial work, which in highly oversimplified terms revolves around the question of the status of the work of art and its relation to reality[36]—in other words, the question of what art (and not-art) *is,* and not about what it *does* in the world—do occasionally build upon Deleuze's brief, parenthetical reference to Warhol in *Difference and Repetition.* As is sufficiently known, Deleuze's engagement with visual art at some point largely shifted to painting and to color as the locus of sensation, especially in his collaborative writings with Guattari and in his solo discussions of Cézanne and Francis Bacon. It is in his earlier, Nietzsche-inspired philosophical work, however, that he explicitly talks about Pop art and "Warhol's remarkable 'serial' series" (*DR,* 293)—an allusion, Stephen Zepke helpfully points out, must, given the book's publication date (1968), "refer to the so-called 'screen-print' paintings Warhol begins in 1962 and developed over the next five years in what is known as the 'Death and Disaster' paintings" (see figures 3.3 and 3.4; see also plate 6).[37]

Zepke takes up this reference to explore what he calls Nietzsche's "onto-aesthetics" in relation to Deleuze's condemnation of any aesthetics that separates art from life. Where Deleuze, echoing Bakhtin, writes that "there is no other aesthetic problem than that of the insertion of art into everyday life" (*DR,* 293), Nietzsche more exuberantly exclaims, "Art and nothing but art! . . . It is the great

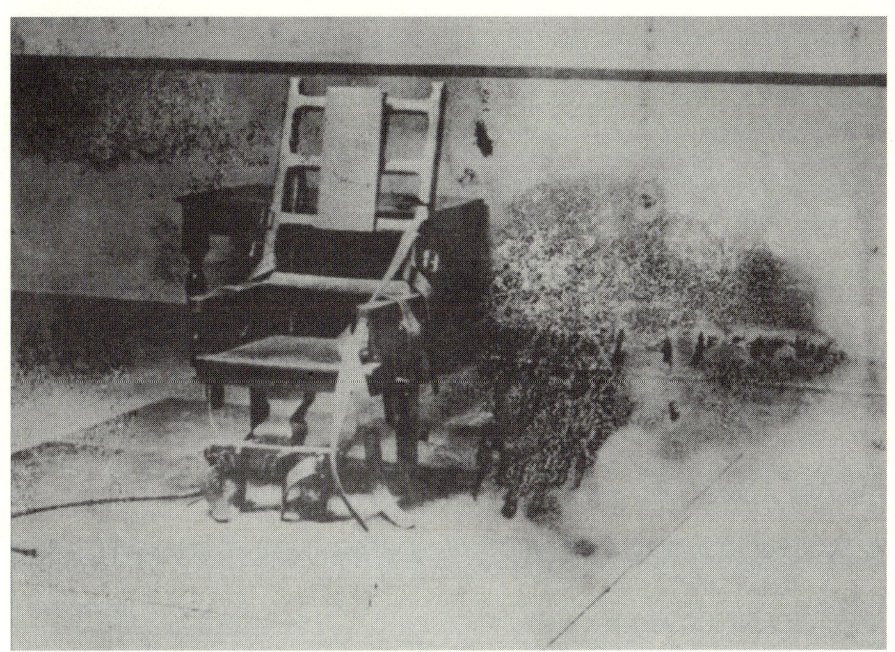

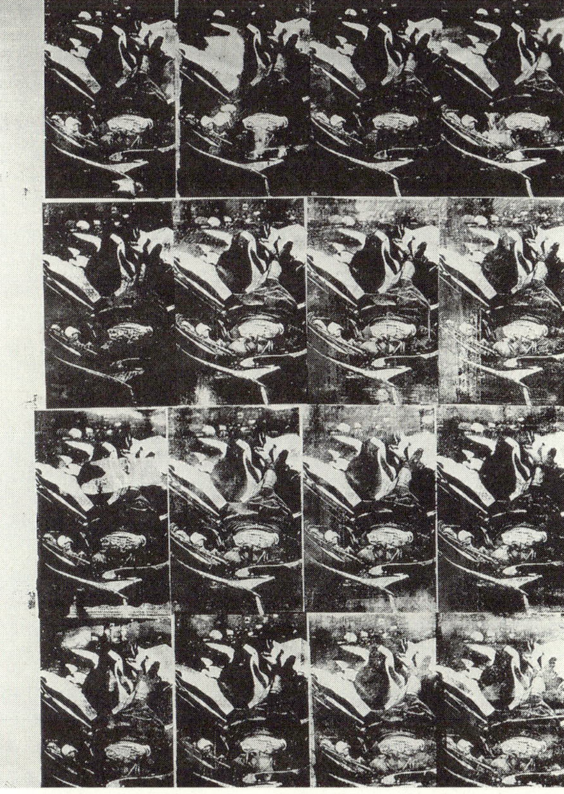

FIG. 3.3 *(top)* Andy Warhol, *Electric Chair,* 1971. Screenprint on white paper, 35½ × 48 in.   © The Andy Warhol Foundation for the Visual Arts, Inc. / ARS, NY

FIG. 3.4 *(left)* Andy Warhol, *Suicide,* 1963. Silkscreen in on synthetic polymer paint on canvas, 111½ × 80⅓ in.   © The Andy Warhol Foundation for the Visual Arts, Inc. / ARS, NY

means of making life possible, the great seduction to life, the great stimulant of life."[38] Zepke argues that Nietzsche's notion of art as "procreative," as both an "affirmative process and the active things it creates,"[39] is at once fundamentally antidialectical, antirepresentational, and radically empiricist. For Nietzsche, the affirmation of life forces is the condition for the creation of art, for the art-work/artwork as an "individuation of the world, an interpretation constructing a singularity in which the will to power is expressed as an evaluation that constructs itself."[40] The artwork, then, on Nietzsche's view, is expression—a "harnessing of forces," in Deleuze's alternative terms—and not a representation of something else because it only exists as an action or activity in an affirmation of forces that escape the Idea (Plato), or the Categories (Kant).

Using a term largely absent from his later work, in *Difference and Repetition* Deleuze follows Nietzsche in defining the modern artwork as a simulacrum or simulacral. He intends the term, however, not in the negative sense of a distorted reproduction (Plato) or, alternatively, as a perversion of reality, a pretense of reality, or as something that bears no relation to reality whatsoever (Baudrillard), but, in contrast, as "systems in which different relates to different *by means of* difference itself." "Essential" for Deleuze is that:

> We find in these systems no *prior identity,* no *internal resemblance.* It is all a matter of difference in the series, and of differences of difference in the communication between series. What is displaced and disguised in the series cannot and must not be identified, but exists and acts as the differenciator of difference. (*DR,* 299—300)

The simulacrum in a Deleuzian sense is therefore not an impoverishment of reality, but the very means by which the world constitutes and renews itself; it is, in Zepke's phrase, the "continued creation of the world, the becoming of a world constructed into a mobile series, differentiating and differentiated."[41] Modern art, having rejected representation in favor of simulacra, is thus the "affirmation of a creative becoming, creating divergent series in which the art-work is continually becoming-other."[42] In Deleuze's own terms, and with specific reference to Pop art:

> Art does not imitate, above all, because it repeats; it repeats all the repetitions, by virtue of an internal power (an imitation is a copy, but art is simulation, it reverses copies into simulacra). Even the most mechanical, the most banal, the most habitual and the most stereotyped repetition finds a place in works of art, it is always displaced in relation to other repetitions, and it is subject to the condition that a difference may be extracted from it for these other repetitions. . . . Pop art pushed the copy, the copy of the copy, etc., to that extreme point at which it reverses and becomes a simulacrum. (*DR,* 293–94)

In breaking down the Platonic dualisms between the copy and the real, between art and life, modern art generally, and Pop art particularly, does not reflect or even constitute a loss of some reality existing outside or prior to the artwork, but rather succeeds in injecting itself into daily life "in order to extract from it that little difference which plays simultaneously between other levels of repetition." In this way, it fulfills the "highest object of art," which for Deleuze is to "bring into play simultaneously all these repetitions, with their differences in kind and rhythm, their respective displacements and disguises, their divergences and decentrings; to embed them in one another and to envelop one or the other in illusions the 'effect' of which varies in each case" (*DR*, 293).

A similarly affirmative take on Pop art in general, on Warhol's iconophilia, and on his "serial series" in particular, is presented by Gary Shapiro within the larger context of his book *Archeologies of Vision* (2003). This study of "Foucault and Nietzsche on seeing and saying" centers on the former thinker's critical interrogation, as it is influenced by the latter's thought on the visual, of the "differential character of various visual regimes," and of the "disparate and possibly conflicting visual practices of a single era."[43] Shapiro takes Deleuze's attempt to reverse Platonic dualism to consist in "replacing a representational image of thought with a form of thinking that understands difference and repetition as primary features of being that need not be traced back to concepts of identity and resemblance"—a revolution in thought that, he goes on to suggest, Deleuze likens to the shift in painting from representation to abstraction: painting "abandons the image, but not visuality, through abstraction."[44] Letting go of the image (but not the visual) means that a space is opened up for a decentered perspective on visuality that transforms repetition from a "dreary succession of the identical" into a "displaced difference,"[45] a mode and notion of repetition that emphasizes multiplicity, change, novelty, the new.

Deleuze's remarks on Pop art suggest that in rupturing the traditional hierarchy between copy and original and, in the case of Warhol, the use of technological means of reproduction, the emptying out of meaning (whether as essence, substance, or reality) effected by such works is neither distressing nor a cause for mourning, but rather to be embraced as a perspective on a space of "displaced difference" in which the spreading of serial simulacra reveal multiplicity with nothing at its center. Within such a regime of the visual, difference and otherness replace the foundational concepts of the original and its (imperfect) copy. "The truth of art," Shapiro concludes, "is not in imitation, but in repetition."[46] And since for Deleuze repetition is always the repetition of difference, that is, the repetition of difference as, in Zepke's formulation, the "compositional principle of modern art,"[47] produces, in Deleuze's own words, an "internal resonance," a "forced movement which goes beyond the series itself," a movement that is pure affect or the "affective charge" (LS, 260, 261) that dissolves the relational identities of subject and object and enfolds them both in the singularity of the expressive event. A Deleuzian onto-aesthetics thus by no means obscures the function of art in its ethical modality because, as Zepke argues, precisely in its "transvaluation of representation," art emerges in its active, affirmative, productive function, as life forces, the "harnessed forces" or "simulacral signs that construct the world."[48]

Not only, then, does a Deleuzian, affirmative approach allow us to perceive the ethical dimension of art, and thereby maintain the possibility of critique, albeit not in its all but exclusively negative mode; it additionally enables us to differentiate Warhol's Business Art from the sad and saddening repetitions of more recent Business Artists[49]—whose commercial and commodified work is, I concede, characterized by the "insolence and arrogance" that Deleuze quite rightly attributes to "people who occupy the impoverished periods." This brings me to the final reason why I prioritize a Deleuzian, or Deleuze-inspired approach to the study of the arts of the present over and above the negative form of critique whose decreasing influence Foster so eloquently bemoans. For however urgent it may be—and such urgency is beyond dispute—this mode of critique also runs the risk of giving so much importance to the dominant figures successfully operating a cultural "period of the desert" that it discourages us, as suggested, from looking for encounters elsewhere, for works of art that affect us, that force us to think in what Deleuze calls "either a parallel circuit for expression, or a black market of some sort," and to ask after what ideas such artworks generate.

To ask after the ideas a work of art generates is not, perhaps, too dissimilar from asking what a work of art does, how it operates in the world, and how it affects its participants, questions that inevitably return us to the ethical dimension of art, albeit in a vein radically different from Foster's negative critique of Hirst and his peers. As I have tried to suggest, in his ambivalent lamentation on the corporatization of some forms of artistic production, Foster, following Benjamin, cannot but ultimately succumb to precisely the kind of nihilism he so obviously deplores. An alternative approach would be to espouse the originally classical procedure also adopted by Foucault, which is to pursue the path of *ekphrasis* and to attempt to describe the visual impression or effect of a particular artwork, or a body of work, to articulate what we see when we look at it, the wonder or astonishment we feel, what is new or unexpected in our observations, instead of trying to determine or understand what the artwork means or represents.

Let me use the final paragraphs of this chapter to explain what I mean by this by focusing on two encounters with very different bodies of work in different media by two contemporary artists—encounters that made me think, each in its own way, and that in effect gave rise to the writing of this chapter in the first place, and hence to the thoughts unfolded herein.

The first was a mid-career retrospective at the Cranbrook Institute of Science in Bloomfield Hills, Michigan, showcasing a range of recent works by acclaimed photographer Richard Barnes, titled *Animal Logic*.[50] One series is of particular interest to me in this context, a series called "Refuge," which consists of a number of interconnected works that focus, according to the exhibition catalogue, on "the 'hybrid architecture' of urban bird nests that incorporate the detritus of human life." The series comprises a total of eleven meticulously finished, large-scale close-up photographs of birds' nests, seven of which are rendered in velvety full color, four in black and white. Every print has its individual title, and the black and white ones are all identified as "Nest" followed by a number and the year in which the picture was taken. The color prints are named after the type of bird whose nest appears in the picture, some in Latin, others in English (see figures 3.5 and 3.6; see also plate 7). Not only do these titles suggest a kind of taxonomic, near scientific identification of the photographic object, the words, as signifiers, also come to stand in for the signified, the nests that in and of themselves operate as signifiers for the living animals that are absent from the pictures. I do not see birds in these images, but intricately crafted nests made up of dead materials (twigs, leaves, thread), and I read the captions, the words, that represent the birds rendered invisible behind the sign at two removes.

The great visual detail with which these artfully constructed animal habitats meet the eye gains momentum in its stark contrast with the solid black background. There is no context but for the black hole from which the photographed object emerges, becomes visible in its two-dimensional presence. Unique as animal artifacts thus captured, framed, and potentially endlessly reproduced, the nests, the longer I look at them, to me become aesthetically pleasing abstractions, representations presented in serial form and inserted into a classifying system that does not sufficiently jar with the fragility of the nests, "shot" as they are within a visual register that appears just as hermetically sealed as the systematic truth discourse evoked by the bird names/work titles. With the empty nests standing in for the living birds, these photographs do not offer me an access point, do not take me into a different realm of experience, leave me no option but to remain anchored in my spectator's subject position, enjoying the aesthetic pleasure provided by beautiful still lifes of lifeless objects.

Second was an ostensibly modest series of drawings by Kathleen Henderson, shown under the lengthy and awkwardly self-conscious title *What if I Could Draw a Bird that Could Change the World?,* in fall 2008 at the Drawing Center in New York.[51] The exhibition comprised twenty-three drawings in oil stick on paper, all between 17 × 25 or 19 × 25 inches in size, the majority untitled, with a few significant exceptions (see figures 3.7 and 3.8). Crudely drawn, mere black lines on white paper, most of the images present what appear to be human figures, but

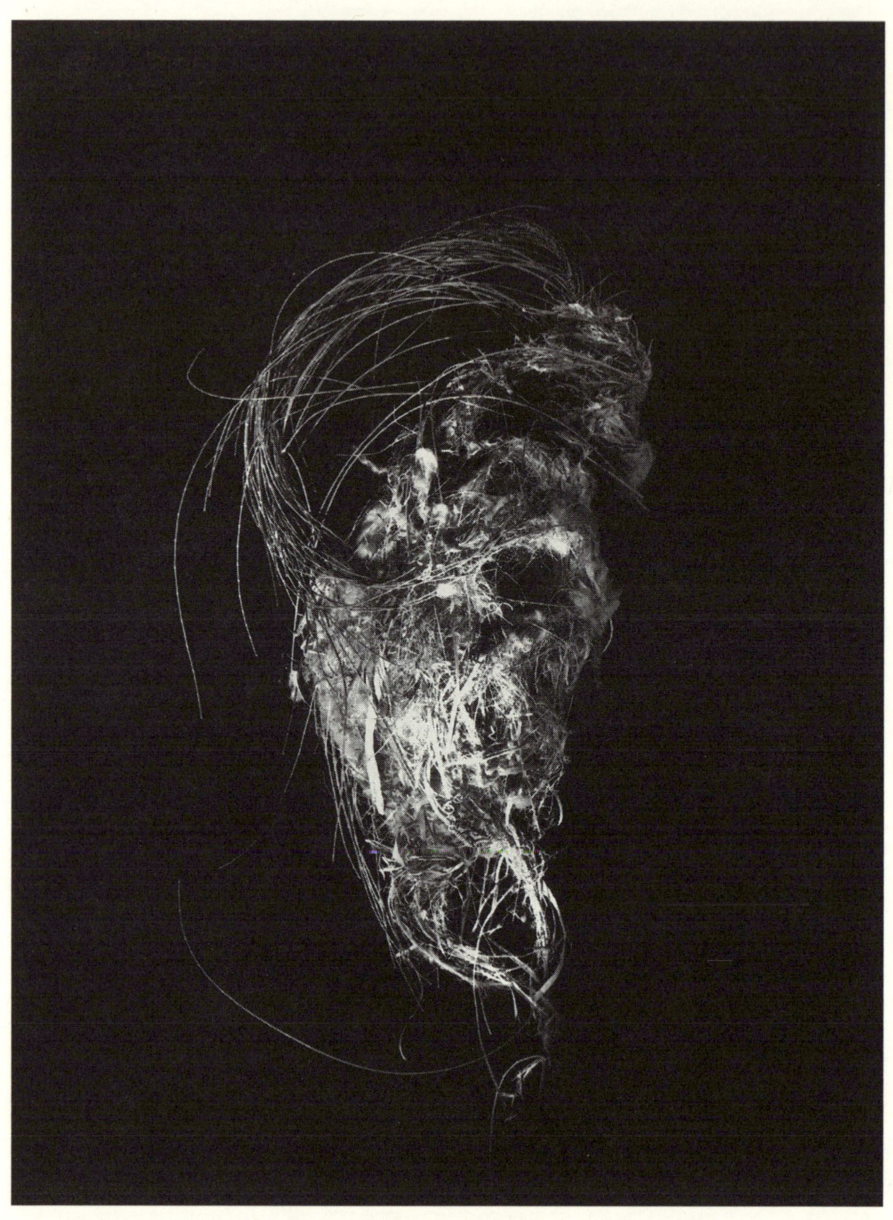

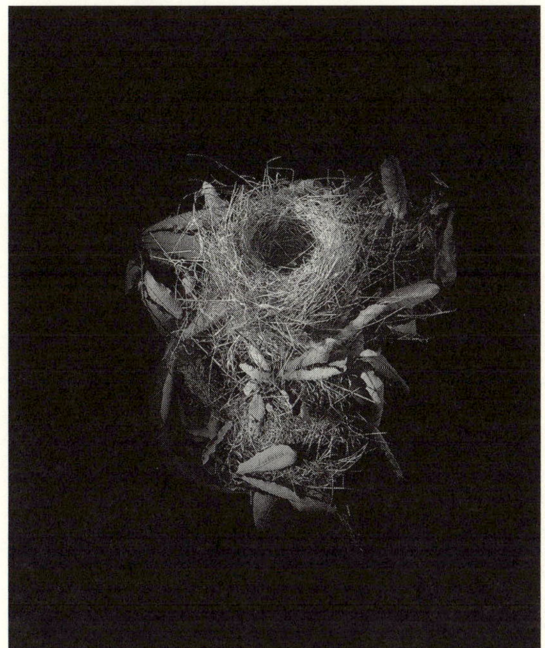

FIG. 3.6 Richard Barnes, *Happy Wren,* 2000. Archival digital C print, 48 × 42 in.   © Richard Barnes

some of them have animal faces while others seem to be wearing masks, showing no facial features other than black dots suggesting eyes, sometimes a nose and a mouth. The figures largely emerge against an empty background, with an occasional big black blot in a corner of the paper (a shadow? an oil spill? a puddle?) or numerous smaller dots that seem to indicate some kind of surface. Most of the figures, however, float in a two-dimensional space of rectangular whiteness. Several of the drawings contain handwritten words, two repeating (several times) the drawings' titles, while the work that gives the exhibition its title integrates what almost strikes me as a kind of mantra: "What if I could draw a bird that could change the world? In a good way, I mean in a good way. I know this is not that bird. I know that" (see figure 3.9).

Though clearly not "narrative" in the traditional sense suggested by Shlomith Rimmon-Kenan, or even by Mieke Bal, these drawings, the clumsy black lines and black dots, appear to be telling me a story, or various stories, but not stories with a beginning, a middle, and an end. As images containing narrative elements, they start in the middle, tracing out into multiple directions, drawings drawing me in and drawing me out into where I may not want to go. The two figures in socks, for example (figure 3.10), are they two men, or a man and a woman? Does

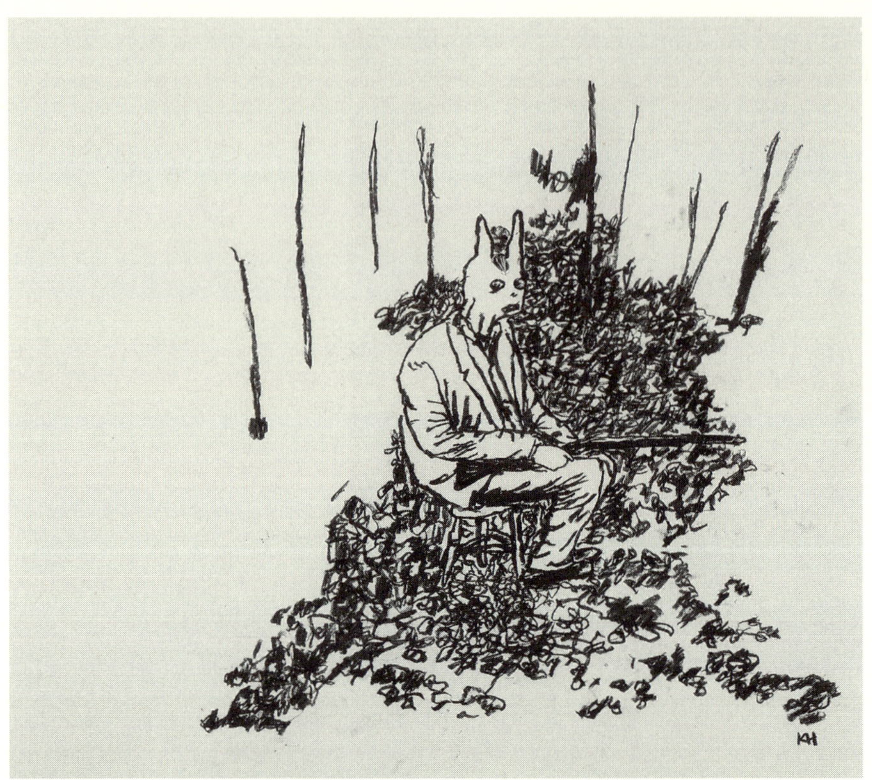

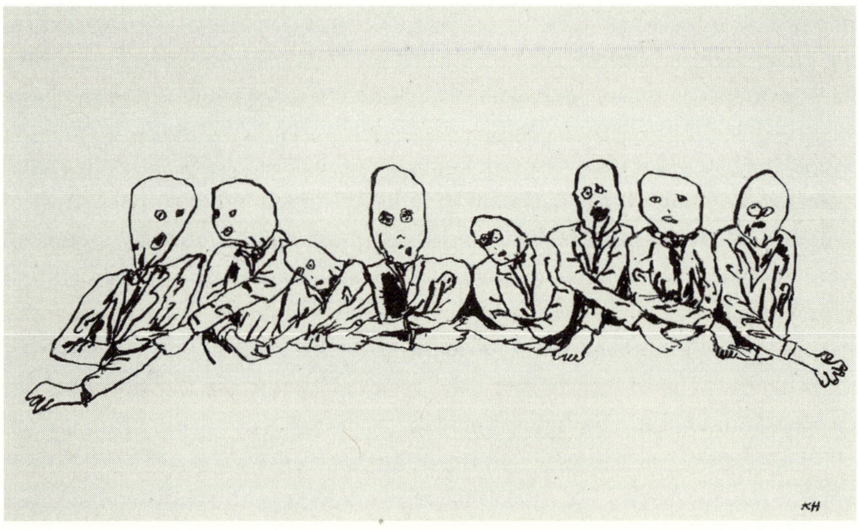

FIG. 3.7 Kathleen Henderson, *Untitled (rabbit in the woods with gun),* 2006. Oil stick on paper, 19⅛ × 21¼ in.   © Kathleen Henderson. Courtesy of the artist and Rosamund Felsen Gallery, Santa Monica

FIG. 3.8 Kathleen Henderson, *Solidarity,* 2006. Oil stick on paper, 19⅛ × 31 in. © Kathleen Henderson

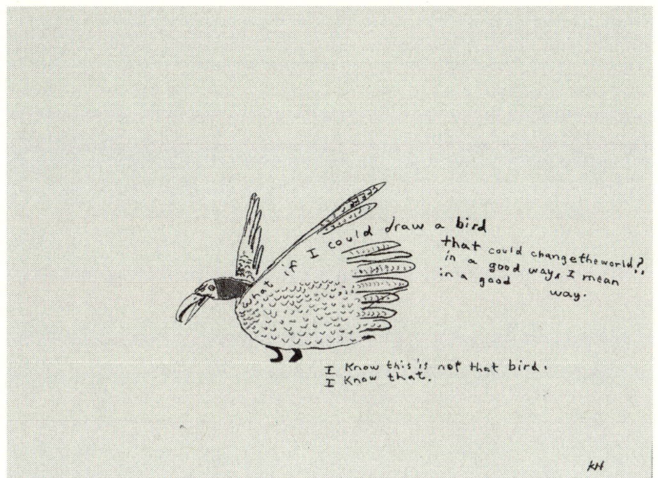

FIG. 3.9 Kathleen Henderson, *"What if I Could Draw a Bird
that Could Change the World?"* 2007. Oil stick on paper, 19 × 25 in.
© Kathleen Henderson

it matter to know this? What is or has been happening here? The smaller figure on the right appears to be jumping, in fear or in fright, onto the lumpy, big, solid figure on the left, but the latter's face and body are turned out, toward me, disconnected, unaffected by the impact of the other's clinging bodily materiality. Why are they in their underwear and wearing socks, and how and why is it that their bag heads, their masked faces, immediately evoke images of the hooded knights of the KKK and their racial hatred and violence? What kind of blatant threat or latent violence is leaping at me from these cartoonish figures, making me flinch, wince?

Or the eerie encounter between the animal-faced figure in full suit (Is it a rabbit? A dog? A cat?) leaning over from his chair to pat a pair of lambs (plate 8). The dark shadows cast by the chair and the lambs render the ambivalence of this image even more pronounced than does the contrast between the figure's lugubrious face, with his pointed ears, one glaring eye, and widely opened mouth, and the symbolic value of the innocent lambs: is he patting the lambs, or is he planning on eating or molesting them? Whence the pronounced sense of violence, of destruction, or self-destruction, that I feel to be implicit in this scene of animal-animal, animal-human interaction, of animated, active assemblage?

And, finally, one of the titled drawings, showing a frail male figure wearing wings, turned away from the viewer, with a distinctive straight haircut that is joltingly explained by the drawing's title "Hitler with Wings" (figure 3.11). A story of horror taking wings, the myriad lines drawing out from the Holocaust, from

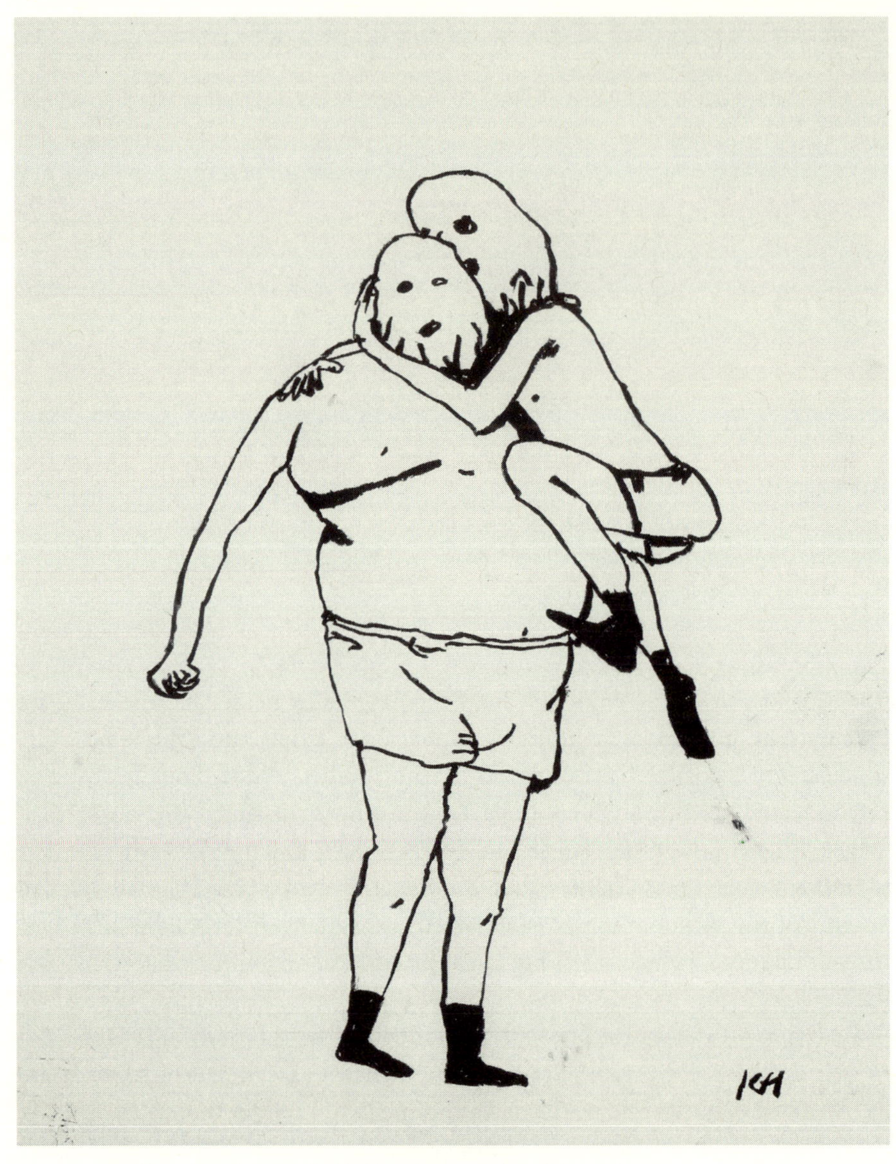

FIG. 3.10 Kathleen Henderson, *Untitled (two figures with socks)*, 2006.
Oil stick on paper, 24 × 19 in.   © Kathleen Henderson. Courtesy of the
artist and Pierogi

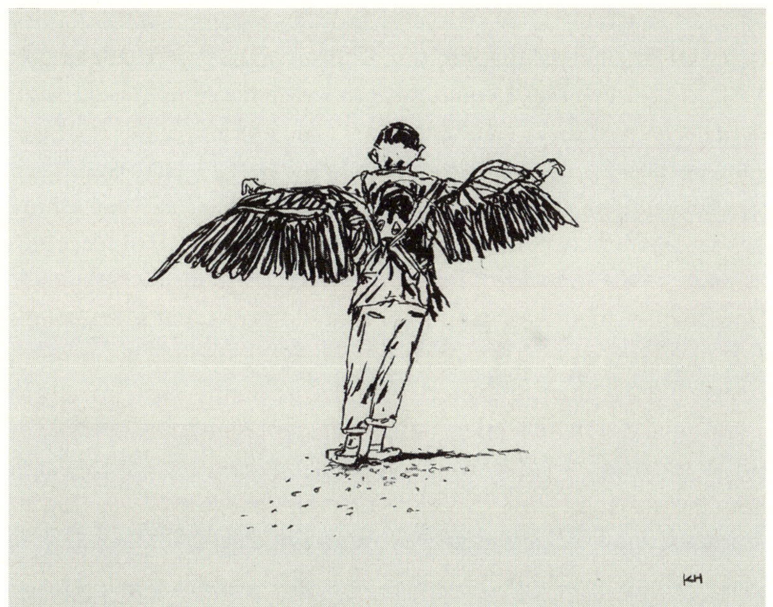

FIG. 3.11 Kathleen Henderson, *Hitler with Wings,* 2006. Oil stick on paper, 17½ in. Collection of Dean Valentine and Amy Andelson, Los Angeles. © Kathleen Henderson

Hitler as the time-proof symbol of evil to angelic beneficence, Christian mythology, Hitler as the angel of death, the harbinger of truth about human evil, and/or the closeness between creative and destructive forces? The clash between the Hitler image stored inside me, in my mind, in my dreams and in my nightmares, woven together of so many visual, narrative, and imaginary strands, and the fragility of this human cherub, dreaming of reaching for the skies, doomed like Icarus, driven by ambitions and aspirations that are, perhaps, not all that different from what drives me, us, individually and collectively, toward imaginary elsewheres, unforeseeable futures?

No more than black lines drawn on paper, Kathleen Henderson's almost childlike figurations do not leave me alone, intact. They uproot me, take me away from where I thought I was, dissolve me as a subject-viewer into a participator in a scene, a space/time or chronotope in which the lines between subject and object can no longer be clearly drawn, an in-between space in which I am necessarily implicated, albeit not as my familiar, subjective self. These haunting images find me, and I steal them, as sites for the possibility of thought; they entangle me in lines of flight whose ethical implications are, just as the work or the operations of these artworks themselves, neither straightforward nor unambivalent. In their tangible, inescapable visibility, these drawings do not teach me anything that I already know; they touch me, they affect me, and they force me to think; they take me up in a violent embrace that profoundly disorganizes me, that compels me to thought, to do work that I could not otherwise have envisaged, that I would not have been urged to do, clandestinely, if I had not sought out and been captured in and by the encounter with these works and been given to the actual, empirical experience of its "effect," be touched by the "zigzag," the "something which passes or happens between two as though under a potential difference."

If such encounters amount to anything at all, if art has anything to offer outside and beyond any practical or utilitarian purpose, it would be precisely as the conditions for work, by forcing us to think. Art, I submit, in the solitude of the office in which I am writing this chapter, is good to think with. Rather than turning to art as social critique or as merely one among many representational practices, the main task for the study of the arts of the present, it seems to me, is to search for such works, perhaps living in the margins of a dominant art world ruled by commercial interests and global market forces, to forge aesthetic encounters in order to ask what art is genuinely creative, and what ideas it generates. For art is not just a weekend activity, but a means of transformation and, as such, it generates its own kind of thought. Admittedly, to adopt such an "affirmative" and empiricist attitude toward art does nothing to contribute to traditional art historical and critical undertakings, such as authenticating, classifying, interpreting, regulating, and judging individual artifacts. Through its power to activate the aesthetic, the autonomy of art emerges in our encounter with it, an encounter that is a partial process of always partial becoming; an "a-parallel evolution" that is always "'outside' and 'between,'" and that moves or flows in another direction. Such an aesthetic praxis cannot evolve from pre-established paradigms or result in programmatic clarity, but it may present us, at times, with a total, radical dissection of orders and lineages, while at other times, perhaps, doing no more (and no less) than allowing us a shy and nervous peering into things.

In the following three chapters, I will pursue these suppositions by seeking out distinct encounters with different bodies of visual art, and I will attempt to suggest more extensively in what ways such an affirmative and empiricist attitude diverges from more traditional models of art criticism, as well as what its experimental practice may afford.

The entire history of representation . . . is . . . traversed by
the fissure of absence, which, in effect, divides it into the absence
of the thing . . . and the *absense* [sic] *within* the thing.

Jean-Luc Nancy, *The Ground of the Image*

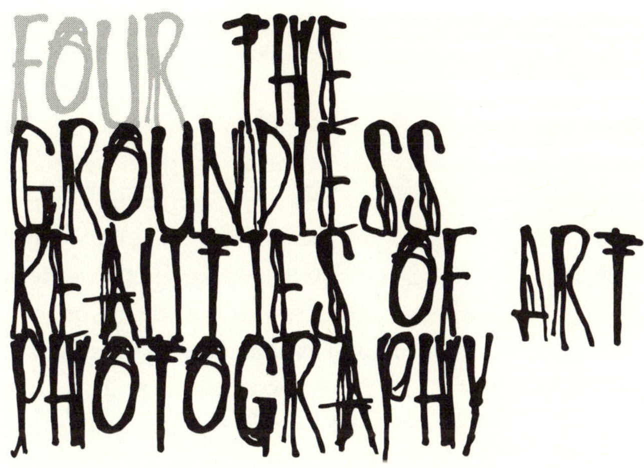

If there is one form of visual cultural production that at once marks the rise of commodity culture and that lends itself to co-optation in and by an increasingly market-driven art world so as to become highly lucrative Business Art, it would be the prototypical mode of mechanical image reproduction: photography. True, the work of photographers like Richard Barnes today unabashedly presents itself in art galleries and museums on a par with more traditional forms of fine arts, such as painting and sculpture, but this is a relatively recent phenomenon. Although the place and function of photography has shifted dramatically since the invention of the new medium in the early nineteenth century and its popularization throughout the twentieth and twenty-first centuries, the still occasionally ambivalent position of so-called art photography—is it art or is it documentation?—finds its origins in an aspect inherent in its function as a visual medium as such. For photography has from its very beginnings incorporated a fundamental ambivalence, a tension between the technological, mechanical nature of the camera and its operations on one hand, and the tool's ability, as well as its users' desires, to create beautiful images on the other. The phrase "art photography" is an expression of this ambivalence, and an appropriately awkward one.

With the modifier "art" (in "art photography"), however, an additional ambivalence is brought, quite literally, into the picture, in that the mechanical medium's mode of (re)production is bound to clash with conventional art historical assumptions about the origins and aesthetic value of artworks, that is to say, with respect to the former, the genius of the individual artist, or his or her personal experiences—indeed, to recall Mieke Bal's take on Louise Bourgeois, her or his personal memories—and with respect to the latter, the notions of authenticity and originality, the work's depth of meaning, its placement in the overall hierarchization of art into high and low forms, of art and craft, and, of course, its market value.

In line with such ambivalence, most contemporary definitions of the term "art photography" happily embrace what literary scholars designate the "intentional fallacy," the error of trying to determine a work of art's success on the basis of the maker's intentions—which, we know since Wimsatt and Beardsley, are neither available nor somehow retrievable from the work itself.[1] Popular reference books list "art photography" as "photography that is done as a fine art—that is, done to express the artist's perceptions and emotions and to share them with others,"[2] or, while duly acknowledging that it is a "somewhat vague term," similarly state that the "underlying idea" of the phrase is that the "producer of a given picture has aimed at something more than a mere realistic rendering of the subject, and has attempted to convey a personal impression."[3] Other sources stipulate the second, more mercantile aspect through which certain material objects in the postindustrial world tend to become recognized as "art" by insisting that art photography distinguishes itself from its more commercial and documentary uses (often referred to as photojournalism) in foregrounding its production and use as "high-quality photographic prints" that are "usually reproduced in limited editions to be sold to dealers, collectors or curators, rather than mass reproduced in advertising or magazines," and that will "sometimes be exhibited in an art gallery" or museum.[4]

It will be clear that within the larger context of this book, my interest in art photography neither concerns the person or genius of the individual maker nor his or her intentions in producing work that may (or may not) qualify as art, nor the work's market value. As before, I do not consider objects of aesthetic creation as primarily the *result* of certain forms of making and doing—even if, in this case, mechanical ones—but as involuntary forces, as forms of making and doing themselves, as expressive materiality with its own immediacy and vitality. It is therefore the ambivalent operations of art photography in the second sense, that is, as large, meticulously produced prints that form part of or constitute exhibitions and which *thereby* come to function *as* art, that will be one of my guiding concerns in this chapter. Let me briefly explain why it is precisely this highly contingent aspect of art photography that is at once key to and that considerably complicates the ambivalence at the heart of the photographic image per se.

Though ostensibly straightforward, the term "exhibition" is in itself ambivalent. As a noun it designates both the act of exhibiting and a collection of things (goods or works of art, etc.) for public display. The former sense relates exhibition to demonstration, manifestation, expression, presentation, and presentment; the latter establishes its connection to exposition, explanation, exposure. Both senses are present in the word's use with reference to art. Yet what the phrase "art exhibition" more importantly conveys is, first, the unbridgeable gap between that which is on display, that which presents, manifests, exposes itself—indeed, that which marks itself off as (the) Other—and the public, the viewing subject, the spectator who finds herself exposed to, if not beholden by, the exhibited goods confronting her. Second, and at the same time, the designation "art exhibition" inscribes the inevitable *rapport* or relation between the two, between Self and Other, between the object and the subject of the display, between artwork/image and recipient/viewer, which is constituted in the event that I call the aesthetic encounter. "Exhibition" thus highlights the separation between the "parties" involved in such encounters, as much as it designates the contracting force field between them, which marks them as actual occasions of experience, of feeling. This ambivalence is perhaps most poignantly expressed in the word's disreputable cousins, "exhibitionist" or "exhibitionism." Here, the act of exposure literally cannot but mark the distance between that which is shown, exposed, put upon display, on one hand, and the involuntary observer of the exhibited goods on the other, while yet equally powerfully inscribing this very act as a form of relation, a *rapport,* the establishment of a contact zone. These interconnected meanings or valences of the term "exhibition" point up my concern with art photography as not necessarily "something more," yet as definitely something different from a "mere realistic rendering of the subject," and they furthermore mark its function as an active, singular, and decidedly modern mode of artistic expression.

All this is by way of introducing my inquiry into the functioning of photography in the context of contemporary art theory, its operations in what I have earlier called the arts of the present and, by extension, and to slightly twist around the title of Jacques Rancière's recent study, the future of the image.[5] My approach to these broader questions runs through selected works of Dutch photographer Rineke Dijkstra (1959–), whose work offers a productive site to explore art photography from a neo-aesthetic perspective, that is to say, as art-work, as a "harnessing" of creative forces that escape both the terms of representation and those of identity or identification.

Dijkstra started out as a freelance photographer, working for journals like *Elle, Avenue,* and *Elegance,* and gained her international reputation as an "art photographer" with large-scale portrait series in color that have been widely exhibited since the beginning of the 1990s. Her photographic approach has been categorized as strictly conceptual, and her portraits have often been associated with those of the German portrait and documentary photographer August Sander (1876–1964), as well as the work of American photographer and writer Diane Arbus (1923–1971), an association about which I will have more to say shortly. Since the mid-1990s, Dijkstra has, in addition to a large-format still camera, been using the camcorder, and has exhibited videos at, among others, the Stedelijk Museum in Amsterdam, the Folkwang Museum in Essen, the Museum of Modern Art in New York, and most recently the Guggenheim Museum and the San Francisco Museum of Modern Art. Her work is quite rightly considered *art* photography in the various senses mentioned above, partly because her portraits move beyond documenting lives and recording moments, partly because they are primarily on display in galleries and museums and reproduced in expensive, limited-print catalogues and art books.[6]

Dijkstra's photographic portraits have fascinated me since I visited her large solo show of the same title ("Portraits") in the Stedelijk Museum in Amsterdam in 2005.[7] I am furthermore drawn to her work because of the variegated, often conflicting critical evaluations it has received from both art historians and other critical theorists. Such confusing, if not confused, responses are not unique to Dijkstra. They equally characterize a large part of the critical engagement with associated contemporary art photographers since photography from the early 1980s began moving away from its journalistic functions and was self-consciously and deliberately to be made to hang in art galleries and museums. Both the philosophical and theoretical interest in art photography today and the controversial place it still occasionally occupies in the world of art criticism suggest something about the importance of the photographic image, as it does about the image more generally, and its changing role in our increasingly visual culture. And, as my opening comments suggest, it is the ambivalence or elusiveness of art photography itself that, more than any other medium of visual expression, testifies to the need to address the function and significance of the image not only outside its representational functions, but also beyond the parameters of Baudrillard's notion of the "simulacrum,"[8] that is, as a perversion or a pretense of reality or as something that bears no relation to reality whatsoever, and beyond Guy Debord's critique of the "spectacle" as a self-fulfilling control mechanism for society, the "*negative expression* of living value" in a commodity culture in which the "perceptible world is replaced by a set of images that are superior to that world yet at the same time impose themselves as *eminently* perceptible."[9] Within a conceptual framework taking its cue from, among others, Whitehead's theory of pure feeling and Deleuze's (Nietzschean) onto-aesthetics, that is to say, an aesthetics of existence as an ontology of pure sensation, the clear-cut distinction between image and reality that the terms "simulacrum" and "spectacle" in this context suggest does not really make much sense. Furthermore, as the central terms in an overall negative critique of contemporary culture, in the sense discussed in the previous chapter, neither "simulacrum" nor "spectacle" allow us to inquire into the actual aesthetic operations of photographic images to address their power in their presentness, in their givenness, as organized activity, in everyday life.

Amidst the expanding range of theoretical and critical perspectives on the visual, on visual culture, and on what Susan Sontag has called the contemporary "image-world,"[10] as well as in the context of current art critical debates, the photograph takes up a privileged position. This is not particularly surprising, because the potential function of the photographic image, not as a representation of something else, but as presentation of itself—in other words, the consideration of photography not as an "objective" medium, but rather as operation of art—has, as suggested, been disputed from its emergence. As early as 1859, Baudelaire, father of modern art criticism, wholeheartedly rejected the modern medium, which he foresaw would put an end to artistic creation as such. As he writes in his commentary "On Photography":

> If photography is allowed to supplement art in some of its functions, it will soon
> have supplanted or corrupted it altogether, thanks to the stupidity of the multi-
> tude which is its natural ally. It is time, then, for it to return to its true duty, which
> is to be the servant of the sciences and arts—but the very humble servant, like
> printing or shorthand, which have neither created nor supplemented literature
> . . . . Let it rescue from oblivion those tumbling ruins, those books, prints and
> manuscripts which time is devouring, precious things whose form is dissolving
> and which demand a place in the archives of our memory—it will be thanked and
> applauded. But if it be allowed to encroach upon the domain of the impalpable
> and the imaginary, upon anything whose value depends solely upon the addition
> of something of a man's soul, then it will be so much the worse for us![11]

Although the shadow of painting would continue to haunt the modern new medium throughout the twentieth century, it is well—perhaps too well—known that Walter Benjamin in his famous essay "The Work of Art in the Age of Mechanical Reproduction" (1936) had already rejected the whole "nineteenth-century dispute as to the artistic value of painting versus photography," which seemed to him both "devious and confused." While he thus forthrightly dismissed photography's struggle to find its place among other artistic media and, indeed, its claim to aesthetic credentials, Benjamin nonetheless attributed great importance to the debate as such, because in his view it pointed up the as-yet-unrecognized transformation of the "entire nature of art" that he believed to have been heralded by the "very invention of photography."[12]

Rosalind Krauss points out that Benjamin had earlier, in a slightly less well-known essay titled "Little History of Photography" (1931), presented the "decay of the aura as a tendency within [the medium's] own history." At that point, however, Benjamin was still primarily concerned with the "contemporary return to the authenticity of photography's relation to the human subject."[13] Accordingly, Krauss suggests that a shift occurred in Benjamin's thought on photography, from the earlier essay, in which he regarded it as an autonomous medium that could claim its own specificity and enabled the "common" people to acquire a clear sense of their social realities, to his view expressed in the later essay on mechanical reproduction, "in all its modern, technological guises," as both "source and symptom of a full-scale demise of th[e] aura across all culture." This, Benjamin foresaw, would profoundly affect art itself, art as "celebrator of the unique and the authentic," in that it would "empty [art] out completely." As Krauss asserts, this shift in his view on the role of photography and of mechanical reproduction generally confirms Benjamin's critical role in turning photography into a theoretical object and thus ultimately, in the dismissal of the "very idea of the independent medium, including that of photography."[14]

In a recent essay on the photographic image, Jacques Rancière duly returns to Benjamin's shifting position on the medium, not in order to argue in favor of one or the other, but instead to maintain that Benjamin in fact turns the early and still ongoing debate over photography as an artistic medium "on its head." Rather than separating the latter's emphasis on photography's genius in establishing the human subject in his or her social context from the medium's function in producing its own obsolescence, Rancière takes these two positions together and places them in the historical context of the early years of the twentieth century. Assuming the rapid commodification of photography at the time to be inseparable from its role in reconfiguring the domain of art as a whole, Rancière maintains that Benjamin at once "made mechanical reproduction the principle of a new paradigm of art," and that he declared mechanically produced images to be the "means toward a new sensible education." Instead of merely initiating its own obsolescence, the photographic medium for Benjamin, in Rancière's gloss, becomes a participant in the "construction of a sensible world where men of the age of the masses could affirm their existence as both possible subjects of art and experts in its use."[15] This dual emphasis, pace Krauss, is as clearly articulated in Benjamin's earlier essay, "Little History of Photography," as it is in the later, more famous one on mechanical reproduction.

In 1931, Benjamin, for instance, refers to Eugène Atget's (1857–1927) Paris photographs as "the forerunners of Surrealist photography."[16] In 1935, in contrast, he asserts that, with Atget's photos of Paris (see figure 4.1), "photographs become standard evidence for historical occurrences, and acquire a hidden political significance."[17] Such optimism about the political significance and social potential

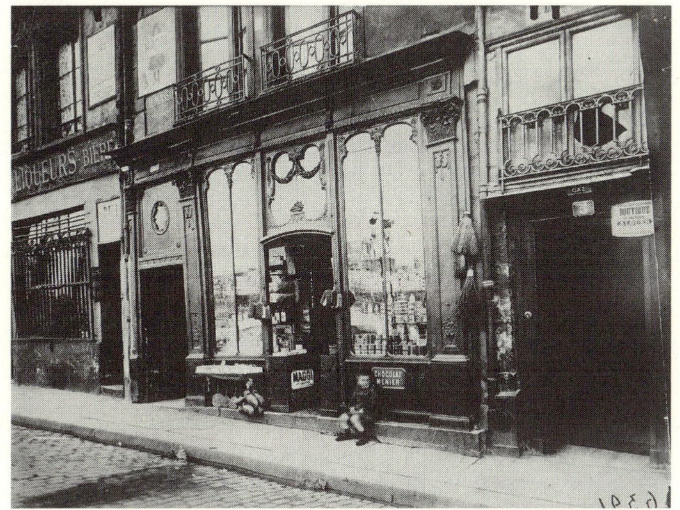

FIG. 4.1 Eugène Atget, *Shop front of "Courone d'or," Quai Bourbon*, 1922. Gelatin silver print, 17.7 × 22.4 cm (6¹⁵⁄₁₆ × 8¹³⁄₁₆ in.). The Metropolitan Museum of Art, David Hunter McAlpin Fund, 1962 (62.548). Image © The Metropolitan Museum of Art. ARTstor Collection, Metropolitan Museum of Art—Images for Academic Publishing

of the mechanical medium, which is conjoined throughout with an appreciation of photography's aesthetic dimension, is, however, similarly pronounced in Benjamin's 1931 discussion of the series of portraits by the progressive photographer August Sander (1876–1964), *People of the Twentieth Century* [*Menschen des 20. Jahrhunderts*] (see figure 4.2): Sander's work, Benjamin argues, underscores photography's revolutionary role, similar to that of psychoanalysis, in making what he defines as an "optical unconscious" available to consciousness,[18] thus enlarging our knowledge of the social world.[19]

Benjamin's optimism, however modified, about the political potential of mechanically reproduced images, and his equal insistence on the aesthetic dimension of the new medium, testify to the inherent ambivalence of the photograph in its very emergence as a theoretical object—in its unique, at least in a predigital age, operation as not only a representation and a connection to the social world, but also as presentation, as creative production. That the former aspect of photography has generally taken precedence over the latter in twentieth-century discussions of the medium may be partly attributed to the fact that its potentially edifying, revolutionary potential can equally readily be used to conservative, if not reactionary purposes, another instantiation of the medium's immanent ambivalence and the widely divergent uses to which it can be put, even in its purportedly straightforward documentary functions. There is, perhaps, no bet-

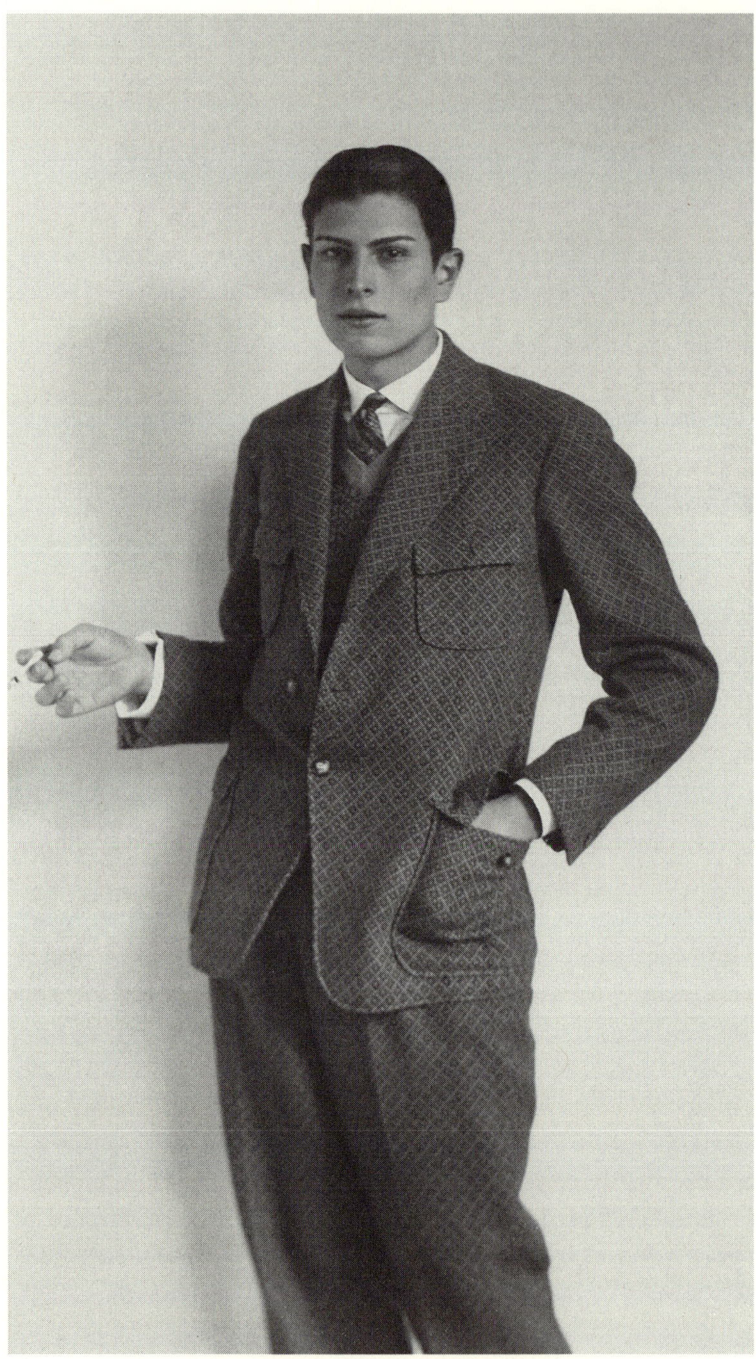

FIG. 4.2 August Sander, *High School Student,* 1926. Gelatin silver print, 9½ ×
5¼ in. (24.1 × 13.3 cm). The Museum of Modern Art, New York. Thomas Walther
Collection, Purchase (1852.2001). ©Die Photographische Sammlung / SK Stiftung
Kultur–August Sander Archiv, Cologne; ARS, New York, 2013 © The Museum of
Modern Art / Licensed by SCALA / Art Resource, NY.

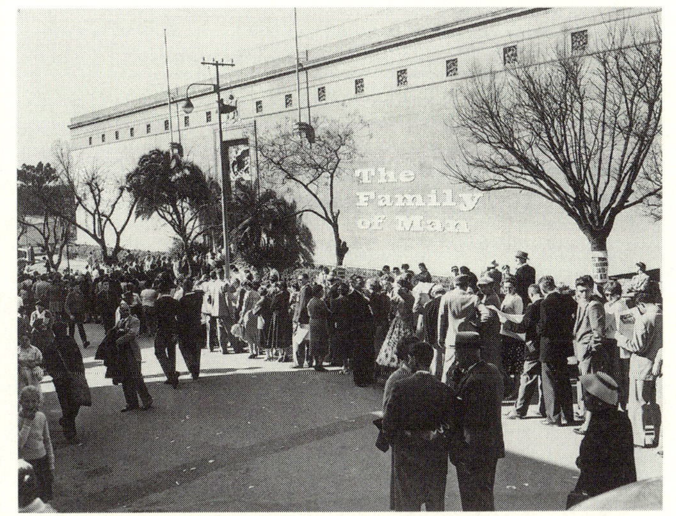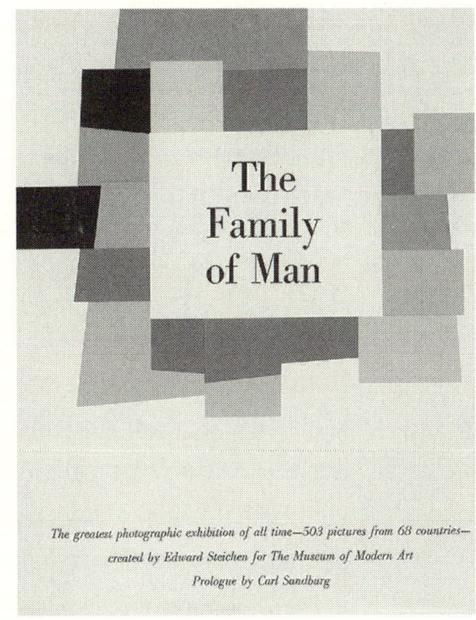

FIG. 4.3 (*left*) Visitors awaiting entry into the exhibition "The Family of Man," organized by the Museum of Modern Art, New York, at Government Pavilion, Johannesburg, Union of South Africa, from August 30 to September 13, 1958; photographer unknown. Permission of the Estate of Edward Steichen. Digital Image © The Museum of Modern Art / Licensed by SCALA / Art Resource, NY

FIG. 4.4 (*right*) Cover of the exhibition catalogue *The Family of Man*, by Edward Steichen. New York, The Museum of Modern Art, 1955. Offset, printed in color, 11¼ × 8¾ in. The Museum of Modern Art, New York. Permission of the Estate of Edward Steichen. Digital Image © The Museum of Modern Art / Licensed by SCALA / Art Resource, NY

ter counterexample to the social, "critical" photography of such leading early twentieth-century photographers as Atget and Sander than that of the mid-century American photographer Edward Steichen.

Ostensibly following in the footsteps of his radical predecessors, and thus in an equally seemingly truly "Benjaminian" tradition, although from a radically different political position, Steichen achieved in 1955 what he considered to be the "culmination of his career" by curating the wildly successful exhibition *The Family of Man* (see figures 4.3 and 4.4). First shown at the Museum of Modern Art in New York, the exhibition subsequently traveled to thirty-eight countries and was viewed by nine million people. Shortly after its opening, *The Family of Man* was turned into a book of the same title, whose fortieth anniversary reprint alone has sold more than four million copies.[20] What was and continues to be the appeal of this immensely successful collection of photographic images?

In the prologue to the first edition of the book, Steichen's brother-in-law, Carl Sandburg, claims that the undertaking of "A Family of Man" constitutes a "camera testament, a drama of the grand canyon of humanity, an epic woven of fun, mystery and holiness." Steichen's aim, Sandburg continues, in collecting

503 photos by 273 photographers, both famous and unknown, in sixty-eight countries, was visually to prove the universality of human experience and photography's role in its documentation: "Though meanings vary, we are all alike in all countries and tribes in trying to read what sky, land and sea say to us. Alike and ever alike we are on all continents in the need of love, food, clothing, work, speech, worship, games, dancing, fun. From tropics to arctics humanity lives with these needs so alike, so inexorably alike."[21] And the photographs are here to prove it. Seen in the context of the global divisions produced by World War II and, no less significantly, Cold War America, as well as in light of the growing racial and gender divisions that marked the U.S. domestic situation at the time, these grandiose claims may neither be surprising nor do much to obscure their author's, if not the entire project's, ideological stance. In their conservatory, if not ultraconservative thrust, Sandburg's comments were taken up by Roland Barthes, in one of his early writings on photography, a scathing critique that formed one of his monthly contributions to *Les lettres nouvelles,* a selection of which would later be published under the title *Mythologies* (1957).

Barthes effectively dissects the "ambiguous myth of the human 'community'" proffered by Sandburg and the "pietistic intention" underlying *The Family of Man* exhibition as a whole. He rejects the projection of what we today would probably call "our global community," which he considers to be based on the "very old mystification which always consists in placing Nature at the bottom of History," a classic humanist mystification that results in the erasure of the real differences that history and culture make on the lives of real men and women. Barthes, in not immediately addressing the function of the photograph in the creation and preservation of this myth, appears to accept its "common sense" definition, that is to say, the photographic image not as reality but as what he elsewhere (a few years later) will describe as the "perfect *analogon*" of reality, as a "message without a code."[22] Interestingly, at least for my purposes here, Barthes does, in the earlier essay, explicitly point up the complicit function of the photographic medium when he goes on to state, "The failure of photography seems to me to be flagrant in this connection: to reproduce death or birth tells us, literally, nothing."[23]

Assuming in 1957 a position that stands in direct opposition to that of Benjamin in 1931, Barthes unceremoniously rejects the photograph's potential as a medium to render the "human subject woven into the network of its social relations."[24] He nonetheless adds a new layer to the photograph's transformation into a theoretical object in a Benjaminian sense, as, in Krauss's terms, effecting both a change in the object, which, due to the "structure of reproduction," becomes more and more available to the masses, and in the subject, "for whom a new form of perception operates" as a simultaneous result of mechanical reproduction.[25] If it is indeed the photograph's political function qua reproduction that Barthes cashiers in this essay in spite of his later, semiotic analysis of it as a "message without a code," it is the earlier argument that he will pursue in his subsequent writing about the medium, which would culminate in his short book *Camera Lucida* (1980; hereafter *CL*),[26] published three years after his mother's deeply mourned death and a few months before his own unexpected death.

Camera Lucida, together with Susan Sontag's *On Photography* (1977), was for many years one of the most influential critical, if not quite theoretical books on photography—Rancière calls it the "absolute reference for thought on photography in the 1980s."[27] Sontag's *On Photography* has lost much of its critical significance, perhaps especially in the digital age, because of its almost absolute dismissal of the controlling, desensitizing, "anaesthetizing" effects the celebrated essayist and political activist attributes to the mechanical medium's operations in its redefinition of reality, its "way of imprisoning reality," as well as for "de-personalizing our relation to the world."[28] The disconnection between the representational subject of an image on one hand, and a presumed, pre-existing referential reality on the other, literally made manifest and enabled by digital imaging/composition, adds to the already quite tenuous nature of the grounds upon which the supposition of a "world" outside our perception, beyond our aesthetic prehension of it, rests, and has rendered Sontag's contribution to the discussion "on photography" decidedly dated.

Camera Lucida, in contrast, continues to provoke discussion even though not just Sontag's but Barthes' ideas as well have been severely criticized since the 1990s, especially, again, because of the increasing untenability of some of his claims in the light of digital technologies. Such criticisms do nothing to detract, however, from one of Barthes' most significant insights into the unique operations of the still strictly mechanical (at the time of his writing) rather than digital medium. For it is in *Camera Lucida* that Barthes elaborates his famous distinction between the *studium* and the *punctum* of the photographic image, a conceptualization that not only inscribes the essential difference between the representational level of the photographic image and its existence as artifact, but also, perhaps even more importantly, one that shifts attention away from the photograph as the work of an individual artist/genius/photographer, or the subject (world, reality) photographed as an object of analysis, to its effect on the viewer or spectator, or, more precisely, on the individual beholder.

In a highly personal account of the profoundly emotional effect of a picture of his mother taken when she was a child—the in/famous "Winter Garden Photograph," the only image he discusses at length but does not reproduce within his text—Barthes defines photography as asymbolic, as irreducible to the codes of language and culture, and as something that acts on the body as much as it engages the mind. In the distinction between the *studium* and the *punctum,* it is the conscious mind that perceives and processes the former. The *studium,* Barthes submits, derives from culture, from a certain form of polite education that generates a kind of "*average* affect"; it is the "application to a thing, a taste for someone, a kind of general, enthusiastic commitment . . . without special acuity" (*CL,* 26). Since the *studium* is a wide field of general interest and of "inconsequential taste," the recognition of its operation in a particular image means to "encounter the photographer's intentions," to understand them and to negotiate one's own position in relation to them (*CL,* 27–28). If we derive any pleasure from the *studium,* it would seem to be the kind of pleasure that Kant defines as "interested," the "barbaric" taste that involves charms and emotions, and not the experience of beauty, the exercise in selfless attention that is essential for "disinterested" aesthetic contemplation. Or, in the alternative terms of a more popular art criticism, the intentional fallacy in Barthes is transformed into the relatively uneventful "average affect"-response, the "demi-volition" mobilized by the photograph that, in its turn, is invested in by the perceiver's "sovereign consciousness" (*CL,* 27, 26), in brief, the photograph in its representational function.

The *punctum,* in contrast, Barthes describes as an element that is neither sought out by the perceiver nor inserted into the photograph by the photographer. It is thus im- or pre-personal. This element "rises from the scene, shoots out of it like an arrow, and pierces" the viewer. The *punctum* additionally interferes with, disturbs the *studium*; it is a "prick" or "punctuation" that "bruises," is "poignant," and that affects the perceiver on the nonconscious level of her or his embodied being (*CL,* 26). This element—in Barthes, the wounding or piercing detail—would appear to produce the kind of agitation that Kant primarily associates with the "terrifying sublime," but what I have, in previous chapters, identified with the prepersonal forces of affect, and, in a more limited, artistic context, described as the force of "uncontrollable beauty." In terms of the founding ambivalence of photography, the *punctum* is what I have designated above as the photograph in its eventness, its presentness, which at once mobilizes and constitutes its affective force, the involuntary operation of some point or mark that—perhaps not unlike what Bakhtin designates the "aesthetic object," which, as we shall see in a later chapter, may equally be connected to the Lacanian *objet petit a*[29]—not having been inserted into the image by the photographer nor sought by the viewer, forges the viewing subject's involuntary relationship with the image itself.

In this model, as in Benjamin's several decades before, the photograph as medium disappears; irreducible to the transmission of knowledge or information, its operation, that is to say, the affective force mobilized by the *punctum,* constitutes, in the words of Rancière, the "transfer of an absolute singularity"—which he defines as the thing or person represented but which I would argue to be the thing or subject presented, qua image—to "another absolute singularity."[30] For Rancière this second singularity is the individual viewer, a suggestion I would like to qualify substantially by claiming that this cannot be the same, "unpunctured" viewer that entered into the aesthetic encounter, but instead the produced, the newly constituted self (re-)organized by the *punctum*'s affective force.

Essential for Barthes' radical distinction between the *studium* and the *punctum* is, it will be clear, first, the condition that the photographer is unconscious of, or at least not in control of, the piercing detail that enters the photographic image: the *punctum* is a detail that was not intended by the photographer but that only obtains in the artifact contemplated by the viewer, in the actualization of the aesthetic event, as organized activity. A second aspect, however, that is essential for Barthes' elaboration on the difference between the *punctum* and the *studium* is the intimate, private, one-on-one situation in which he assumes the viewer to observe, study, dwell in and with the photographic image, and for Barthes this especially, if not exclusively, pertains to photos of human beings. *Camera Lucida* has often been denounced for its many internal contradictions, if not for its blatant sentimentality. With the advent of the digitization of the image, and, no less importantly, with the invasion of photography into art museums and exhibitions, it is on account of these two central underlying premises that Barthes' model of photography itself has become increasingly problematical, even if the two aspects of his distinction between the *punctum* and the *studium* do not come in for the same criticism or raise the same problems.

Some critics have claimed that the digitization of photography, and with it the photographer's almost unlimited control over the image, her powers of manipulation over what we see in it, irrespective of the referent, diminishes, in the words of Geoffrey Batchen, "our collective faith in the photograph's indexical relationship to the real." While this discussion, as we have seen, started much earlier, with Benjamin, it is with this latest technological development that, Batchen maintains, people have generally come to fear that photography will cease to exist as an "autonomous medium." In line with this type of lament, others have claimed that that which Batchen calls our current, "post-photography" moment, not only entails the disappearance of photography as an independent entity, but also renders Barthes' notion of the *punctum* obsolete. His argument against such lamentations, which is that we may have reached a moment after, but not beyond, photography, in that the photographic "as a rich vocabulary of conventions and references lives on in an ever-expanding splendor" across a range of artistic practices, strikes me as persuasive.[31] I simultaneously concur with James Elkins' assertion, made in the context of a debate with Michael Fried on the nature of the medium, that photography's digitization has nothing to do with the operation of the *punctum.* Since the discovery of the piercing detail, the event of the *punctum,* occurs on the side of the viewer, it remains unaffected by the evolution in the medium's technology.[32]

The second central aspect of Barthes' model of photography, however, his emphasis on the privacy of photographic contemplation and the idiosyncrasy of the perceiver's affective responses, seems less impervious to the changes of time or to technological developments. Having not so much to do with photographical and reproductive technologies per se, but rather with the ways the photographic functions, shows itself, and operates in the world, this aspect may seem to be fundamentally compromised in the postphotographic era, where the photographic obtains within a shifting configuration of social, artistic, and economic "conventions and references."

The battle between painting and photography over their respective aesthetic credentials, starting in the nineteenth century and resulting in a gradual turning of the tables with what Krauss identifies as the "triumphal convergence of art and photography that began in the late 1960s,"[33] appears to have come to a (provisional?) close at the dawn of the twenty-first century. Photography currently assumes a leading role in the world of art and design, increasingly blurring the boundaries between itself and other media, and, as already mentioned, appearing on the walls of a growing number of museums and art galleries from the 1980s onwards. By moving into the public sphere of the museum, where large-format photographs assume the status of monumental paintings and take up their place among video and other installations, contemporary art photography significantly complicates the notion of the *punctum.*[34]

Equally important, however, is that the expanded purview of the photographic has not remained restricted to the domain of art photography or been confined to the walls of museums and art galleries. The digitization of the image has similarly profoundly affected the way news, fashion, and other forms of "documentary" photography, as well as what Elkins calls "vernacular" photography, meaning the private, personal, domestic, and domesticated pictures that Barthes, at least in *Camera Lucida,* is primarily concerned with, appear and function in the world. What is still sometimes called photojournalism is no longer a mode of image production restricted to venues such as newspapers, television, and other traditional media; "news" and "informative" images are increasingly likely to show up across a range of media, while fashion photography additionally often crosses over from one branch of the postphotographic into the other by making its way from magazines and store websites into art shows and galleries. Nor can "vernacular" photography be any longer considered strictly personal or domestic, because most of us have learned to share all these precious, "captured," and formerly largely private moments across a similarly wide range of semipublic domains such as Flickr, Tumblr, Facebook, and so on, succinctly referred to as Web 2.0 social media.

Rather than the undermining of the significance of or the dislodging of the distinction between the *studium* and the *punctum* itself, it is, I suggest, because of the attenuation of the indexical relation between the photographic image and the real, and the move of photography away from its traditionally private and/or medium-specific sites into the complex, multimedia contexts of our increasingly visual and visualizing culture, that the digital revolution can be argued to have landed us in what Batchen's defines as a "post-photography" moment. This "moment" clearly invites a reconsideration of the function and effects not only of the photographic image, but of the image as such. Still, since my overall interest in this book lies with a more narrowly defined realm of visual art (and aesthetics) after representation and not with new media culture as a whole, I will in this and the following chapter limit my focus to different manifestations of the photographic image "post-photography." I turn to Rineke Dijkstra, whose work, as suggested earlier, offers a provocative venue for a reconsideration of art photography today, while allowing me further to unfold a nonrepresentational model of aesthetic inquiry.

Dijkstra's best-known and probably most widely exhibited and distributed work comprises various series of imposing portraits of otherwise indifferent individuals, featuring awkward-looking teenagers on various beaches in Europe and the United States (see figure 4.5), young mothers holding their recently born babies, toreadors after their first bullfights, male and female Israeli soldiers, a French young man at various stages in his career in the Foreign Legion, a female asylum seeker gradually blending into the culture of her adopted country.

All these portraits are carefully posed. The photographed subjects look straight into the camera. They appear fully aware of being seen, of being looked at by the photographer for the precise purpose of being captured in a picture/by the camera. They do not therefore offer the inadvertent traces of the real many early photography critics believed to be captured by the most popular form of "vernacular" photography, the snapshot.

Susan Sontag, for instance, dismisses the leveling and demeaning effects of everyday amateur photography, but at the same time insists that "photographic images are pieces of evidence in an ongoing biography or history . . . photography supplies not only a record of the past but a new way of dealing with the present." Cameras, unlike brush and paint, she goes on to argue, "establish an inferential relation to the present (reality is known by its traces), provide an instantly retroactive view of experience."[35] On this view, the snapshot is not something that may "bruise" or "wound" the perceiver in his or her private contemplation, as Barthes would like us to believe, or, to put it slightly differently, it is not a site or locus

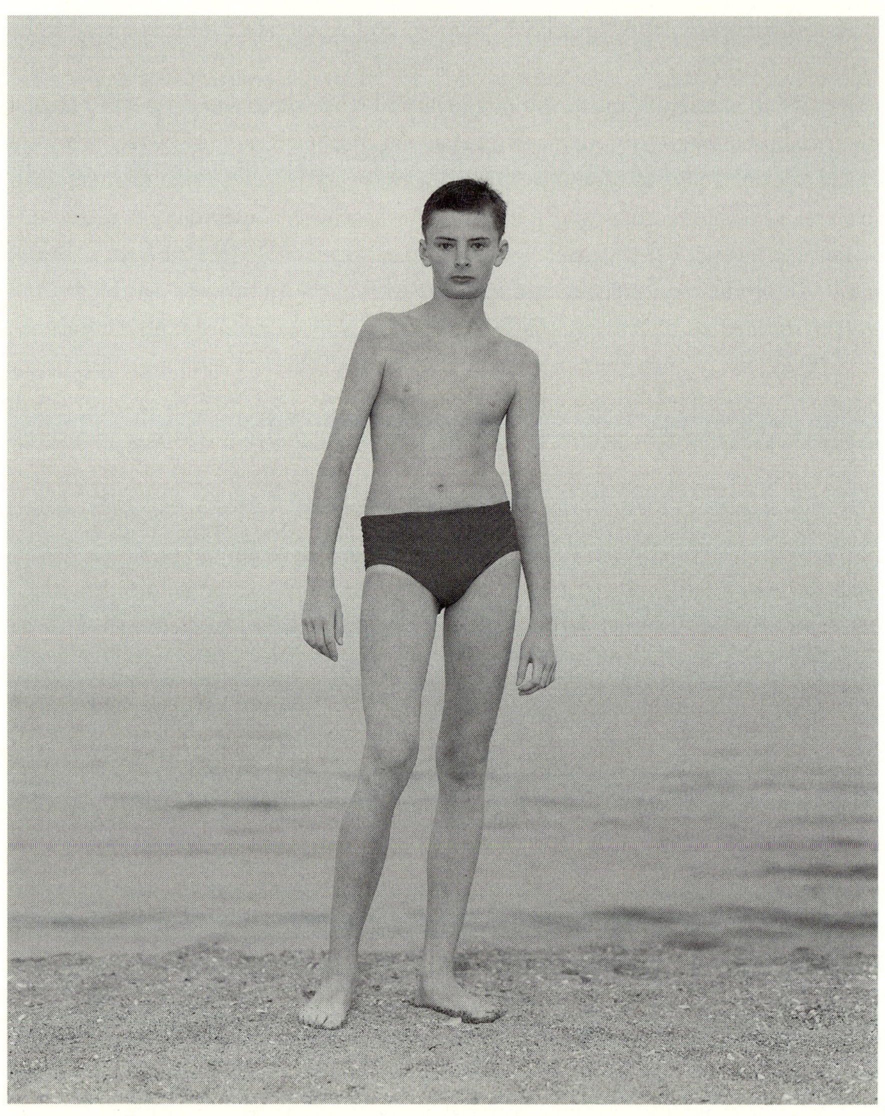

FIG. 4.5 Rineke Dijkstra, *Odessa, Ukraine, August 4, 1993.* Chromogenic print, image: 117 × 94 cm; frame: 153 × 129 cm, edition of 6. Image: 35 × 28 cm; frame: 62 × 52 cm, edition of 15.   © 2013 Rineke Dijkstra. Courtesy of the artist and Marian Goodman Gallery, NY

of aesthetic experience itself. In Sontag's discussion, "vernacular" photography rather becomes a quintessentially twentieth-century phenomenon of alienation, the proof, the manifestation, the inscription of everybody's everyday existence at one remove, after the event; it is a private existence that in the digital age would appear to have removed itself even more from our everyday experience, becoming virtually public by being shared through a variety of ubiquitously accessible social media. Functioning as works of art, Dijkstra's portraits, I argue, do not aspire to provide any such evidence, whether of private or public existence, nor do they reveal a trace of the real. As images presenting themselves to my view, they do not offer an inferential relation to an external reality, past or present, and they do not inscribe histories or biographies—not even in the series of individual subjects captured at different, consecutive moments of their lives (in social reality). Instead, they constitute carefully composed beings of sensation that invite me, urge me to "become with them" (*WP*, 177).

Of colossal proportions, meticulously finished, and largely static in their composition, these portraits do not operate as representations of something else, a record of the past, nor do they offer a "new way of dealing with the present." They do not pretend to be anything but pictorial monuments, but not monuments in the traditional sense as solid, permanent, material objects that commemorate and celebrate important events or exceptional people in the past. Surely they may be seen as carefully marked moments in time. Such moments, however, in their very singularity as visual materiality, as expressive matter, become insignificant, indifferent almost, interchangeable; the socio-historical dimensions of space and time are merely inscribed in the works' titles, which consist of date and place and sometimes include the subject's proper name, but never in the images themselves. The reality of these portraits, their presentness as images, does not refer to an underlying, pre-existing, or ulterior social reality, or past present. On the contrary, their reality is the reality of the pictorial surface, and it is the pictorial surface that functions as a monument in the sense suggested by Deleuze and Guattari, that which is preserved in the work of art, the percepts and affects that become materially expressive, pass into sensation, and address us as a "bloc of present sensations that owe their preservation only to themselves" (*WP*, 167).

Put in different terms, Dijkstra's teenager in a green swimsuit on a Polish beach, for instance (figure 4.6), evokes other images, other "blocs of sensation," such as Botticelli's or Ingres' "Venus," or the latter's "Spring" (see figures 4.7 and 4.8), rather than documenting the life of a social subject, whether in the politically progressive tradition of August Sander or following the trajectory of the "pietistic," universalizing efforts of Edward Steichen.

Instead of presenting a humanistic typology of "the family of man," Dijkstra's series of beach portraits, for example, insert themselves into, revive, and—because

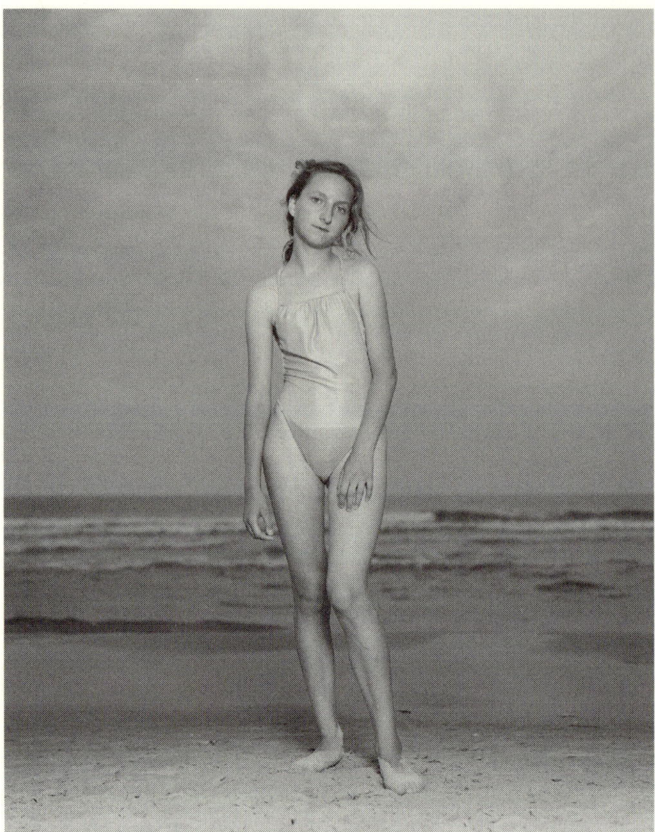

FIG. 4.6 Rineke Dijkstra, *Kolobrzeg, Poland, July 26, 1992.* Chromogenic
print, image: 117 × 94 cm; frame: 153 × 129 cm, edition of 6. Image:
35 × 28 cm; frame: 62 × 52 cm, edition of 15. © 2013 Rineke Dijkstra.
Courtesy of the artist and Marian Goodman Gallery, NY

of their undeniable mechanical reproduction—also transform a long-standing
pictorial tradition that seemed to have been overthrown by the new objectivism
of earlier twentieth-century and especially documentary photography. As photographic images, they appear to partake of both traditions, complicating them,
questioning, if not unraveling them, opening them up to new becomings, rather
than enacting what Rancière describes as the "rediscovered union between two
statuses of the image that the modernist tradition had separated: the image as
representation of an individual and as operation of art."[36]

In their latter function, as what I have called the photographic image as an act
of creation, in its eventness, its presentness, and thus as operation of art, Dijkstra's portraits neither typify, typologize, nor document, despite the suggestion of
documentation evoked by their titles—which we *read* rather than *see.* This does

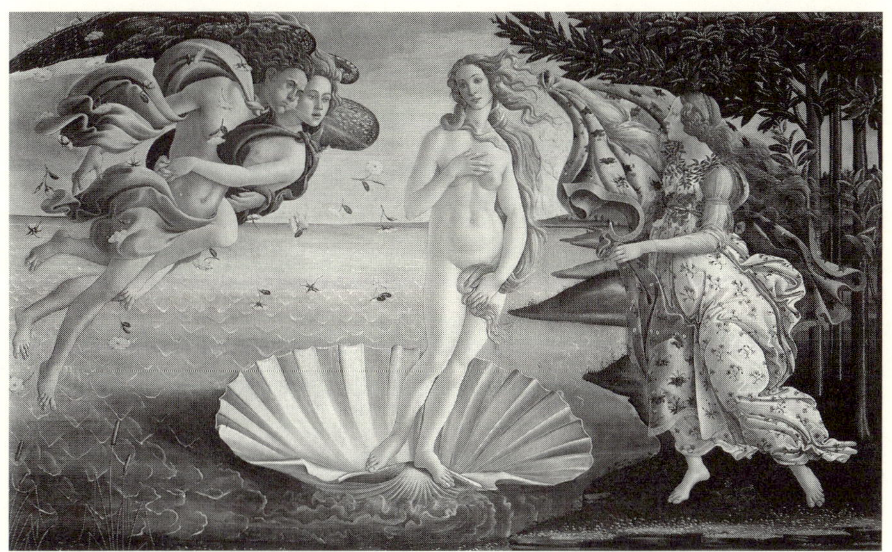

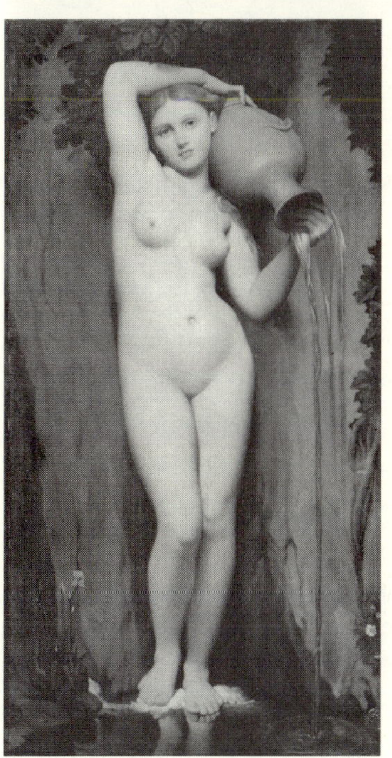

FIG. 4.7 (*above*) Sandro Botticelli, *The Birth of Venus*, post-restoration, ca. 1484. Tempera on canvas, 68 × 109⅝ in. (172 × 278.5 cm). Uffizi, Florence. SCALA / Art Resource, NY

FIG. 4.8 (*left*) Jean Auguste Dominique Ingres, *The Source*, 1856. Oil on canvas, 163 × 80 cm. Musée d'Orsay, Paris. Erich Lessing / Art Resource, NY not mean, however, that they do not also present individuals, even if, as portraits, they do not function in the tradition of twentieth-century social photography, that is, by making an "optical unconscious" available to consciousness and thus enlarging our knowledge of the social world. The differences in attire or location, the idiosyncrasies of their posture, and corporeal self-presentation notwithstanding, the subjects in these photographs are present at the same time that they are ultimately dispossessed of their social identities. Functioning simultaneously as portraits and as pictorial surfaces, the photographic images themselves participate in the construction of, in Rancière's words, a "sensible environment" that reaches "beyond its own specificity."[37] The affective force they mobilize is thus both similar to and different from that of the *punctum*: similar in that their "piercing" or "bruising" effect, their poignancy, cannot be reduced to the intentions of the photographer nor to the will or desire of the perceiver, but is something that arises from the scene of the aesthetic encounter or event; different in that this scene is neither personal nor private but rather a momentary convergence of affective forces actualized in an event that is both impersonal and presubjective. Whereas the effect of the aesthetic encounter with Dijkstra's portraits is perhaps adequately captured in Rancière's earlier cited phrase—the "transfer of an absolute singularity" to "another absolute singularity"—this transfer is divested of any personal, subjective, or social significance and instead comprises "beings of sensations," beings, in Deleuze's and Guattari's terms, "whose validity lies in themselves and exceeds any lived" (*WP*, 163).

By foregrounding the ways in which these portraits present themselves to me first and foremost as pictorial surfaces, as monuments in a Deleuzian-Guattarian sense, and not as representations of something else, I deliberately distance myself from art historical appreciations of Dijkstra's work that focus on the spectator's possibilities for identification or that perceive in these works, as Canadian critic Thérèse St.-Gelais does, "potential collective—or even communitarian—affinities that can be detected in certain signs and characteristics."[38] Such "readings" of these monumental works do not focus on their presence as images, or even as images per se, but instead on their potential meanings, which are erroneously assumed to be somehow retrievable, or "read off" of what St.-Gelais boldly claims to be the artist's "desire."

Not only does St.-Gelais fall headlong into the trap of the intentional fallacy, she actually goes a step further in depriving Dijkstra's works of their uniqueness qua works of art by insisting on placing the artist in a photographic tradition that stretches from Sander to Arbus. In doing so, however, she is forced into a twisted argument, asserting that Dijkstra's work expresses an attempt to show "what is universal in the common," that is to say, that the photographer's desire is a kind of reversal of Arbus's equally putative intention to reveal the "uncommon

in the common"[39]—a curious move that additionally returns us to a "pietistic"
humanist tradition à la Steichen, detected and effectively rejected by Roland
Barthes as early as 1957.

In trying to avoid such reductive readings and move toward a nonrepresentational and what I would call, admittedly awkwardly, a post-Baudrillardian and
post-Debordian approach of contemporary art photography, I take my cue not
only from Deleuze and Guattari, but I also find a rich conceptual resource in
Jean-Luc Nancy's alternative philosophical (rather than art historical) writings,
especially his collection of essays on images and visual art, *The Ground of the
Image* (2005; hereafter *GI*).

The image, Nancy boldly proclaims, is "always sacred," in the sense that it is
separate, cut off, set aside, at a distance. Since the term "sacred" carries too many
religious overtones, however, and religion is precisely the "observance of a rite
that forms and maintains a bond," he decides to call the sacredness of the image
"*the distinct.*"[40] The distinct is always marked off by a trait or a line, "no longer of
the order of touch," yet "not exactly untouchable . . . but rather an impalpable."
The distinct may be at a distance, set apart, in two ways: it is "separated from
contact or from identity," and/or "it does not touch, and it is dissimilar." This,
then, according to Nancy, is the nature of the image:

> It must be detached, placed outside and before one's eyes (it is therefore insepa-
> rable from a hidden surface, from which it cannot, as it were, be peeled away: the
> dark side of the picture, its underside or backside, or even its weave or its subjec-
> tile), and it must be different from the thing. The image is a thing that is not the
> thing: it distinguishes itself from it, essentially. (*GI*, 2)

Nancy goes on to point out that the distinct may well be set apart, impalpable,
but that it is nonetheless also a force, an "energy, pressure, or intensity . . . not to
say a violence." What needs to be explained, then, is the way the image—always
marking itself as image, distinguishing itself through a trait, puncture, or inci-
sion—both gives itself by such a trait and "how what it thus gives is first a force,
an intensity, the very force of its distinction" (*GI*, 2).

Nancy's exposition of the image in its ostensible simplicity—a thing that is
not the thing—is in the first place helpful in attempting to approach Dijkstra's
portraits as operations of art, as organized aesthetic activity. It is nonetheless
his emphasis on such distinctness as a force, a force that "has no use . . . and is
not presented in a manifestation," that allows me to reflect upon the ways these
portraits affect me as what I tried to articulate in my introductory comments
on the term "exhibition," that is, as simultaneously that which is shown, on
display, and that which shows itself as essentially Other, and that to which I am
simultaneously, voluntarily or involuntarily, exposed, that which draws me into

their composition, into the "compound of percepts and affects" that make me, to recall Deleuze and Guattari, "become with them" (*WP*, 177). It is as instantiations or actualizations of exhibition/exposure, as distinct from their representational function, and thus emphatically not as sources of potential recognition and/or identification that I find Dijkstra's portraits to mark themselves off most forcefully, or poignantly, as sites of intensity or a violence.

As the other of form, Nancy's concept of force in relation to the image is the "intimate and its passion," that which has withdrawn in and upon itself and is distinct from all representation. To re-evoke Barthes' notion of the *punctum,* it is the puncture or trait that marks the image as sacred; the distinction of the distinct is its separation, and its tension or intensity is "that of a setting apart and keeping separate which at the same time is a crossing of this separation" (*GI*, 3). In other words, only by being set aside, by separating itself off from representation, by withdrawing into itself, and by becoming impalpable, the image sets up a force field into which I may enter, in which I may grasp the passion or violence of the image, without the establishment of continuity. There is no possibility for identification between me, the perceiving subject, in my exposure to the pictorial surface of the image, and its subject, that which is represented in the image. Rather, to cite (and slightly pervert) Rancière's phrase again, there is "transfer of an absolute singularity" to "another absolute singularity," which is not something that obtains between individual subjects or between subject and object, but which is the "work of sensation" (*WP*, 191) To put it differently, in my exposure to what shows itself in the image, qua image, I am subject to a certain "energy, pressure, or intensity . . . not to say a violence," which is unequivocally not the violence of representation. Rather than forging or maintaining a bond, the force field of the image constitutes a contact-zone in which I may experience shock, confrontation, or embrace, but my crossing of that zone does not obviate the distinction of the image. In Nancy's terms: "An intimacy is thus exposed to me, but for what it is, with its force that is dense and tight, not relaxed, reserved, not readily given" (*GI*, 3).

In the world of things, as much as in the realm of representation, continuity operates through making connections, the indistinct being bound together in a homogeneous space: recognition, identification, typification, all belong in this realm. In the heterogeneous realm of the distinct, however, the "unbound" or, indeed, the "unbindable" prevails. The force of the distinct, the way the image gives itself through the trait that sets it apart, ultimately "transports us to . . . its very unbinding" (*GI*, 3). Such unbinding, and the violent, if not violating force of the distinct, which is at the same time the force of the passion of the image, its intensity, I experience most powerfully in my encounter with a particular series of Dijkstra's portraits titled "Julie," "Tecla," and "Saskia," three young Dutch mothers clutching their newly born babies to their visibly violated postnatal bodies.[41] (As an aside, natural childbirth is the rule in the Netherlands.) The subjects in these pictures stare at me directly, frontally, unreservedly; their bodies' nakedness and the inexpressible intimacy between their own and their infants' bodies in this postpartum moment are exposed to me, but not readily given. The exclusivity of that corporeal bond, "placed outside and before my eyes," to which I find myself exposed in my encounter with the image—impalpable yet passionate—both inscribes the distance between us (Other/Self, object/subject) and forges the *rapport* between us, engages me in the violent embrace of the force that transports me to its "very unbinding," into the actual occasion of un/becoming that is constituted in the aesthetic event. The singularity of each of these images, in their inescapable presentness, in their distinctness, violently draws forth an intimacy, pulling and extracting something from me, precisely by withholding it, and thereby exert its deterritorializing force.

As Nancy points out, the word "portrait" is etymologically linked to the Latin verb *pro-trahere,* to draw forth. His elaboration of this aspect—he calls the portrait the "image of the image in general"—enables us to see how Dijkstra's photographs touch us while remaining impalpable; their force extracts an intimacy while remaining at a distance, setting up a relation of discontinuity. Their force is that of a calling-forth, an unbinding, a violence even, or, to use a Deleuzian term, a line of flight, a becoming-other. This is perhaps, paradoxically, most strikingly evident in the two series of photographs that follow their subjects through different stages of their lives: those of "Olivier," captured at different intervals through his career in the French Foreign Legion (see plates 9 through 11), and those of "Almerisa" (see plates 12 through 14), marking her various transmutations through a life as, respectively, a refugee, an asylum seeker, and an immigrant in the Netherlands.

Rather than tracing a line of continuous becoming, of natural, social, or professional development, these portraits, in their individual separateness, their distinctness, pull me into their force field by throwing their force in front of me, projecting a line, a tracing, that instantiates a discontinuity, the distinct jumping toward the indistinct without ever linking up with it. Looking at these portraits (admittedly, over and over again), I am exposed to their presentness, entangled in their intensity, but their force is the force of withholding; the photographic image cannot but mark its unbinding, or deterritorializing force. As such, all these portraits mock Steichen's mystification of a "family of man" as much as they implode any easy or reassuring notion of communion. Dense and tight, reserved, and not readily given, their intimacy precludes identificatory continuity, which can only occur on the plane of the indistinct. As instantiations of the transfer of an absolute singularity to another absolute singularity, my repeated encounters with them over time are, moreover, never the same from one viewing to the next. Simulacra in the sense suggested by Deleuze, they are "systems" or "series" in which I find "no prior identity, no internal resemblance . . . what is displaced and disguised in the series cannot and must not be identified, but exists and acts as the differenciator of difference" (*DR*, 299–300). Presenting themselves in their spatiotemporal separateness, each moment of exposure, the actual occasion of my experience of them, reinscribes the ambivalence marking their operation as works of art, as acts of creation. Their intimacy violently confronts me with the unbridgeable gap between that which exposes itself, that which is (the) Other to my Self, and, at the same time, calls forth the contracting force of the encounter, takes me up in a ceaseless process of becoming-other, of discontinuous transformation, and produces me anew.

In its actualization, the aesthetic encounter with Dijkstra's portraits defies any notion of artistic intention, as much as the works themselves resist signification and definition. It is in this sense that Dijkstra's portraits, and that of several other contemporary photographers, mark themselves off as art and forfeit photography's earlier documentary or informative functions. And it is this kind of photographic work that, by extension, offers itself up as a productive site to rethink the function and effects of the postphotographic image and critically reflect upon its future. That such reflection, pace Barthes, by no means needs to be restricted to images of one or more human beings, but rather encompasses the postphotographic "vocabulary" as such, will be a central supposition of my discussion on "ruin porn" in the next chapter.

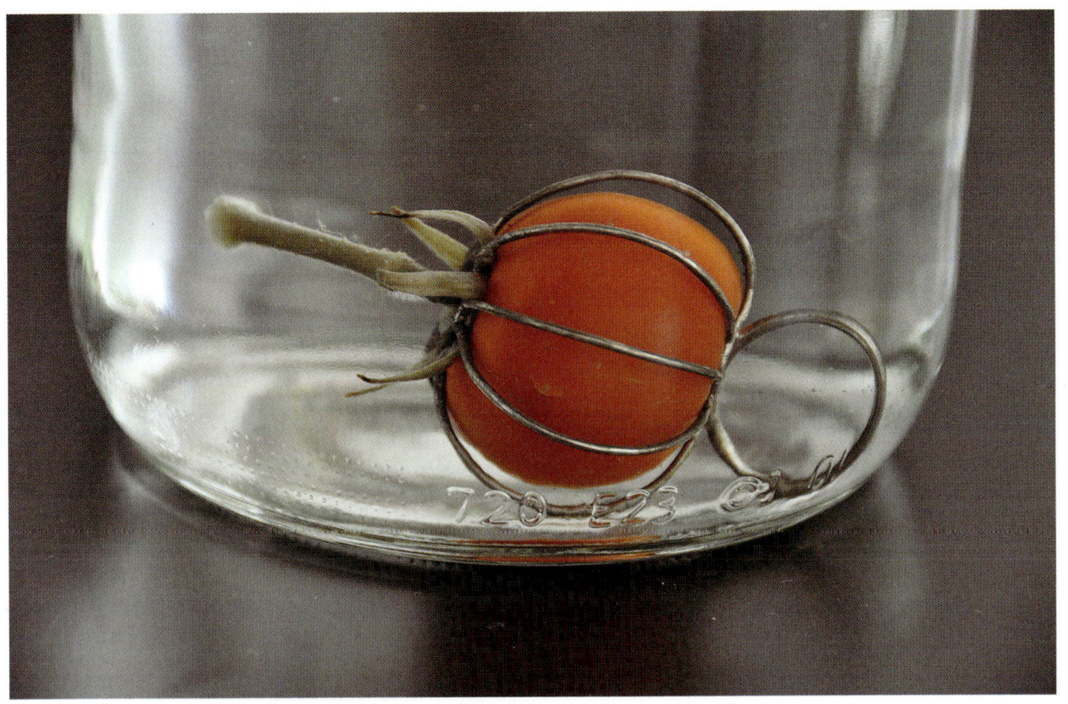

PLATE 1 Hilde de Decker, *For the Farmer and the Market Gardener,* 1999. Gold, silver, vegetables, 12 × 12 × 17 cm © Hilde de Decker. Photo: Michiel Heffels

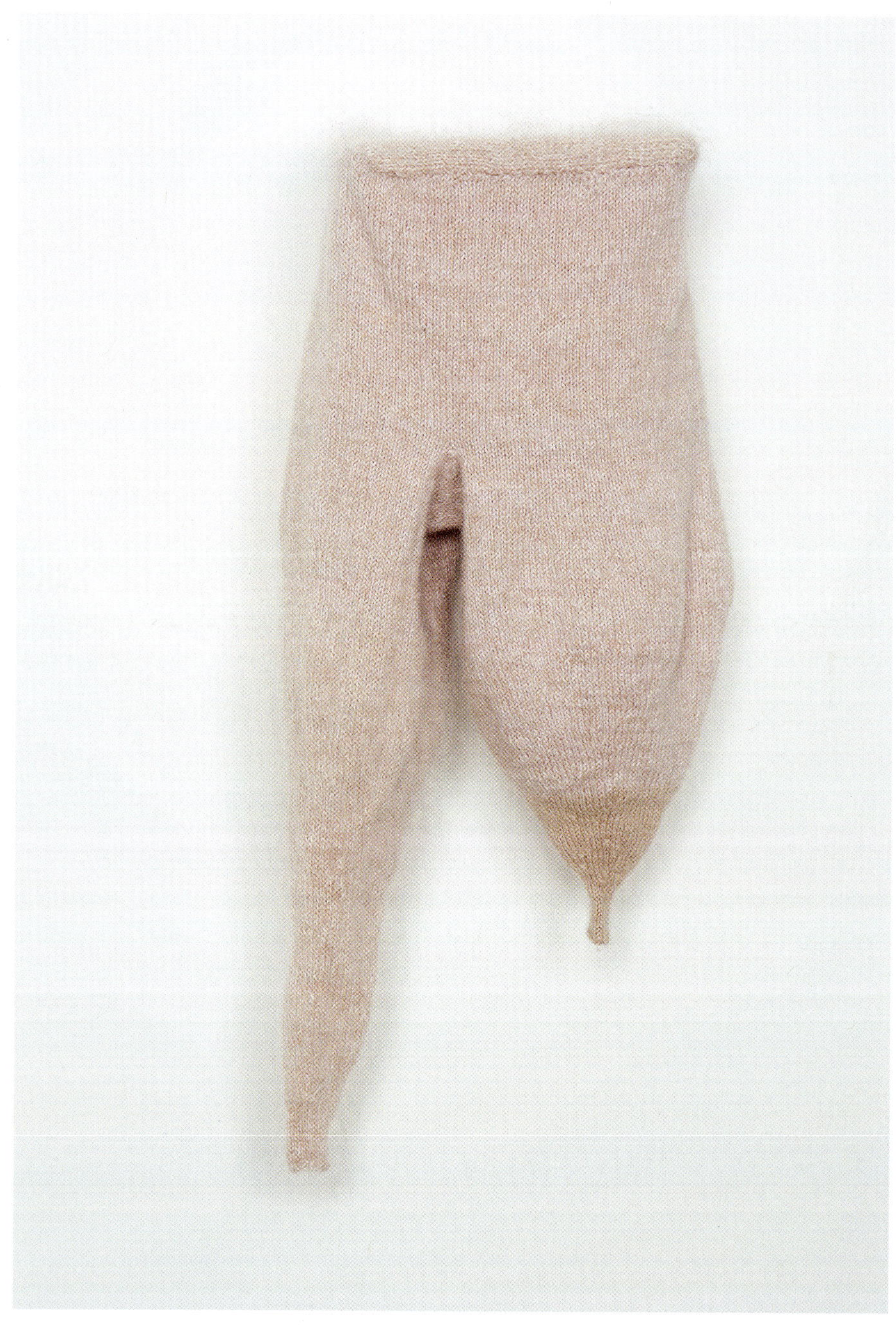

PLATE 2 Iris Eichenberg, *Broek,* from the series *Pink Years Later,* 2009.
Boiled wool, 15 × 10 × 25 cm © Iris Eichenberg

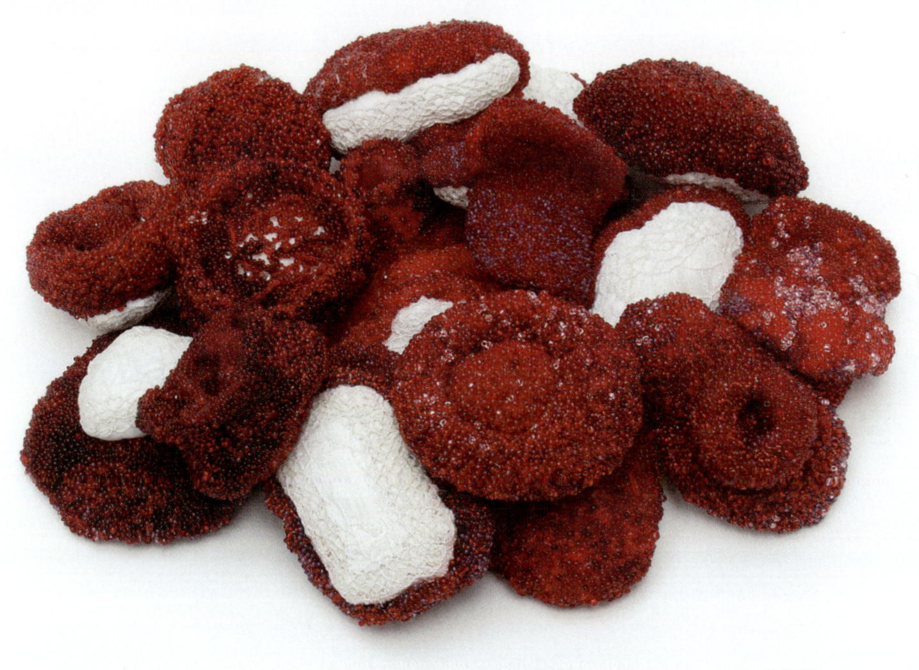

PLATE 3 Célio Braga, *Untitled* ("Rubros" collection, 14 pieces), brooches/objects, 2001/2002. Handmade felt, cotton, silk, and glass beads; sizes and dimensions variable. Collection Stedelijk Museum Amsterdam

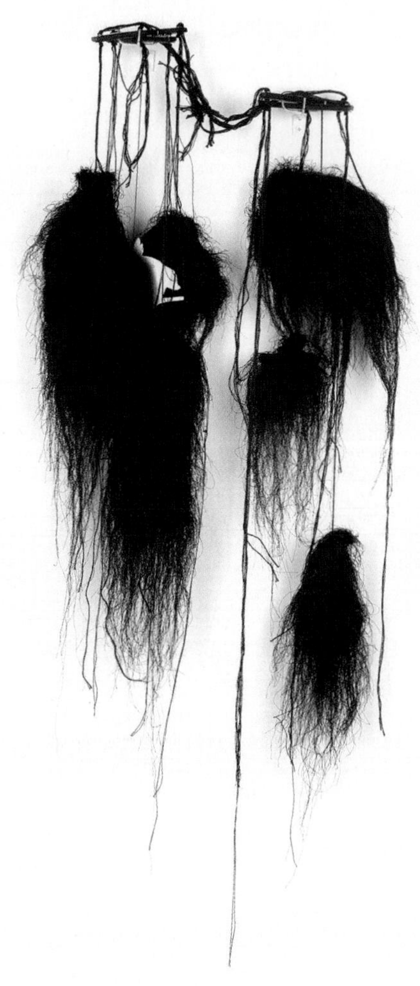

PLATE 4 Seth Papac, *Tangle, necklace*, 2008. Silver, wool, cotton, wood. 100 × 70 × 15 cm © Seth Papac

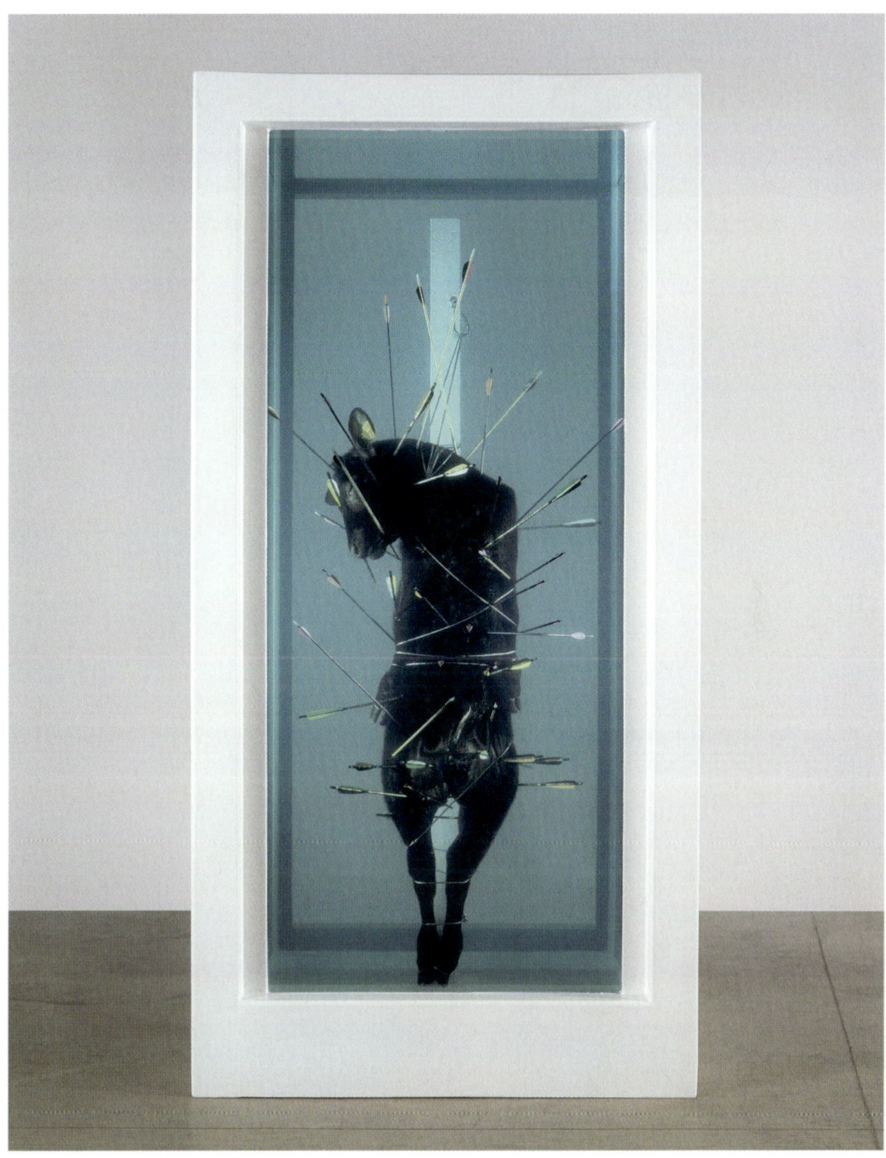

PLATE 5 Damien Hirst, *St. Sebastian, Exquisite Pain,* 2007. Glass, steel, bullock, arrows, crossbow bolts, and formaldehyde solution, 126⅝ × 61⁵⁄₁₆ × 61⁵⁄₁₆ in. (321.6 × 155.8 × 155.8 cm). © Damien Hirst and Science Ltd. All rights reserved, DACS 2013 / ARS NY. Photographed by Prudence Cuming Associates Ltd.

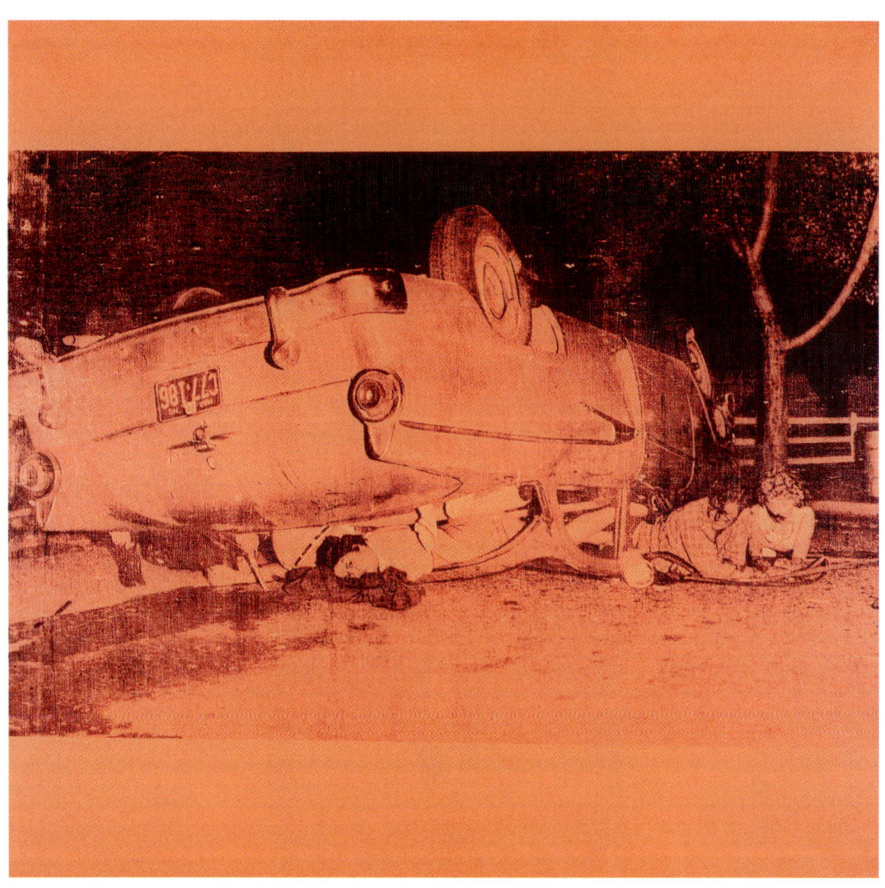

PLATE 6 Andy Warhol, *Five Deaths on Orange (Orange Disaster)*, 1963.
Silkscreen ink on synthetic polymer paint on linen, 30⅙ × 30⅛ in.
© The Andy Warhol Foundation for the Visual Arts, Inc. / ARS, NY

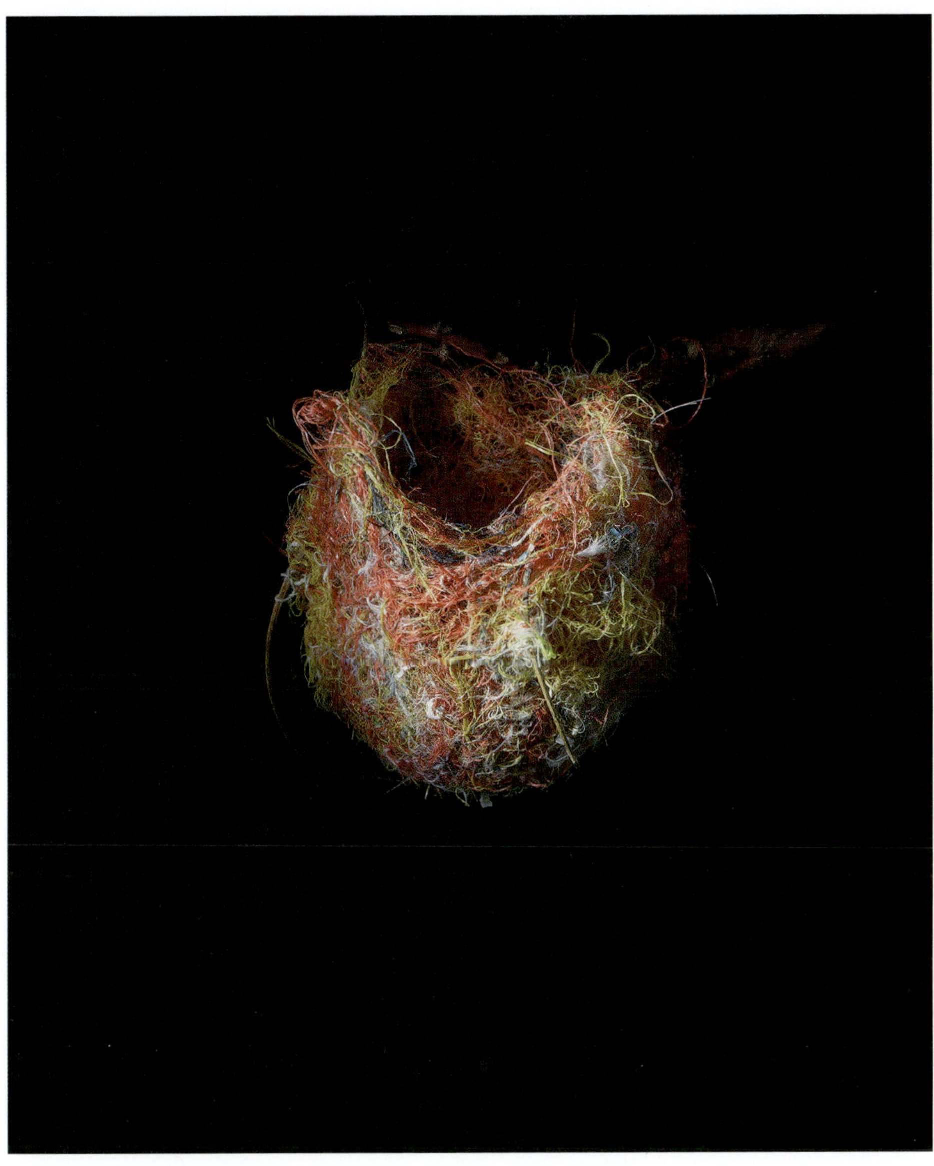

PLATE 7 Richard Barnes, *Northern Oriole,* 2000. Archival digital C print, 48 × 42 in. © Richard Barnes

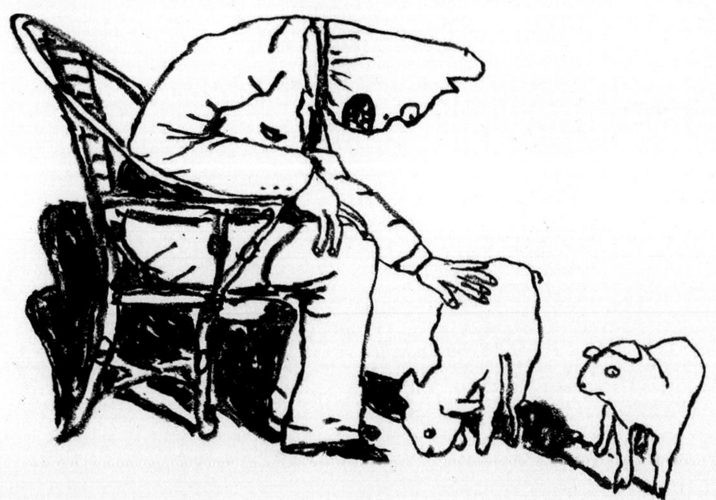

PLATE 8 Kathleen Henderson, *Untitled (figure with two lambs)*, 2006.
Oil stick on paper, 17 × 20⅛ in. Private collection, Beverly Hills. © Kathleen
Henderson. Courtesy of Rosamund Felsen Gallery, Santa Monica

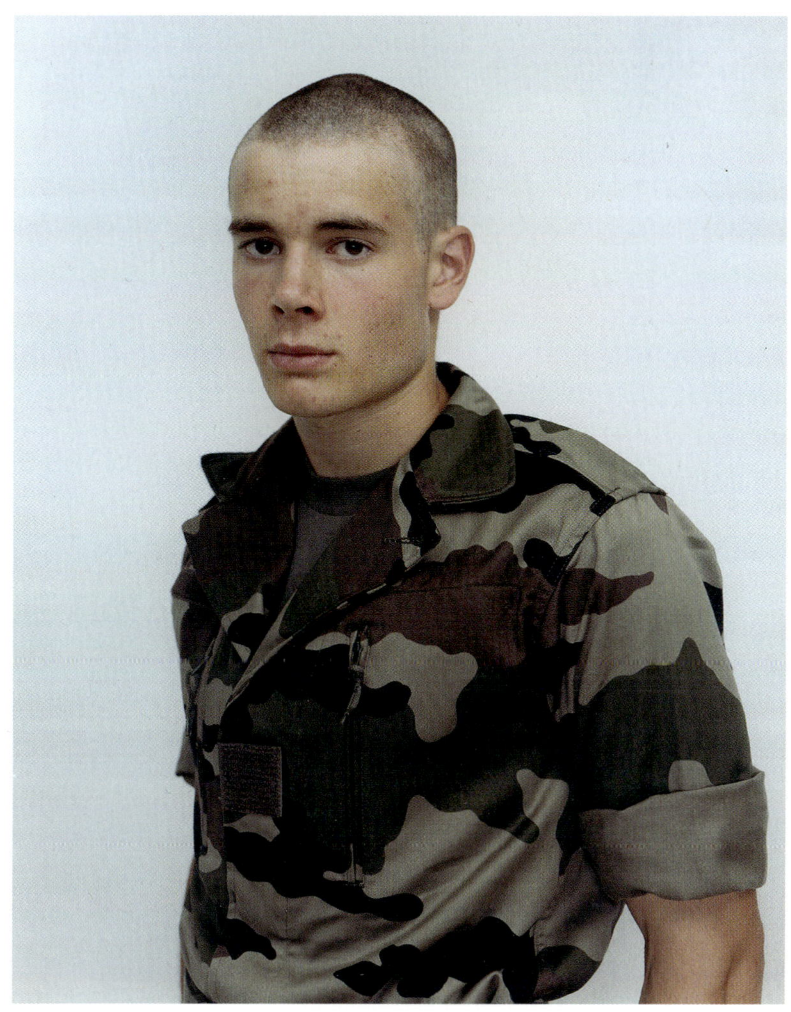

PLATE 9 Rineke Dijkstra, *Olivier, Quartier Viénot, Marseille, France, July 21, 2000*. Chromogenic print, image: 90 × 72 cm; frame: 126.5 × 108.5 cm, edition of 10.   © 2013 Rineke Dijkstra. Courtesy of the artist and Marian Goodman Gallery, NY

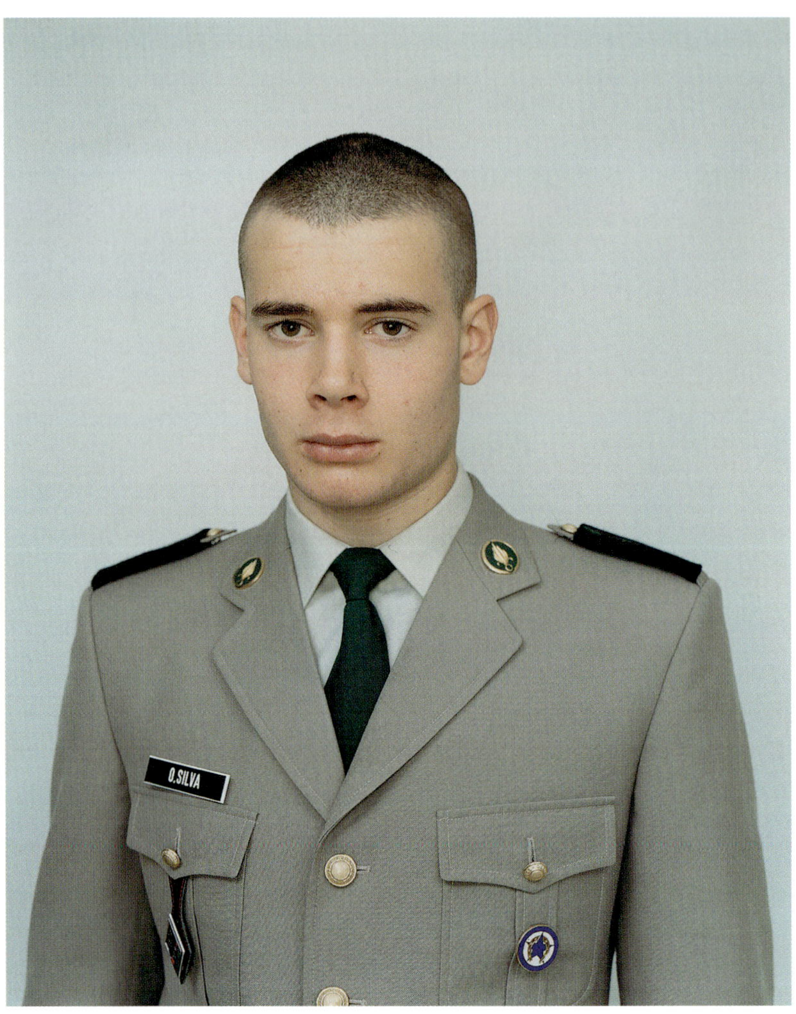

PLATE 10 Rineke Dijkstra, *Olivier, Quartier Viénot, Marseille, France, November 30, 2000*. Chromogenic print, image: 90 × 72 cm; frame: 126.5 × 108.5 cm, edition of 10. © 2013 Rineke Dijkstra. Courtesy of the artist and Marian Goodman Gallery, NY

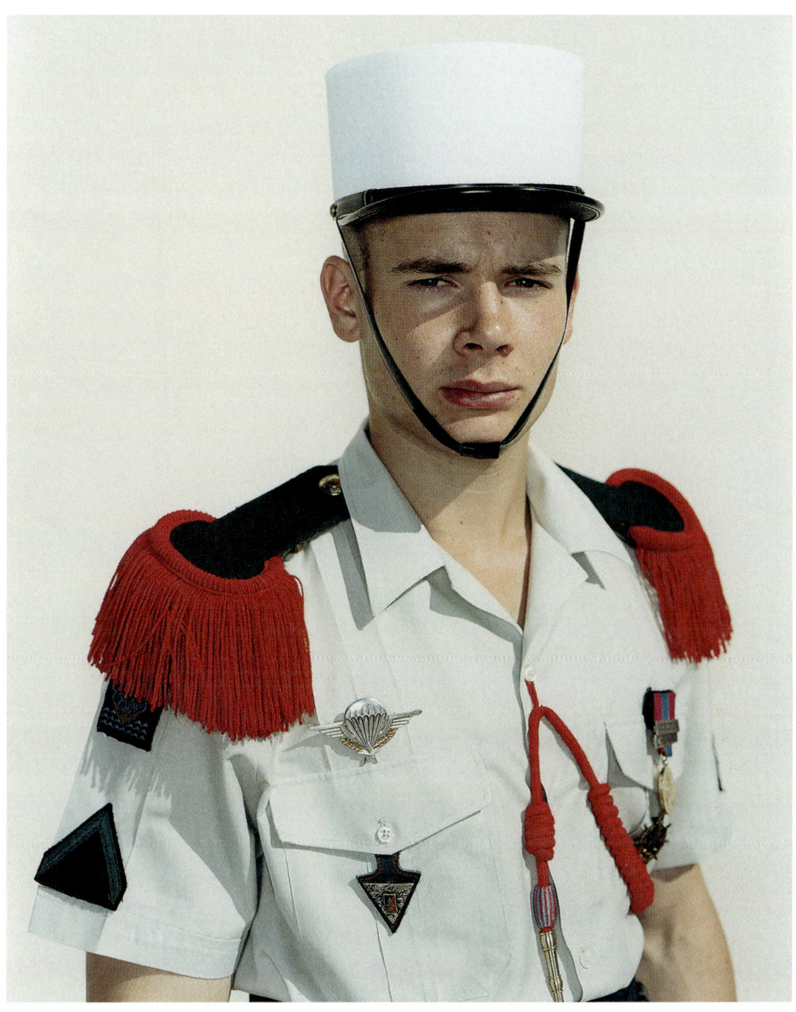

PLATE II Rineke Dijkstra, *Olivier, Camp Raffalli Calvi, Corsica, June 18, 2001*.
Chromogenic print, image: 90 × 72 cm; frame: 126.5 × 108.5 cm, edition of 10. ©
2013 Rineke Dijkstra. Courtesy of the artist and Marian Goodman Gallery, NY

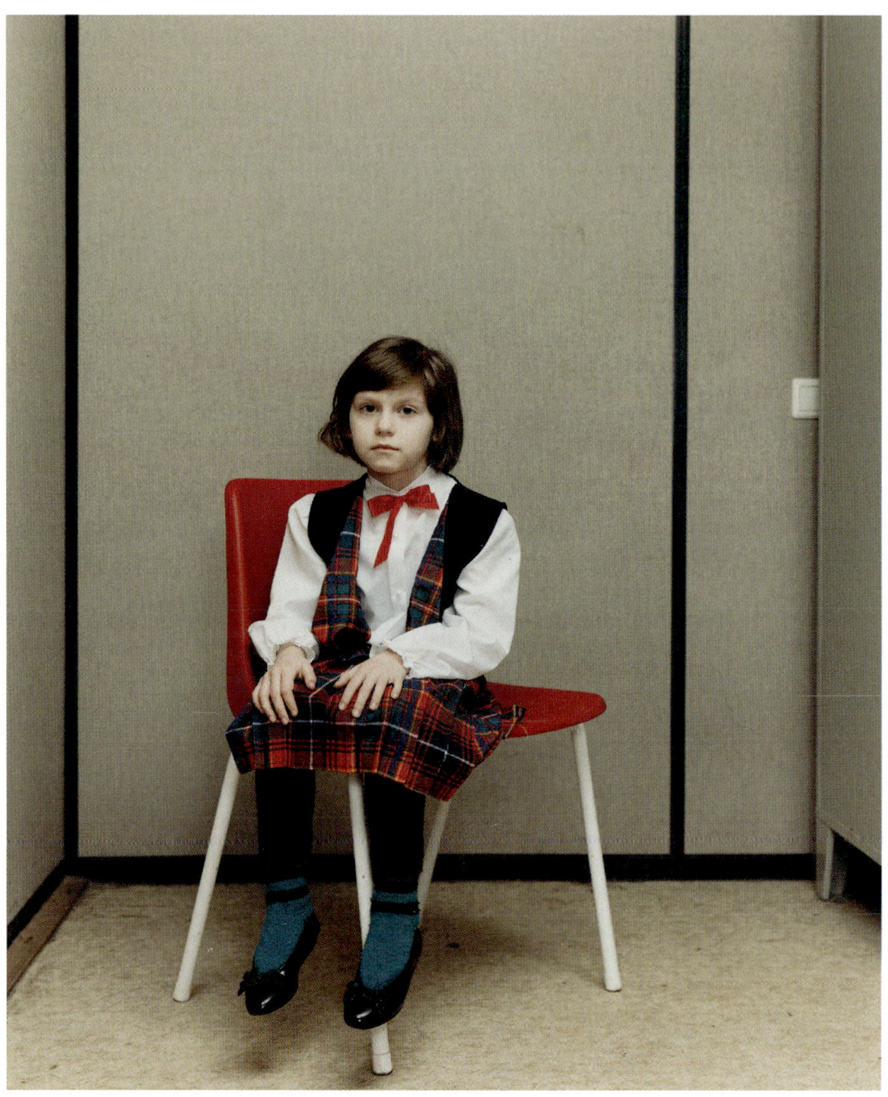

PLATE 12 Rineke Dijkstra, *Almerisa, Asylum Center Leiden, Leiden, Netherlands, March 14, 1994*. Chromogenic print, image: 94 × 75 cm; frame: 129 × 109.5 cm, edition of 6. Image: 35 × 28 cm; frame: 62 × 52 cm, edition of 15. © 2013 Rineke Dijkstra. Courtesy of the artist and Marian Goodman Gallery, NY

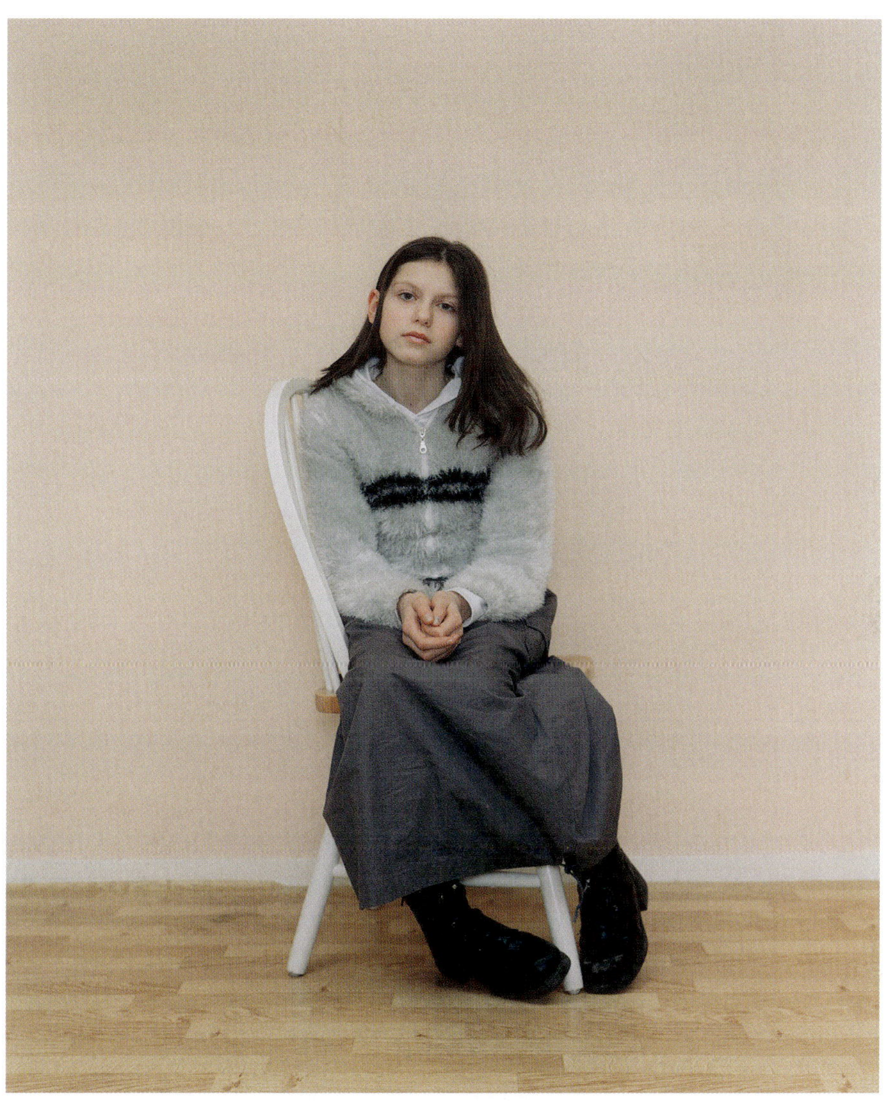

PLATE 13 Rineke Dijkstra, *Almerisa, Leidschendam, Netherlands, March 19, 2000*.
Chromogenic print, 94 × 75 cm; frame: 129 × 109.5 cm, edition of 6. Image: 35 × 28 cm;
frame: 62 × 52 cm, edition of 15. © 2013 Rineke Dijkstra. Courtesy of the artist and
Marian Goodman Gallery, NY

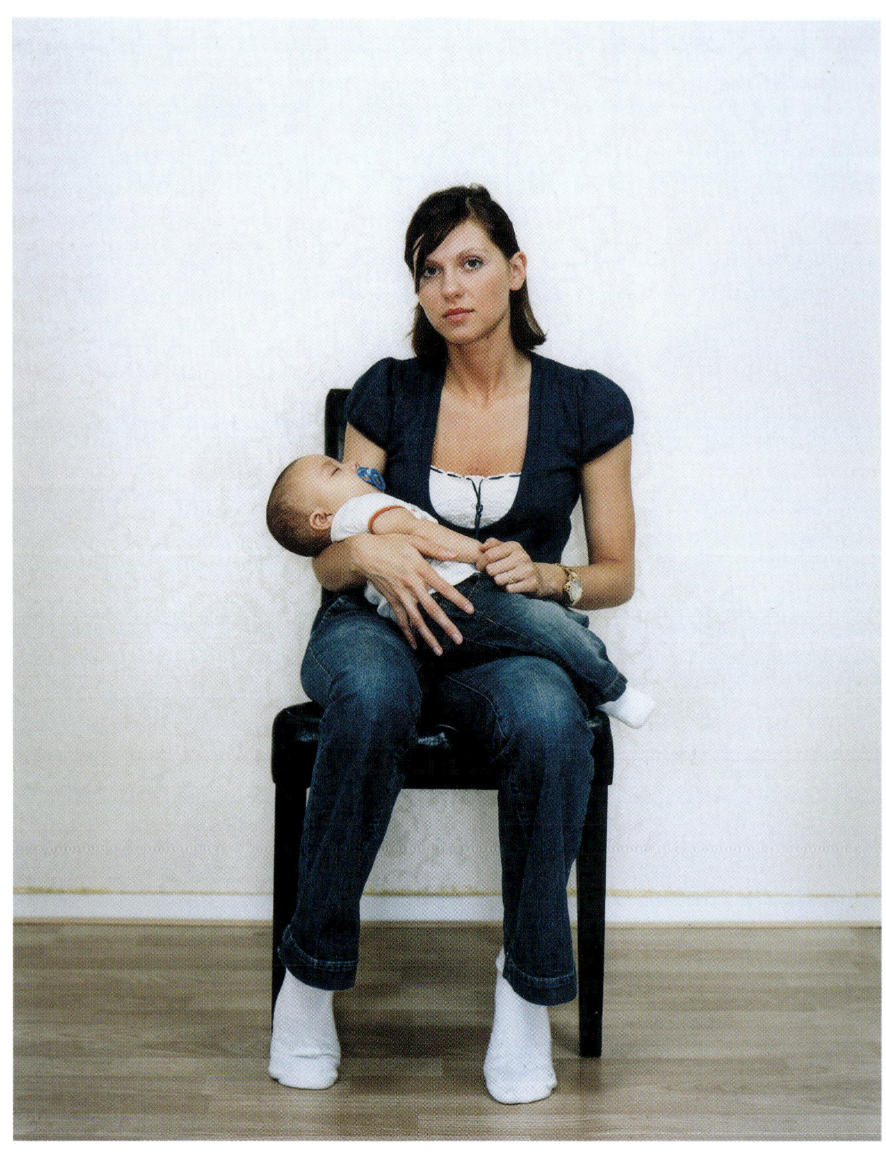

PLATE 14 Rineke Dijkstra, *Almerisa, Zoetermeer, Netherlands, June 19, 2008*.
Chromogenic print, image: 94 × 75 cm; frame: 129 × 109.5 cm, edition of 6.
Image: 35 × 28 cm; frame: 62 × 52 cm, edition of 15.   © 2013 Rineke Dijkstra.
Courtesy of the artist and Marian Goodman Gallery, NY

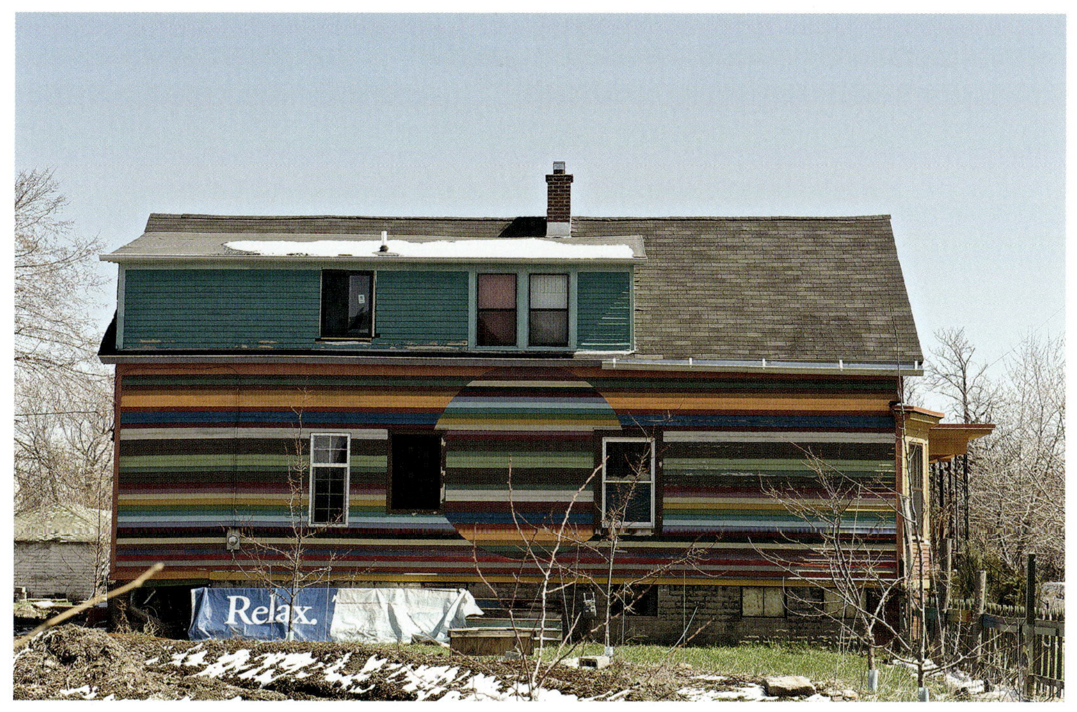

PLATE 15 Julia Reyes Taubman, *East Detroit* (2005–2011).
© Julia Reyes Taubman

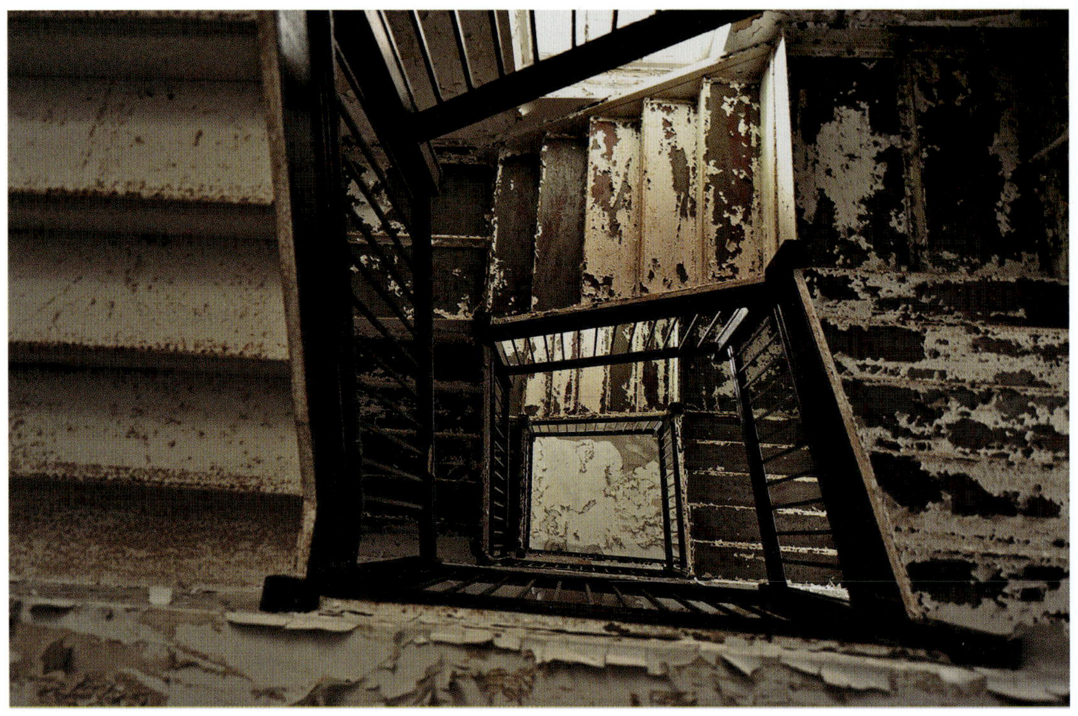

PLATE 16 Julia Reyes Taubman, *West Detroit* (2005–2011).
© Julia Reyes Taubman

But skepticism is precisely what I've been talking to you about: the difference between believing and seeing, between believing one sees and seeing between, catching a glimpse—or not. Before doubt ever becomes a system, *skepsis* has to do with the eyes. The word refers to a visual perception, to the observation, vigilance, and attention of the gaze during an examination. One is on the lookout, one reflects upon what one sees, reflects what one sees by delaying the moment of conclusion. Keeping the thing in sight, one keeps on looking at it. The judgment depends on the hypothesis.

Jacques Derrida, *Memoirs of the Blind: The Self-Portrait and Other Ruins*

FIVE · THE RUSE OF THE RUINS, OR: DETROIT'S NONREAL ESTATE

In the summer of 2009, *Time* launched "Assignment Detroit," the media conglomerate's yearlong reporting project on what was hailed as a "city in crisis—but with potential for a big comeback." The project ended on November 11, 2010, with a final blog installment titled "The Future of Detroit: How to Shrink a City." A quote from John Huey's exuberant editorial of September 24, 2009, suggests something about the nature and purposes of the undertaking, which appeared both in print and validated its own interactive space on the magazine's website:

We did something a little out of the ordinary for us or, frankly, for anybody: we bought a house in Detroit. As houses go, it's nice enough—three stories, five bedrooms, 3½ baths with a yard and a basement. We paid $99,000, about $80,000 above the average price of a house in the city limits. Why would we ever do such a thing? Because we believe that Detroit right now is a great American story. . . . As a story, Detroit has been misunderstood, underreported, stereotyped, avoided and exploited for decades. To get it right, we decided to become stakeholders. . . . The house will be a gathering place and a clearinghouse; we've already had Mayor Dave Bing over for dinner and thrown a lawn party to greet our new neighbors.[1]

Huey sees and believes in Detroit as a story, a story he is convinced the dozens of journalists, photographers, videographers, and bloggers from TIME.com, Fortune.com, CNNMoney.com, even *Sports Illustrated,* all eagerly flooding the D-zone, will be able to get "right." For more than twelve months, the stories coming out of this lofty enterprise kept being spewed onto *Time*'s "The Detroit Blog"[2]—as Huey zestfully exclaims: "After spending a couple of days here, we found that you could not throw a rock in Detroit without hitting a good story." Whether Detroiters (or readers for that matter) maintain the same standards of what is a "good story" as journalists do is a question for debate, unless it is some of the more amusing anecdotes about Detroit, such as French TV crews vainly searching for the wild deer that reputedly range the pampas of the city's downtown area, or, on a more positive note, breathless reports on the successfully spreading enterprise of urban farming.[3] It seems safe to say, however, that it is not so much the stories of Detroit, but its images, the visual imprint of its ruins, the horrifying pictures of its material disintegration, that form the most abiding impression of the city today, not only in the United States but around the world.

In a sour mood, one might say that both the upbeat stories and the horror images of Detroit function as cheap entertainment for the gringos. Still, my point here is not to assert or contest the veracity, the helpfulness, or the political and social viability of these stories and images, nor to examine the integrity or, as the case may be, the questionable intentions of the rock and lawn party throwers who largely produce them. My interest primarily lies in the widely disseminated photographs of the by now in/famous Detroit ruins in their irresistible beauty, as on one hand markers of the irreversible loss of modernity and its founding premise of infinite progress, of the destruction and decay of a bygone industrial era, of complex and ongoing racial and class struggles, and on the other the operations of these photographs, not so much as inscriptions or traces of a past reality, but rather, in the words of German philosopher Lambert Wiesing, as images, which "alone make the artificial presence of things possible . . . present[ing] things as exclusively visible, released from the laws of physics."[4] As such, the ruse of these ruins not only consists in their function and operation as runes, whose significance at once lies in, but cannot be reduced to, the visualized objects themselves, but also—and more spectacularly—in their ubiquitous "presentness" as images, as instantiations of the phenomenon of pictoriality as such. The photographs of its ruins thus produce, in and of themselves, what I would like to call Detroit's "nonreal estate" in its pure visibility.

"Assignment Detroit" and *Time*'s reporters' undoubtedly well-meant exhortations for the city to become "smaller, greener, and thriftier," may now, a few years later, appear a stale, old story. The interest in what has come to be known as "ruin porn"—a phrase that a recent Internet search suggests is practically synonymous with Detroit—has, however, by no means subsided. Since Huey and his crew left Detroit to find "good stories" elsewhere, the city has become "hot," which means that it has emerged as a cool, hipster city in some sections of the mainstream media. The indignant blogs, rants, and more serious online rejections of its visual presence in these same media as "ruin porn"[5] nonetheless suggest a tension, an ambivalence, or perhaps an indissoluble contradiction inherent in the images of the ruins themselves and in the imaging of Detroit through them. It is this tension that I would like to address in this chapter as, in the first place, a question of aesthetics, and thus as a question of central concern to my inquiry into the nonrepresentational operations of the visual in our current, postphotographical moment.

I had been thinking and writing about the visualization of Detroit for some time, when I was invited to chair a panel session at a recent American Studies conference at Wayne State University in Detroit, Michigan's only urban public research university in the heart of the city's cultural center.[6] The panel, titled "Getting Beyond 'Ruin Porn': The Politics and Aesthetics of Deindustrialization," evidently intended to denounce and get away from—indeed beyond—the supposedly insidious fascination of so-called outsiders with the all-pervasive visual representation of Detroit as no more than a bunch of burnt-out, half (or wholly) demolished buildings, what insiders prefer to call "urban blight." Clearly, these two phrases do not refer to the same things (as the panel's subtitle, perhaps unintentionally, suggests). The latter evokes the deterioration or collapse of Detroit as a modern industrial city, with all the social, political, economic, and cultural consequences thereof in their appallingly concrete, everyday reality. The former, in contrast, pertains to something that is decidedly real and concrete, but not material or everyday in the same way. A brief comparison between so-called regular porn and what is accurately called "ruin porn" should help to clarify the difference.

Regular porn, most of us know whether we "consume" porn or not, involves sometimes written, but increasingly primarily visual materials that explicitly represent or portray sexual subject matter and that serve the purpose of sexual arousal. Crucially, though, it does so at more than one remove. Pornography is always at a distance, always mediated, in the sense that the term applies to the depiction of sexual acts, not to the acts themselves. Such distancing or detachment is not only critical for porn to produce the desired effects, but is additionally further extended in its actual use. Indeed, the last thing those of us who read, watch, and enjoy porn want is to be in the room with the people (animals? objects?) that enact the titillating scenes of sexual activity, to be a player in those scenarios ourselves. The essence of porn, in other words, is the pleasure derived from observing something that is not actually there, from an encounter with a two-dimensional (nowadays usually a screen) surface, a visual reality without any real-life or social depth, an image or imaginary realm without the *presence of the real.* Porn thus points up what could be argued to pertain to any image, that is to say, that vision and the production of images can never exhaust, never fully capture the totality of reality, and that that is precisely the point, the image's magic, if you will. To put it differently, it is in the nature of the image (which need not be visual)—if it is not in fact its essence—to do the opposite of capturing reality. Porn, and its operations, can only be successful if it accomplishes its task of derealization.

The same holds true for what is commonly decried as "ruin porn." The phrase itself—as much as the remarkable ease with which it has caught on, particularly with reference to Detroit (apart from suggesting that looking at images of ruins is, to say the least, a dubious if not embarrassing pastime)—strikingly brings to the fore the ambivalence at the heart of the image, and especially of the photographic image, that is, its simultaneous presence qua image, as pictorial surface, and its potential representational or semiotic functions. It equally underlines its operations to be, first and foremost, aesthetic in nature. This very ambivalence suggests that as objects of perception or, more precisely, as data or givens that may or may not provoke our concern, images cannot be expected to do the work of social critique. They are able to invite or incite us to initiate social action, to fight the blight, to combat the reality of the decay of Detroit, but images as such cannot do that work and cannot be expected to. Where urban blight, in other words, evokes Detroit in depth, the phrase "ruin porn" cannot but pertain to a pictorial surface. The problem, of course, especially when we are dealing with photographic images, is that the separation between the two is sometimes hard to make.

The fact that it is not always easy to separate the semiotic operations of the photographic image from its existence as phenomenological object is the direct result of the hegemony of the metaphysics of presence, firmly rooted in Western culture since Plato and prevailing with particular vengeance since the Enlightenment. Within the metaphysics of presence (a term originally used by Heidegger), seeing is not so much believing, as St. Thomas suggests, as it is the privileged road to knowledge, to understanding, to cognition, on the assumption that even the most complex ideas first appear to us in their visible shape. Having evolved in a variety of forms, the foundation of dominant modes of positivist or Enlightenment epistemology is that vision is not only the "noblest of senses," as Plato assumed, but also that it makes everything present, that it allows for a detached and objective perception of the world in its totality—for, literally, *comprehension.*

I am not drawing attention to the privileged position of vision in our ocular-centric culture to critique the oppressive effects of dominant organizations of the visible, such as in terms of gender, race, class, and sexuality, nor even to evoke such critiques in deconstructive terms. I am not interested in rehearsing familiar (and convincing) arguments that the realm of vision is, by definition, not given but constructed, and that there is thus no "view-from-nowhere"—which is an ideological construct that primarily serves dominant groups (modern science, corporate capitalism, white straight middle-class males). My interest in Western culture's ocularcentrism in relation to the visualization of Detroit as "ruin porn," at least in the larger project of this book, is of a more narrowly defined, yet fundamental theoretical nature. My central concern in this chapter is the photographic image in the context of the proposed neo-aesthetics of existence, that is, the function of the visual for a metaphysics of becoming in which art assumes a privileged function.

On the face of it, the photographs featured in most discussions of Detroit-as-"ruin porn,"[7] for instance Andrew Moore's *Detroit Disassembled* (2010) and Yves Marchand and Romain Meffre's *The Ruins of Detroit* (2010), would appear to fulfill the requirements of "art photography"—in its ambivalent distinction from photojournalism—as I have described them in the preceding chapter. Presented as something more than "mere realistic renderings" of their subjects, these mostly large-scale photographic works tend to be exhibited in art galleries and museums as the unique productions of individual photographers, to be collected and published as expensive, beautifully finished, limited-edition art books.[8] Their operation in the world, however, the work they do in their singularity and difference as organized aesthetic activity, is undeniably markedly dissimilar from that of the type of work produced by, say, Richard Barnes and Rineke Dijkstra, or similarly "recognized" art photographers and/or media artists. The latter invite us to approach the photographic image in its interrelations with and divergence from more traditional modes of artistic visualization (such as painting), and thus force us to reflect upon its function in its presentness and its self-presentation as art. "Ruin porn," in contrast, confronts us much more powerfully and, judging by the outraged responses to its in/famous manifestations, inescapably with the photograph's simultaneous and originally primary documentary function, or at least with its appreciation and theorization as such. This is the paradox of the mechanically produced and endlessly reproducible image, the type of image that the Czech-born writer, philosopher, and journalist Vilém Flusser (1920–1991) designates the "technical image."[9]

In common parlance, the paradox of the technical image tends to be cast in the reductive terms of a variety of related binary oppositions, such as the distinction between surface and depth, the visible and the invisible, or appearance and reality. The interplay between surface and depth as it emerges in and from the technical image (even if it pervades the field of aesthetics more generally) comes poignantly to the fore in the imaging of Detroit, where the photograph functions at once as a representation of the sociomaterial reality of urban blight and, no less compellingly, as an aesthetic surface with a distinctly affective, captivating power. In order to be able to say something about the former, it is the latter aspect that needs to be addressed first.

To shift the attention from the enduringly disputed aesthetic credentials of photography and yet maintain my focus on Detroit "ruin porn" as aesthetic object, I wish to move away from the all-too-familiar examples that have given the phenomenon its name, fame, and notoriety.[10] My comments in the following paragraphs therefore do not pertain to any of the earlier mentioned "art photographers," or even to any image in particular, but instead refer generally to a recent collection of photographs, monumentally published under the title *Detroit: 138 Square Miles,* by local documentary photographer Julia Reyes Taubman.[11] These photographs have not (at least not as far as I know) been exhibited in any museum or art gallery, and they present themselves self-consciously as an attempt at "documenting Detroit," as the title of Elmore Leonard's foreword to the volume suggests, an effort reflected in the sheer range and number of photos (the hefty tome counts almost 500 pages and contains 454 individual images). We find a great number of by now familiarly depressing shots of the empty, abandoned, or burnt-out interiors of both commercial and residential Detroit buildings (figures 5.1 through 5.3; plates 15 and 16). A variety of street views across the enormous expanse of the city offers us a sense of the extent of its decay: whole blocks are boarded up (figure 5.4) or have been virtually razed, with the exception of one or two forlorn-looking houses still suggesting what the neighborhood might have looked liked before its ultimate demise (figure 5.5). The tragic fate of the Grand Central railway station, by now perhaps the most frequently photographed and reproduced icon of postindustrial disintegration, poignantly emerges from the contrast between its grand design and its current appearance as a spooky void, its empty windows, the dilapidating wall tiles (figure 5.6). The photos also show the "other side" of Detroit; its "can-do" spirit as the capital of the American automobile industry is palpable from the many powerful images of its remaining plants and factories (figure 5.7), the persistent sense of community emanates from churches, stadiums, bars, and park gatherings. Still, rather than inscribing itself in either a "pietistic" (à la Steichen) or in a critical tradition of social photography (à la Sander), it is precisely the apparent effort at full coverage, the seemingly exhaustive visual presentation of the "reality" of Detroit in this designated documentary work, that powerfully points up the impossibility of presenting the totality of any reality by representational means. Even such a wide range and large number of images can never offer us more than a glimpse at an imaginary world, an imaginary Detroit that here merely exists in its visuality. It is

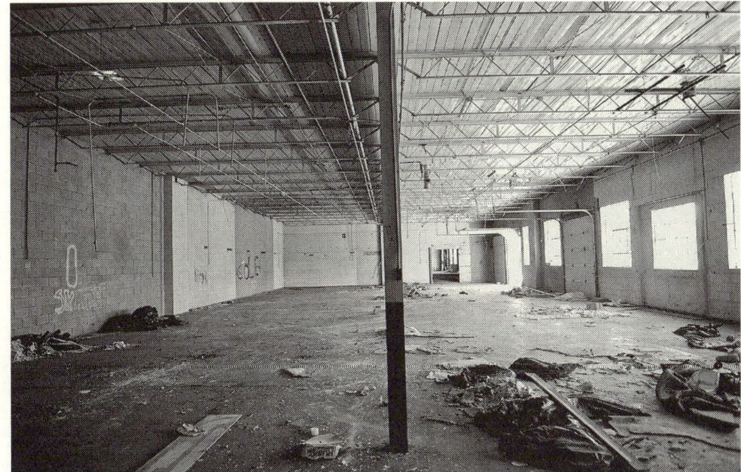

FIG. 5.1 Julia Reyes Taubman, *East Detroit* (2005–2011). © Julia Reyes Taubman

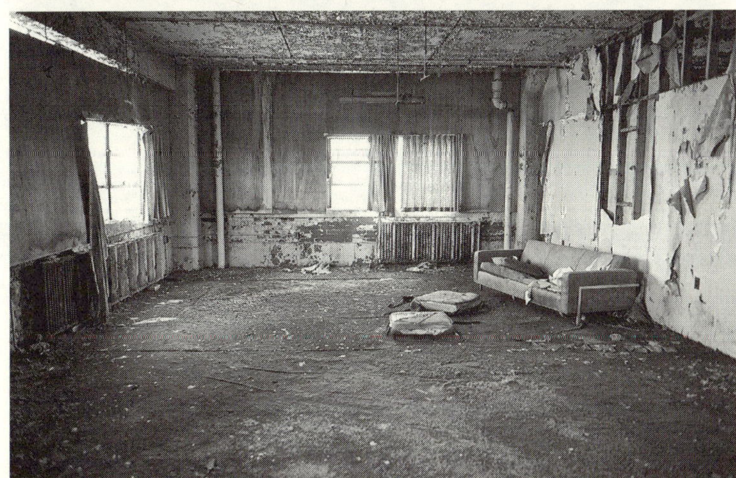

FIG. 5.2 Julia Reyes Taubman, *Highland Park Plant* (2005–2011). © Julia Reyes Taubman

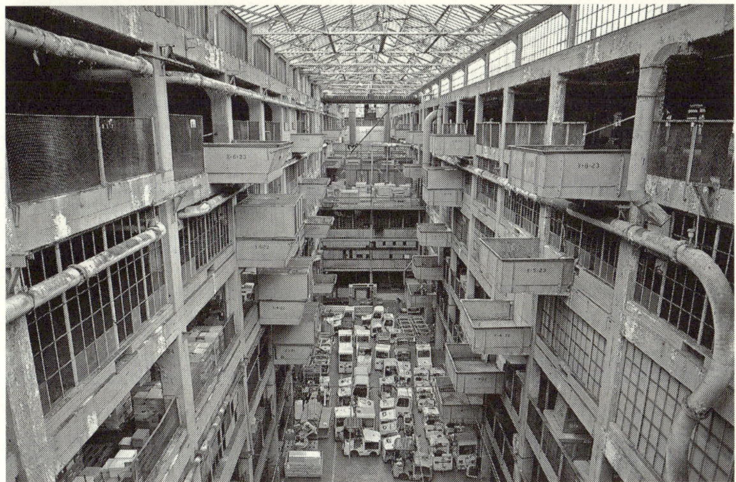

FIG. 5.3 Julia Reyes Taubman, *Highland Park Plant, Craneway* (2005–2011). © Julia Reyes Taubman

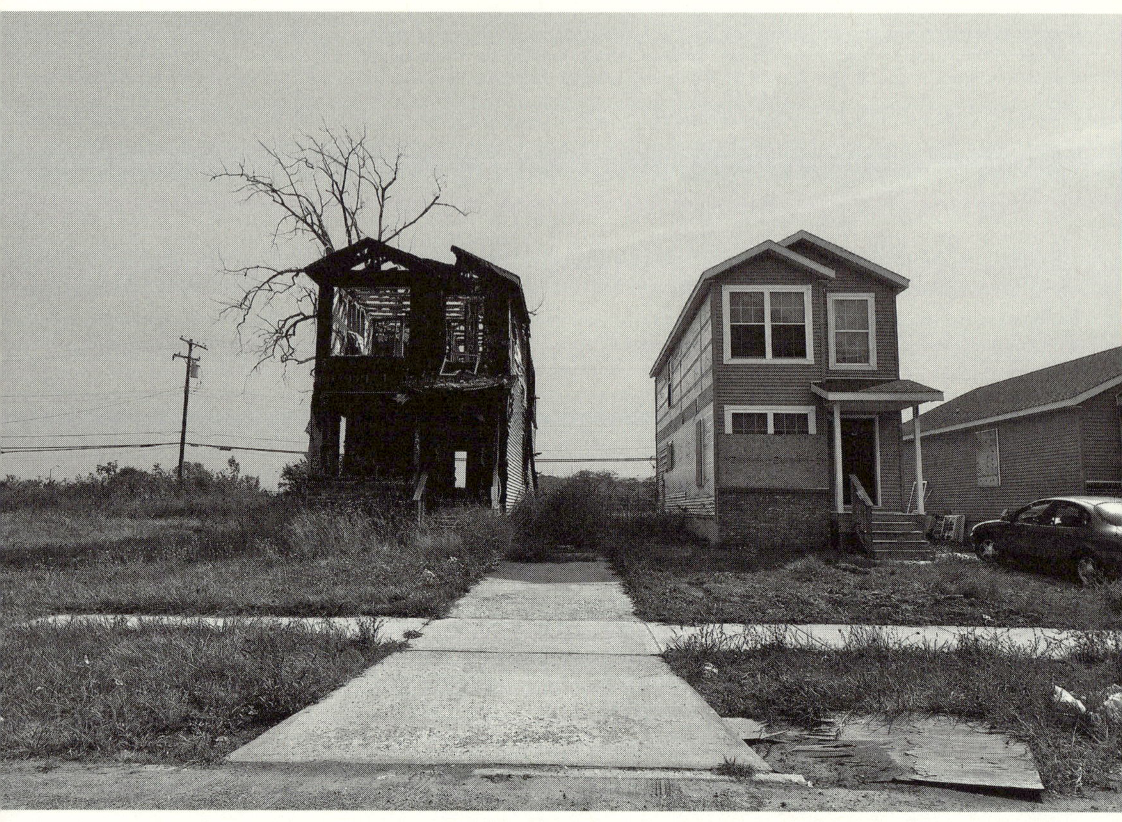

FIG. 5.5 Julia Reyes Taubman, *Central Detroit* (2005–2011). © Julia Reyes Taubman

thus this same effort at comprehensiveness that equally forcefully puts into effect the ambivalence at the heart of the image, specifically of the postphotographic, technical image, and which therefore requires the adoption of a different route of theoretical exploration than the one pursued in the previous chapter.

I have earlier expressed my reservations about phenomenological approaches of the aesthetic. Within an overall aesthetics of sensation, or a theory of feeling, along the Bakhtinian/Whiteheadian/Deleuzian lines pursued thus far, the subject does not exist prior to, but is born anew in each fresh encounter with an object (whether physical or mental). As Whitehead succinctly puts it, "The word 'object' . . . means an entity which is a potentiality for being a component in feeling; and the word 'subject' means the entity constituted by the process of feeling, and including this process. The feeler is the unity emergent from its own feelings" (*PR*, 88). For Whitehead, there is thus neither a subject, as there is for Kant, who "projects" the world, from which the world "emerges," nor is there a subject, as there is for phenomenologists, who "intends" the world. With Whitehead, I reject the presupposition of the existence of a consciousness that intends the identity of an

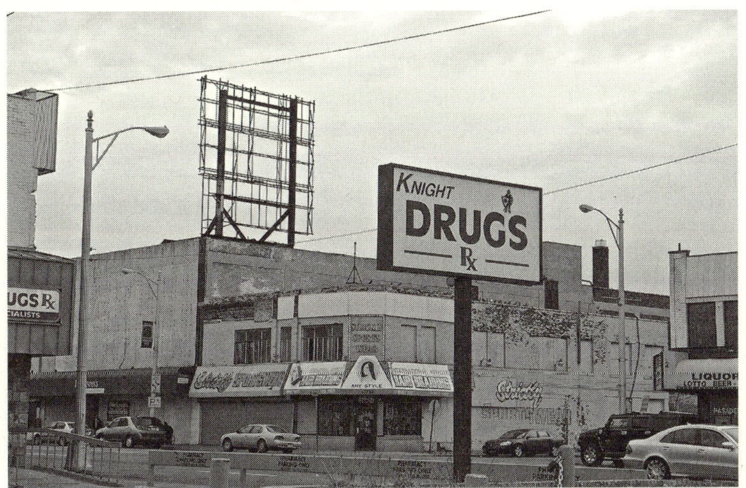

FIG. 5.4 Julia Reyes Taubman, *Woodward Avenue* (2005–2011). © Julia Reyes Taubman

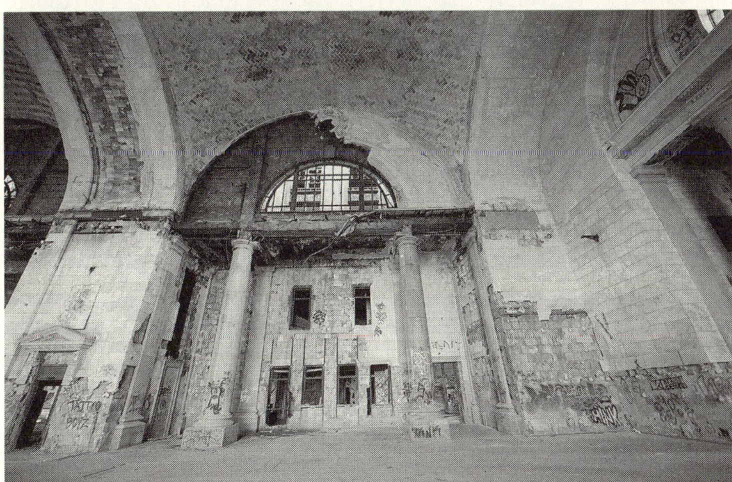

FIG. 5.6 Julia Reyes Taubman, *Central Detroit* (2005–2011). © Julia Reyes Taubman

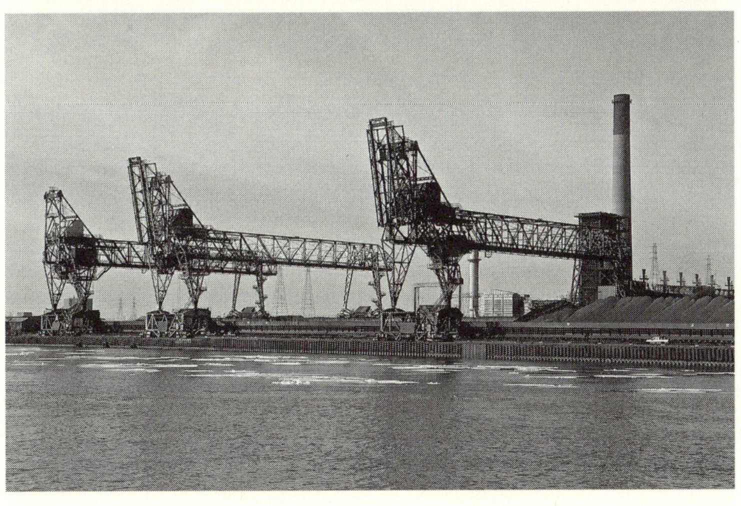

FIG. 5.7 Julia Reyes Taubman, *Zug Island, U.S. Steel* (2005–2011). © Julia Reyes Taubman

object, or of a perception, and I follow him, Bakhtin, and Deleuze in recognizing the constitutive or *poietic* function of the aesthetic event, as creative activity, as a process of becoming that critically hinges on the nonpersonal, or presubjective nature of affect. I nonetheless wish to approach the visualization of Detroit and the question of "ruin porn" more generally, from a phenomenological, or rather from a phenomenologically inspired perspective. My reasons for doing this are, first, that the photographic ubiquity of Detroit cannot be denied its function as phenomenological presence, and second, because the two theorists cited earlier, Wiesing and Flusser, who both write within a phenomenological philosophical framework, offer particularly helpful suggestions—some of which I will read oppositionally—about the function and operation of a visual aesthetic in the narrow sense I am attempting to bring into focus, that is, a form of visuality that specifically obtains in the photographic image.

While Wiesing's strictly philosophical concern is with the image and with image theory more generally, Flusser writes specifically about the technical image from a combined philosophical and a media theoretical perspective.[12] This difference in positioning may explain the fact that despite their shared phenomenological orientation on visual media, the latter presents an overwhelmingly negative critique of technical images and of their effects upon our world and our selves, whereas the former foregrounds the enabling and enriching function of visual mediation and the production and circulation of images. This contrast neatly expresses the profoundly divergent appreciations of Detroit "ruin porn," as much as it illuminates the vehemence with which the ceaseless dissemination of these photos tends to be rejected as socially destructive and unethical, and equally ceaselessly consumed in the form of gallery shows/museum exhibitions and art books. The very phenomenon of Detroit "ruin porn" thus testifies to the need for a theory of the technical/photographic image that adequately addresses, even if it cannot ultimately resolve, such conflicts as they play out on both the level of social reality and on what I must imprecisely call the reality of the image per se.

Flusser opens his concise treatise *Toward a Philosophy of Photography* (2000; hereafter *PP*) with a discussion of the image in its distinction from and struggle with writing. Images, he states, are "significant surfaces" the space and time of which are "none other than the world of magic." Writing, in contrast, is the world of historical consciousness, the world of cause and effect, of linearity, of consequences. "Structurally different" from this world of meaning and interpretation, in the world of magic images "replace events and translate them into scenes" (*PP*, 7, 8). While prehistorical—what he calls "traditional"—images are supposed to have provided people with the mediation required to render an inaccessible reality comprehensible, technical images, Flusser writes, do not so much succeed as they factually replace that other revolutionary transformational invention, "linear writing," which marked, on his view, the "beginning of 'historical consciousness' and 'history' in the narrower sense" (*PP*, 10).

Technical images, Flusser claims, were invented at the very moment when texts became themselves "incomprehensible," which was at the height of a nineteenth-century "textolatry" with which history "c[a]me to an end" (*PP*, 13). He numbers Marxism, Christianity, and a specialist scientific discourse as examples of such "textolatry, of 'faithfulness to the text.'" Written accounts up to that moment served to interpret ideas. With the invention of photography, Flusser goes on to suggest, technical images, which are endlessly reproduced and distributed on a global scale, become increasingly conceptual. Photography allows for the generation of ideas that are taken at face value as truth and no longer as something that requires interpretation or decoding. Whereas they were supposed to be "maps" that enable humans to negotiate their relation to the world, they turn into "screens":

> Instead of representing the world, they obscure it until human beings' lives finally become a function of the images they create. Human beings cease to decode the images and instead project them, still encoded, into the world "out there," which meanwhile itself becomes like an image—a context of scenes, of states of things . . . the technical images currently all around us are in the process of magically restructuring our "reality" and turning it into a "global image scenario." (*PP*, 10)

Thus, even if the technical image was primarily invented to make the world of texts comprehensible again, Flusser notes that such images gradually have become abstractions of the "third order," in the sense that they "abstract from texts which abstract from traditional images which themselves abstract from the concrete world" (*PP*, 14). To be sure, the clear distinction Flusser makes between so-called traditional images and technical images may not be altogether convincing; both the earliest known images, such as cave paintings, and photographic images, at least up until the digital moment (and, as we have seen, beyond that moment) share a principal mimetic function and have and continue to be regarded as, at least potentially, indexical. The inference he draws from this distinction is nonetheless noteworthy. The reason technical images are difficult to decode, Flusser maintains, is that they appear to wear their significance on their surface, to be "objective" renderings of the world, so that they do not operate symbolically but rather "appear to be on the same level of reality as their significance." People who look at photographs hence tend to see them "not as images but as windows," and they do "not criticize them as images, but as ways of looking at the world . . . their criticism is not an analysis of their production but an analysis of the world" (*PP*, 15).

Flusser's use of the words "window" and "screen" as if they were interchangeable is confusing; I will come back to this in a moment. Yet the strength of his analysis of the operation of the technical image lies in the fact that it, first, forces us to think about the power of images in their presentness as significant surfaces, surfaces that "translate everything into states of things," and to recognize that their "magical effect" consists in enticing "those receiving them to project this undecoded magic onto the world out there." Technical images, with their capacity for being endlessly reproduced, ever more widely disseminated, and easily distributed, to a large extent determine the "way in which we experience, know, evaluate and act as a function of these images" (*PP,* 16). If we do not learn to look critically at these images, at the ways they function in the world, and the ways they work on our selves, Flusser warns us, we lose the ability to think conceptually, to produce ideas that allow us to think productively about the kind of "magical spell" we are under. His avowedly "apocalyptic perspective" thus urges us to take the "problem" of photography, in its various political, ideological, and ethical dimensions, seriously, and it alerts us to the dangers of a rising illiteracy owing to an uncritical faith in photography's "reality."

Second, Flusser's method of approaching the photographic image through its three main aspects—the Apparatus (camera), the Functionary (photographer), and the Technical Image (photographic surface)—allows us to consider the contemporary, no longer merely "mechanically," but digitally reproduced image in its specificity and its distinction from both traditional images and from previous modes of visual mass mediation. If, as he suggests in *Into the Universe of Technical Images* (2011; hereafter *UTI*), the invention of photography has led to a "mutation of our experiences, perceptions, values, and modes of behavior, a mutation of our being-in-the-world" (5), then certainly the advent of the digital age validates the assumption that yet another such mutation has already happened or is in the process of taking place. Flusser, for one, was fully aware of this; although he wrote his two studies on the technical image before the digital revolution truly took off, he nonetheless clearly envisioned the development of a "future society that synthesizes electronic images," a "fabulous society where life is very different from our own" (*UTI,* 3).

Considering the growing theoretical importance of media and Flusser's work in the field, it is, as Mark Poster mildly puts it in his introduction to *Into the Universe of Technical Images,* "disappointing that the major cultural theorists of the 1970s and 1980s tend to overlook media theory and almost completely ignore the thought of Flusser."[13] It is clearly partly this neglect that has spurred growing numbers of more recent cultural thinkers to direct their attention to new media in both their technological and social operations from a primarily theoretical and/or philosophical perspective and to make the thought of Deleuze and Guattari, among others, relevant for the "fabulous society" we undeniably (albeit sometimes uncomfortably) inhabit.[14] The transformation of our visual universe from a technical to a technological one has additionally given rise to more sustained theoretical reflection on the nature of the image per se. It is as a representative of the latter that Lambert Wiesing takes up the question of the image and of image studies, and to whose repeatedly mentioned book *Artificial Presence* (hereafter *AP*) I presently turn to further examine Detroit "ruin porn," not so much as a mediated image in the narrow sense, but instead as an aesthetic object in the sense that has been the focus of my inquiries in preceding chapters.

Wiesing tentatively differentiates the project of what in German is called *Bildwissenschaft* and what in English, as noted in the introduction, appears under the names "image studies," "visual studies," or "visual culture," respectively, from both more established disciplines, such as philosophy and art history, as well as from interdisciplines such as cultural and media studies. He suggests instead that "image studies" may not be a discipline at all, but rather denotes a field in which various reflections from different disciplines, each with its own content and method, converge. The premise of his own collected studies of the image is nonetheless that the "concept of the image" is a problem that "can only be solved philosophically," that it is the "task of *image theory*" (*AP,* 5). Rejecting anthropological and semiotic approaches alike, Wiesing takes his cue from nonsemiotic philosophies such as Konrad Fiedler's (1841–1895), and especially that of the principal founder of phenomenology, Edmund Husserl (1859–1938), to opt for a theoretical position toward the image that is based on perception.

In Husserl's terminology, the problem of the image revolves around the theoretical distinctions between the depicting material, which he calls "image carrier" [*Bildträger*], and the referential object or the "image subject" [*Bildsujet*]. What is "decisive," however, according to Wiesing, is the name Husserl suggests for the "depiction that visibly appears in the image," which he speaks of as the "image object" [*Bildobjekt*] (*AP,* 18–19). Husserl's purpose in identifying the depiction in the image as an object, instead of a sense or content, is to give depiction, Wiesing asserts, a "special ontological status": depiction is a "special object that becomes visible in an image," and that which thereby distinguishes itself from a real object. As he continues in his characteristically refreshing, straightforward terms: "The image object is not a real object; it is exclusively the object that is described when someone says what he or she thinks he or she sees on an image carrier" (*AP,* 19).

The suggestion to describe that which becomes visible in an image as an object rather than as sense or content notably allows for a distinction or, more precisely, for a specification of different forms of presence. There are real objects in the world, materialities or substances that are subject to the laws of physics, Wiesing submits, whose presentness requires or combines with "substantial attendance [*Anwesenheit*]." He complicates what at first sight appears to be a simple adherence to a traditional metaphysics of presence, however, by making a distinction between different modes of such substances' "realness." It is precisely because the presence of such materialities and substances can be defined as "real"—as he laconically points out, "to speak of real presence is not a pleonasm"—that there can also be a "nonreal, an artificial presence—a presence, precisely, without substantial attendance." An image object is a presentness the particular kind of being-an-object of which consists in the fact that it exists only and exclusively in its "pure visibility"—"pure," that is, in a Kantian sense, as opposed to "attached." Things in images are exclusively visible; they cannot be touched, smelled, heard, or tasted, and hence they are not connected to any substance that can be so perceived. Wiesing infers from this that the "implication of presence and substantiality dissolves in the image" and, furthermore, that images can thus be understood as a medium "with which it becomes possible to produce a nonphysical yet still visible object *sui generis* (even though this object is addressed differently, as image object, imaginary thing, pure visibility, or false unity" (*AP*, 20).

By describing the depiction in the image "not as a form of sense or content, but as a kind of object" (*AP*, 19), Husserl provides us with what Wiesing defines as a "decidedly antisemiotic counterconcept" to common determinations of image reception in terms of meaning and interpretation. Still, Wiesing's Husserlian theory of the image does not so much run against the commonly held belief that every picture tells a story. The artificial presence of things in and through images does not obviate the latter's function as signs. What it does do, however, is point up the ontological differences between the image carrier, the image subject, and the image object and, in contrast to semiotic approaches to the image, Husserl's phenomenological perspective, centering as it does on the "artificial presence" of things, on the image object in its ontological status distinct from both the depicting material and from the real or referential object, poses the question of whether images must always be representation and thus must always refer to something else. Put slightly differently, and more assertively, whereas a semiotic view assumes that images can and should be read, Husserl's notion of the image object suggests that when we look at an image, we are not reading but seeing, and that we are, hence, "dealing with a sensual consciousness of the presentness of something" (*AP*, 22) that does not necessarily refer, that does not necessarily give meaning or content, but that is pure visibility. Images, of course, like everything else, can become signs, carriers of meaning, can tell stories requiring interpretation as well, but they need not do so; that is to say, in Wiesing's own concise terms, "What resembles does not have to refer" (*AP*, 23).

In its distinction from both the image carrier and the image subject, the notion of the image object additionally points to a difference lodged in the equivocation of the concept of the image per se, a difference that in the case of photography has often been articulated in terms of "double exposure," that is, to indicate the photograph's dual function in terms of what I have earlier called its documentary capacity and its operation as a medium of artistic creation, its "nonreal presence" qua image object. This ambiguity accounts for the fact that a photographic image can but need not function in significatory terms and that it does not do so in our actual encounter with it. Being exposed to a thing, looking at it, even studying it, does not, Wiesing aptly points out, "turn this thing into a sign, does not give meaning to it" (*AP*, 23). Following Husserl, Wiesing evidently deviates from Whitehead and Deleuze—who both, we recall, reject phenomenology—in that he presupposes a consciousness, a someone for whom an image object appears as such. He nonetheless reaches a similar conclusion about the ways an image does its work as, first and foremost, an object of perception, an aesthetic object. For it is, he submits, only after the image object has been "brought into appearance [*Erscheinung*]" that it can (but need not) be *used* as a carrier of meaning, as a sign, and thereby become a signifier (*AP*, 35).

Wiesing's theory of the image fundamentally questions the supposition that a photographic image, even in its most ostensibly documentary appearance, in and of itself necessarily operates as a carrier of meaning, as a phenomenological object whose referential or real object we can infer or read off of its significant surface. Husserl's notion of the image object in its artificial or nonreal presence additionally allows Wiesing effectively to problematize a metaphor we have already encountered in Flusser (if only to be simply rejected), which is the idea of the photographic image as a window onto the world. Harking back to the Renaissance artist and theoretician Leon Battista Alberti, as Wiesing helpfully reminds us, the metaphor of the open window has profoundly marked the philosophical reflection not only on technical images but on images generally. In one sense, Wiesing concedes, the comparison should be considered accurate:

> The look we take at the image, as well as the look we take through a window, directs our attention toward things and events that are not in the same space. By means of a window, we normally look out of a house at the outside; by means of an image, we see an image object in an imaginary space. Images and windows make it possible to look at something other than themselves. (*AP*, 80)

In another sense the metaphor must nonetheless be firmly rejected, for we look through a window into an existing world, whereas we look at an image into an imaginary one. Even if, as Husserl himself admits, we may *feel* as if we are in the presence of a person when we look at a portrait, this is clearly not the case. Indeed, a "thing depicted in an image 'appears' in the way in which an actual physical thing appears, but in conflict with the actual presence [*Gegenwart*] that conflict-free perception brings about."[15] Our empirical experience of images,

Wiesing hence infers, confirms that the window metaphor does not in fact work at all: "Hardly anyone will look at an image and then greet the person depicted there because he or she presumes that person to be present" (*AP*, 81). The appearance of the image object cannot possibly be confused with the appearance of the thing itself. Furthermore, the limitations of the window metaphor not only show up in relation to the framed painting or photograph, but become equally manifest when we consider the "screen windows" associated with both old and new media. Such screens may well offer a "display for the presentation of things," but the things they present are either necessarily elsewhere, at a distance, as in the case of television, or the things are both "visible and in attendance," yet not real but "virtual things," as is the case with computer screens (*AP*, 85).

The two aspects of Wiesing's theoretical reflections on the image—much more extensive than I can discuss here—that I have foregrounded, first, the erroneous idea that when we look at a photograph we are looking as if through a window into an actual, existing reality, rather than into an imaginary one, and second, the supposition that every image in and of itself functions as a carrier of meaning, as a sign, are particularly helpful in thinking through the complex operations of "ruin porn." More specifically, the photographic visualization of Detroit brings the difference lodged in the equivocation of the concept of the image strikingly to the fore. When addressed in their representational or referential function, that is, as signifiers or signs, it is the image subject of such images in its relation to the image object, rather than the latter in relation to the image carrier, that is at stake. In other words, it is not the "real thing," the actual dilapidated or burnt-out building in the street, but the immaterial object of perception in its artificial presence that is called upon to tell its story about that which it is, in and of itself, not. The question, then, becomes what *are* these objects, and what kind of skepticism is at play in the "difference between believing and seeing" the ruins not only in their significatory function, as runes, each with its own magical significance, but also in their artificial presence, as imaginary things, pure visibility, or false unity? What is the nature, to evoke Derrida's words, of the "glimpse" that we catch—or not—of Detroit in its real presence when we look through the picture window into an imaginary world, at a pictorial surface that appears to act as a transparent plane and thus denies it own existence as a medium? And what would or could be the "hypothesis" upon which to base our "judgment"—aesthetic, ethicopolitical, or otherwise—of these images?

Are the endlessly reproduced images of urban decay the work of "vultures picking at the bones again," as Ron Williams, media-writer and president of 3rdWhaleMobile (a small green tech company based in Canada), maintains?[16] In his 2010 article on "Green Detroit," Williams follows a by now familiar argumentative trajectory in his denunciation of "ruin porn." The foreign and out-of-state photographers coming to Detroit are not considered to be sufficiently knowledgeable about the Motor City to produce "authentic" images of its streets, let alone of its people, who are essentially, Williams correctly points out, largely abjected from Detroit's horrible beauty. The mainstream media coverage of Detroit is furthermore, he continues, "messed up," and misses the fact that "D-troit is the truth . . . [that] D-troit is the end result of a global economic system . . . the deadly consequence of capital freely moving across the planet," as well as of the "utter lack of *vision* (and too often *integrity*) on the part of the local business and political leadership." By no means do I wish to downplay Williams' outrage about Detroit's decline (which is heartfelt) or deny that his identification of its causes bears further discussion. The question, however, is what kind of work the images of the Detroit ruins are supposed to be doing—or not to be doing, as the case here seems to be? If "D-troit is the truth," how might its "authenticity" be captured in any image, in precisely that which, to recall Wiesing's expression, "alone make[s] the artificial presence of things possible . . . present[ing] things as exclusively visible, released from the laws of physics"?

If, as Derrida suggests in the passage from *Memoirs of the Blind* cited at the beginning of this chapter, *skepsis* has to do with the eyes, and judgment of what one keeps looking at depends on the hypothesis, what does Williams believe he is seeing when he dismisses the mainstream visualization of the Detroit ruins/runes for their lack of authenticity, their failure to capture Detroit as "the truth"? What is the hypothesis underlying this judgment? What would happen to our prehension of these images if we accept the hypothesis that photography, as a medium, can be used not only, or even not so much, to picture or visibly *reproduce* but instead to form or visibly *produce* something in its artificial presence? In light of the phenomenological insights explored in the preceding paragraphs, it appears to me that we must follow Derrida in order to begin to think about the function of these photographs through the difference lodged in the equivocation of the concept of the image itself, to try to account for what we see when we look at the depiction of "ruin porn" as "pure visibility, or false unity," and to reflect upon what we see by "delaying the moment of conclusion."

As image objects, and thus as objects of perception or aesthetic objects, the Detroit ruins neatly fit into what Andreas Huyssen calls "The Ruin Craze," the contemporary obsession with ruins in the "countries of the northern transatlantic," which, he submits, "hides a nostalgia for an earlier age that had not yet lost its power to imagine other futures."[17] Huyssen situates the current nostalgia for ruins at the tail end of the history of modernity, whose trajectory, "all the way into postmodernism," he perceives to be "overshadowed by a catastrophic imagination and imaginary of ruins."[18] While the Western fascination with ruins can be traced back to the Renaissance, during which, as Brian Dillon points out, the "ruin was first of all a legible remnant, a repository of written knowledge,"[19] it is only with the "advent of a modernity that conceives itself in relation to the remains of the past," as Dillon elsewhere puts it, that the ruin becomes an "essential aesthetic concept and recurrent image in Western art."[20] Huyssen sees the twenty-first-century fascination with ruins as a form of nostalgia for modernity itself, a "modernity that dare not speak its name after acknowledging the catastrophes of the twentieth century and the lingering injuries of inner and outer colonization."[21] This supposition allows him to couple the "concreteness of ruins" with the equally historically specific, in casu, modern concept of "authenticity." Whereas he does not deny that the "authentic ruin" as a particular conceptual and architectural configuration finds its origins in the beginnings of modernity in the eighteenth century, it is in the twentieth century, more precisely in the "age of mechanical reproduction," that, Huyssen argues, the "fear of inauthenticity, the lack of existential meaning, and the absence of individual originality" produces the idea of and fascination with "authentic ruins," that is to say, with real ruins of different kinds that come to "function as projective screens for modernity's articulation of asynchronous temporalities and fear of and obsession with the passing of time."[22]

To be sure, the concern with originality and uniqueness predates Benjamin's in/famous elaboration of the aura of the work of art in terms of authenticity, but as Huyssen persuasively suggests, it is only in the early twentieth century that a "gap opens up between intellectual insight into the obsolescence of authenticity and the life world's desire for the authentic—cuisine, clothing, identity."[23] This desire is undoubtedly romantic, aimed at the promise of something that does not exist or is no longer there. The paradox of the "romantic ruin" for Huyssen is therefore that what is "allegedly present and transparent . . . is present only as an absence." The modern ruin, then, posits the "problem of a double exposure to the present and past" whereby "its temporality, which points to past glory and greatness," is clearly different from the "claims of plenitude and presentness invariably at stake in the discourse of authenticity." Rather than accepting the "ruin craze" to be the result of a false belief in an authentic and glorified past, which he considers merely to promote the need for "further mythmaking," Huyssen posits the "idea of the authentic ruin as a product of modernity itself," as an "architectonic cipher for the temporal and spatial doubts that modernity always harboured about itself."[24]

Huyssen conceives of the ruin as an instance of the "double exposure to the present and the past." Dillon, in the first of the essays cited above, traces the trajectory of the ruin from its eighteenth-century function as an "image both of natural disaster and of the catastrophes of human history"—which he admits are hard to tell apart because it is precisely the simultaneously emerging "aesthetics of the sublime" that serves to name the "confusion that comes over us with wholesale destruction," whether natural or man-made—through the romanticization of the ruin as a "symbol of all artistic creation," and the nineteenth-century imagination of nature itself "as already ruined," up to the modern ruin as "always, to some degree, a palpable, all-too-real remnant of the future."[25] In his historicization of its development, Dillon thus at first glance appears to follow Huyssen in his reading of the contemporary ruin craze. But he actually takes the argument a step further by emphasizing that the ruin, "still with us after six centuries of obsession," is not a "simple nostalgia for modernity."[26] The endlessly reproducible and endlessly reproduced images of industrial ruin, the vacant malls and abandoned theaters, the defunct railway stations, the silent foundries, the dilapidating bunkers, and amputated subway stations disseminated across thousands of websites, appearing in hundreds of lavishly produced art photography books, to him indicate a "mourning [of] the loss of the aesthetic itself." Always "totter[ing] on the edge of a certain species of kitsch," contemporary ruins, he maintains, "show us again—just like the kitsch object—a world in which beauty (or sublimity) is sealed off, its derangement safely framed and endlessly repeatable."[27]

In their respective readings of modern ruins generally, and of postindustrial ruins particularly—both marked by a profound nostalgia and firmly embedded in contingent structures of affective memory and longing, yet posing different questions—Huyssen and Dillon equally foreground both the function and the problem of the ruin as at least in part, if not primarily, an aesthetic one. From their discussions of various forms of both premodern, modern, and postmodern ruins, it does not become clear, however, whether they are talking about actual, existing ruins in the world (irrespective of their "authenticity"), or if they are concerned with visual presentations of such ruins, in the form of "mechanically reproduced" or technical images, or in the more traditionally defined artistic forms of painting and drawing. When Huyssen, for example, asks "how we can speak of a nostalgia for ruins as we remember the bombed out cities of World War II," or the "decaying residues of the industrial age and its shrinking cities" (a listing in which the "abandoned auto factories of Detroit" evidently cannot remain unmentioned),[28] one can only assume that he is not addressing the remnants and rubble of these ruinous disasters as they are, or once were, actually present in the world, in what Wiesing would call their "real presence," but instead addressing images, visualizations, as image objects in their artificial presence, most likely in the form of technical image carriers. Moreover, Huyssen's dual emphasis on the "concreteness of ruins," the "ruin in its emphatic sense," and the notion of the authentic in modern art and thought does not prevent him from visually organizing his text exclusively around the etchings of the eighteenth-century Italian artist Giovanni Battista Piranesi, whose work he introduces and discusses as "one of the most radical articulations of the ruins problematic within modernity" (see figure 5.8).[29] And even if Dillon's essay opens onto Dimitrios Constantinou's photograph of *The Temple of Zeus,* thereby suggesting that it is actual ruins that are at stake, albeit necessarily present only in the form of technical images, all the subsequent illustrations accompanying his argument are reproductions of paintings from various historical periods, imaginary ruins even further removed from the imaginary world presented in a photograph.

By neither acknowledging or even problematizing the different forms in which ruins do, or at least *can* exist, that is, as real objects in the world, subject to the laws of physics, as distinct from their "nonreal," artificial presence as image objects, Huyssen and Dillon, whether unwittingly, intentionally, or conveniently, gloss over the tension inherent in the "ruinous imaginary" of modernity as a spectacular instantiation of a post-Kantian "horrifying sublime." And it is precisely this tension, stemming from the ambivalence lodged in the equivocation of the concept of the image per se that, as I have suggested, renders the problem of the contemporary "ruin craze" into a problem of aesthetics.

In Wiesing's phenomenological terms, the "serious equivocation" at the heart of the image, the difference between the image carrier and the image subject on one hand and the image object on the other hand, is that the first two exist materially in the world, whereas the third is a "nothing, not part of the world but an object for consciousness." How exactly an "image carrier is able to produce in the viewer the consciousness of an 'image object presently presenting itself'" is, Wiesing concedes, "at least for the moment, inexplicable" (*AP,* 36). The very fact that an image carrier, as a physical object without significatory powers in and of itself, is a necessary precondition for the image object in its artificial presence, in its visible-only existence, to come into appearance, and as such need not acquire its function as a sign, points up the necessity—theoretical, political, critical—for a theory of the image that at once allows us to account for the visible givenness of the image object and that decisively complicates its potential operation as a signifier. Whether "read" as a signifier of destruction and decay, of nostalgia and loss, of the ruthless exploitation of an ulterior and displaced "truth" or "reality" or, alternatively, "merely" seen or perceived in its "uncontrollable beauty," the fact remains that the image subject can only "presently present" itself in our encounter with the image, in its simultaneously real and nonreal presence, that is, as at once image carrier and image object. In Husserl's phenomenological terms: "The physical image awakens the mental image, and this in turn presents something else, the subject."[30]

For Flusser the technical image is a "blindly realized possibility, something invisible that has blindly become visible," a possibility that is realized by the apparatus. Media, on his account, are apparatuses that "grasp the ungraspable,

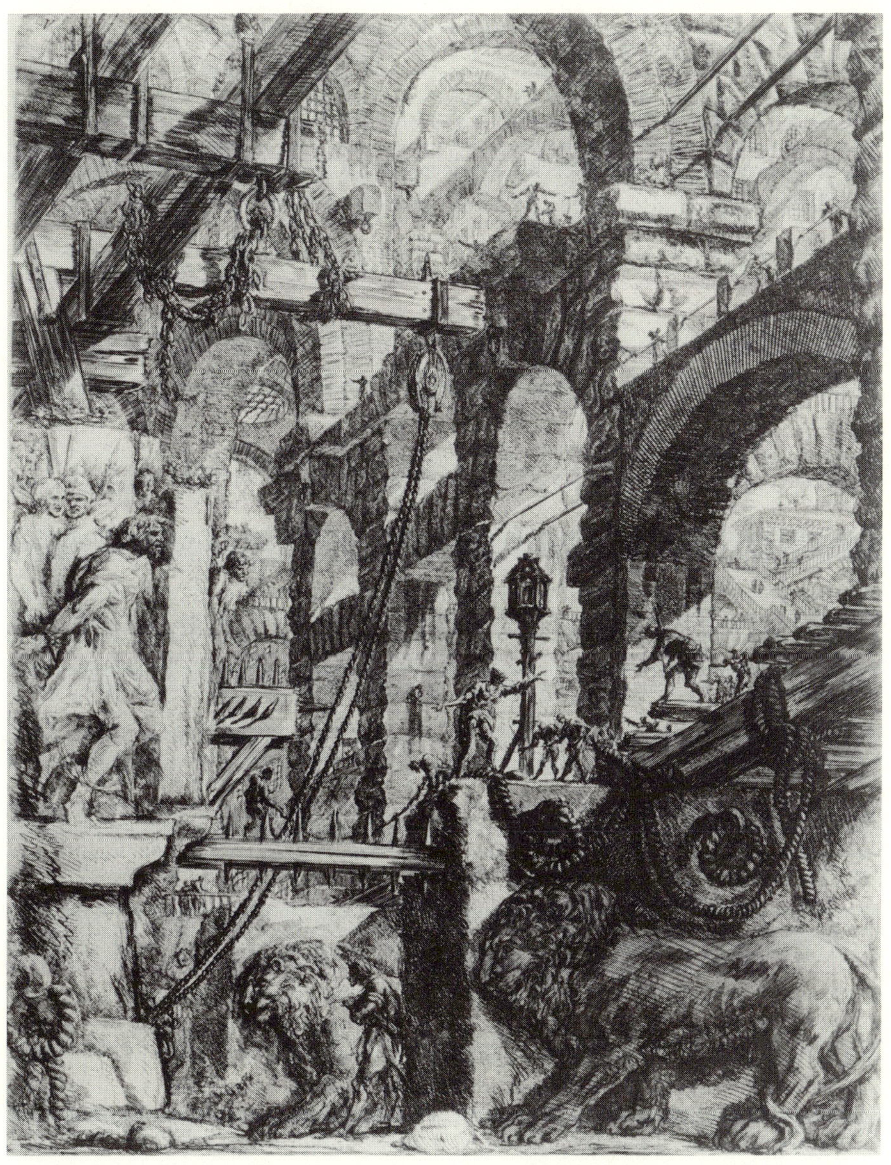

FIG. 5.8 Giovanni Battista Piranesi, *Prison,* 1745. From *Le Carceri*, no. XIV (1st state), 1/5, etching. Photo: bpk, Berlin / Joerg P. Anders / Art Resource, NY

visualize the invisible, and conceptualize the inconceivable" (*UTI*, 16). Technical images are "envisioned surfaces" from which we necessarily keep our distance: "On close inspection they all prove to be . . . computed from particles" (*UTI*, 33). It is for this reason that technical images "arise from completely different kinds of distancing from concrete experience" than do what he calls traditional images (*UTI*, 7). Visualization is radically different from depiction. Yet even if Flusser understands technical visualization as essentially a surface (or superficial) phenomenon, it is the "concrete experience, the adventure, the information that the visualization communicates that is interesting" (*UTI*, 36) to him; in other words, his focus remains on the image surface as sign. Wiesing, in his turn, concludes his musings on media by defining the camera as a "visibility isolation machine: it separates visibility from the present physical substance of a thing." Media, he writes, are the "only means humans have to disempower physics" in that they offer us the possibility to "think and perceive physical impossibilities" (*AP*, 132). This is, for him, the quintessential function of media: "Because there are media, humans live not only in physical nature but also in a culture, and they therefore owe their human existence to the employment of media" (*AP*, 133). Media, that is, that produce images that can but need not function as signs, since any image's only exclusive validity is its visibility. Despite these different emphases and the valuable insights they each provide into the function of images, technical and otherwise, both theorists implicitly assume the pre-existence of a viewing subject, a consciousness already fully immersed in and configured by a culture in which what is "inconceivable" and "ungraspable" is defined in relation to its opposite, the comprehensible, visible, and the possible. They thus confirm, as mentioned earlier, what holds true for phenomenologists generally, which is that the "coming-to-consciousness" of an image object is a question of intention; the "mental image" that is awakened by the physical object, the image carrier, is always an object *for* a consciousness, even if, as Wiesing emphasizes, the image object's "visibility logically precedes its legibility" (*AP*, 37).

On Whitehead's much more radical view of perceptual experience, however, consciousness "with its dim intuitions" (*AI*, 267) is "in general . . . negligible." He pursues: "Blind physical purposes reign . . . blind prehensions, physical and mental, are the ultimate bricks of the physical universe" (*PR*, 308). The content of an occasion of experience nonetheless plays itself out "under two contrasted characters—Appearance and Reality," but this contrast (or "dichotomy") is only important for the functionings of the "higher phases of experience, when the mental functionings have achieved a peculiar complexity of synthesis with the physical functionings." It is only in these higher phases of experience that the contrast between Appearance and Reality—rather than the more fundamental ones, the contrasts between the mental and physical pole itself and between the object prehended and the subjective form of the prehension—dominates "those factors of experience which are discriminated in consciousness with particular distinctness" (*AI*, 209).

Whitehead not only subordinates the contrasting characters "appearance and reality," that is, the two components in the metaphysical conception of reality, to the two other pairs of opposites exhibited in experience, he also rejects the Platonic idea that reality is genuine as opposed to deceptive and that the ultimate realities are things that are intelligible and explicable, hence objects of knowledge or of cognition. In contrast, for Whitehead the "distinction between 'appearance and reality' is grounded upon the process of self-formation of each actual occasion." The initial reception of the given, the "real antecedent world" as it exists for each new occasion, is followed by an intermediate phase in which a certain affective evaluation occurs. These "qualitative" or "conceptual feelings" derive from "qualities illustrated in the primary phase" and merge with the prehensions of the physical pole to enter into new relations with each other and to produce the "how" of the occasion, that which Whitehead calls the subjective form. In the higher types of actual occasions, the mental pole, which also derives its objective content by "abstraction" from the physical pole, provides the "propositional feelings" that integrate with the "conceptual feelings" to fulfill the "aim of the new occasion" (*AI*, 210). The integration, or rather the hybridization of the various feelings it directly or indirectly generates, constitutes the "appearance" for the occasion. More succinctly, appearance is the "effect of the activity of the mental pole, whereby the qualities and coördinations of the given physical world undergo transformation." This means that there is no metaphysical principle that can determine how in any occasion "appearance differs from the reality out of which it originates" (*AI*, 211). Conscious perception is the effect of a process of increasing distinction and what appears as reality is the result of certain sociohistorically contingent modes of coordination: "When the higher functionings of mentality are socially stabilized in an organism, appearance merges into reality" (*AI*, 212). The difference between appearance and reality is thus not an absolute one, in the sense that it is ultimately determinable, but rather a qualification of experience in a complex sensual trajectory of differentiation, specification, and transformation. This trajectory is, moreover, not fixed once and for all, but dependent on the social configuration in which it functions.

In addition to complicating the phenomenological assumption of a consciousness for whom an image appears, as well as the clear distinction between the image object as mental image, which in its turn presents a real subject, Whitehead's account of the formation of "high-grade occasions" of experience (*AI*, 211) dramatically shifts the terms of the interrelations among truth, authenticity, and reality that feature so prominently in the heated debates on Detroit-as-"ruin-porn."

Truth, Whitehead, claims, is a narrower, less fundamental concept than beauty. Truth concerns the relations between appearance and reality; it is the "conformation of Appearance to Reality." Beauty, however, is the "internal conformation of the various items of experience with each other, for the production of maximum effectiveness." Beauty is thus a wider concept than truth because it concerns both the "inter-relations of the various components of reality," the "inter-relations of the various components of Appearance," as well as the "relations of Appearance to Reality" (*AI,* 365). This does not mean, however, that truth has no significance for Whitehead. There is a "blunt force" about truth, he writes; it carries a "sense of directness" with it, which can (but need not: truth can be ugly or evil) function in the service of beauty, realize "some hidden, penetrating Truth with a keenness beyond compare" (*AI,* 266). When this kind of a "truth-relation" establishes itself, "Appearance summons up new resources of feeling from the depths of Reality," but the truth thus generated is neither a truth of understanding or cognition, nor of language or "verbalization," but essentially a truth of feeling. And it is art, as the "purposeful adaptation of Appearance to Reality," which has the dual aim of perfecting such "Truthful Beauty" (*AI,* 267).

In its ability to adapt appearance to reality, art, if it succeeds, engages the higher phases of experience. Though never not integrally related to the sensa—the sensa as "qualifications of affective tone," which gives them their "immense aesthetic importance" (*AI,* 245)—it is consciousness, Whitehead asserts, that "renders Art possible." Consciousness, he writes, is "like everything else . . . in a sense indefinable." It is "just itself and must be experienced." Yet consciousness is not simply a given, but rather "that quality which emerges into the objective content as the result of the conjunction of a fact and a supposition about that fact" (*AI,* 269). Consciousness is a form of attention: it "provides the extreme of selective emphasis" within the mass of "blind prehensions," both physical and mental, that make up our overall animal experience. Every fresh prehension may find its way toward consciousness and produce ideas available to our conscious attention. Art plays a crucial role in this specialized mode of "high-grade" experience. In exhibiting a "finite fragment of human effort achieving its own perfection within its own limits" (*AI,* 270), art offers us occasions for novelty, for new forms of feeling, but it is precisely because of its "adventurousness" (*AI,* 268), its relative freedom from categories and from cognitive systematicity, that art must be both finite and artificial. Art encompasses an artificiality, which is its "essence." While consciousness, Whitehead posits, is the "weapon which strengthens the artificiality of an occasion of experience" (*AI,* 270), the "secret of art lies in its freedom," in its ability to re-enact feelings and elements of experience divorced from the moments of necessity in which they first emerge and to make them newly and differently available within the artificiality of its own being.

In an earlier chapter, I advanced the idea that art is good to think with. Whitehead's elaboration of the essence of art in its finiteness and artificiality, as much as in its adventurousness, its freedom, and its ability to purposefully adapt appearance to reality, encourages us to engage the images of the Detroit (and other postindustrial) ruins in their "uncontrollable beauty" as both occasions for embodied, aesthetic experience and as the "high-grade" occasions of conscious attention, as the higher type of actual occasions where propositional feelings prevail. Such an approach will not necessarily provide us with the "truth" of Detroit, nor reveal the city's, its ruins', or its stories' "authenticity." It does not preclude the possibility, however, for the generation of thought, for making interesting propositions about them. And as Whitehead boldly proclaims, "It is more important that a proposition be interesting than that it be true," for it is a proposition's interest and importance that gives it its "emotional lure" (*AI*, 244).

Rather than reflecting a nostalgia for a lost power to imagine possible futures, as Huyssen would like us to believe, the images of the Detroit ruins in their "doubly exposing" function as documents and as, in Deleuze's phrase, "blocs of sensation," do not so much, as Dillon in his turn suggests, operate as a "means of mourning the loss of the aesthetic itself." On the contrary, Detroit "ruin porn" exposes the aesthetic as an operational force—a force, for sure, that is just as subject to history and thus just as political, ethical, and ideological as the history of ruins in which the contemporary craze with Detroit "nonreal estate" inscribes itself. Yet it is such a neo-aesthetic that cannot but insist on the kind of skepticism that Derrida introduces into his reflections upon self-portraits and other ruins: a *skepsis* that "has to do with the eyes," with "keeping the thing in sight," while "delaying the moment of conclusion." Our judgment will depend on the hypothesis.

For a minute or two she stood looking at the house, and wondering what to do next, when suddenly a footman in livery came running out of the wood—(she considered him to be a footman because he was in livery: otherwise, judging by his face only, she would have called him a fish)—and rapped loudly at the door with his knuckles. It was opened by another footman in livery, with a round face, and large eyes like a frog; and both footmen, Alice noticed, had powdered hair that curled all over their heads. She felt very curious to know what it was all about, and crept a little way out of the wood to listen.

Lewis Carroll, *Alice's Adventures in Wonderland*

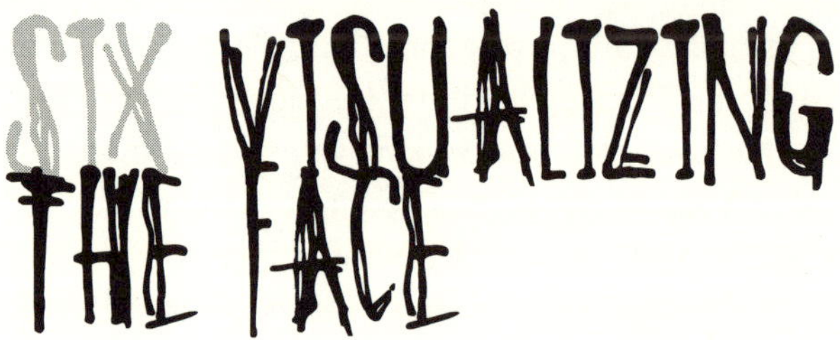

face value and *dévisage*

In her encounter with the liveried footmen in chapter 6 of *Alice in Wonderland* (see figure 6.1), Alice, with her usual yet uncanny perspicacity, returns us to the paradox of visual reality, of the actuality of our experience in a world that is at once, and primarily, perceptible and yet, albeit it not necessarily, potentially intelligible as well. Defying St. Thomas's earlier cited claim that seeing is believing, Alice raises the question of meaning and being as it plays out in her contradictory desires for both spectacle and knowledge, between what she sees—or, to use Whitehead's more precise term, between what she "prehends"—and what she is trying to read, understand, *com*prehend. The paradox of visual reality is here enacted in the appearance of two indecipherable creatures, part human, part animal, a fish-faced and a frog-faced footman facing each other. Alice's curiosity, her desire to know, is simultaneously aroused by and deflected from the spectacle of the two other-faced figures. Rather than trusting her eyes, her immediate perception of the figures' faces, Alice allows her attention to be redirected toward their attire and, furthermore, to the sealed envelope, the letter at the center of the transaction taking place between them. In the play of sense and nonsense that is Alice's Wonderland—in what Deleuze calls the "chaos-cosmos" or chaosmos of Lewis Carroll's work (*LS*, xiii)—that which arouses Alice's curiosity is both con-sealed in and eludes the letter, the event of language.

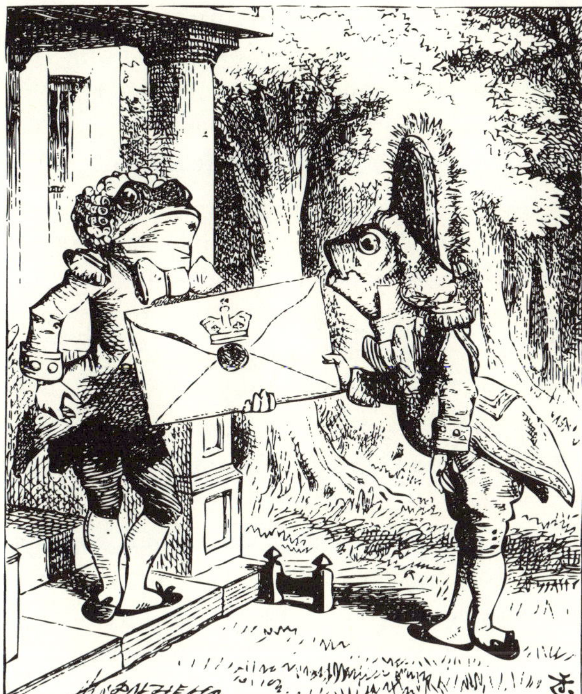

Language, Deleuze maintains, "fixes the limits (the moment, for example, at which the excess begins), but it is language as well which transcends the limits and restores them to the infinite equivalence of an unlimited becoming" (*LS*, 3). Carroll plays havoc with the everyday coordinates of language by placing Alice's private considerations, the articulation of her perceptual reality, in parentheses. He thereby draws our attention to the peculiar capacity of written language to externalize what in actual experience remains hidden, inaccessible both to others and also largely to ourselves, that is, a human being's conscious and unconscious thoughts. Conventionally regarded as a more profound level of "truth" in a story's imaginary reality, the character's "interiority" is nonetheless subordinated to that which is clearly visible, a reality that is in this instance equally produced exclusively in language. Alice in her turn creates a virtual chaosmos, in that she literally reverses the terms of reference of Platonic dualism by disregarding the immediacy of her perceptual reality, the pictorial surface of the footmen's animal faces, in favor of the overlay of social meaning in their liveried bodies.

Central, then, as language or the "great letter, nearly as large as [the fish-footman] himself," appears to be in this scene of curious desire, it is nonetheless Alice's act of reading, or misreading, or, indeed, of her reading against the grain of the bodies-cum-faces of the fish-footman and the frog-footman that points up the centrality of the visual, of the image, if not of the imaginary in the fixing of meaning. It simultaneously points up its function as the "moment at which the excess begins," as the site of unfixing, the moment that restores the signifying and identifying operations of language to the "infinite equivalent of becoming," which, needless to say in the context of *Alice's Adventures in Wonderland,* is also the site of unbecoming.

In its irreducibility to either the perceptual (spectacle) or the intelligible (knowledge), the scene of Alice's encounter with the fish-footman and the frog-footman succinctly, and brilliantly, articulates the central question I wish to explore in this chapter, which is the paradox of visuality and visualization in the context of documentary film. Continuing various lines of thought developed previously—in my engagement with the photographic image as at once pictorial surface, as an expressive event, and the potentiality for an occasion of partial becoming—my concern with documentary film similarly focuses on this form of mediated visual expression in its complex functioning, its ambivalence, as at once representation and presentation, an extraction and organization of the real and hence something that is subject to procedures of understanding or comprehension, on one hand, and as an artistic creation, the site for an "aesthetic event" (Bakhtin), an "encounter" (Deleuze), or an "occasion" of prehension (Whitehead) on the other. I will argue that the paradox of technical visualization, of the production of a visual reality in film, finds its culmination in the imaging, the cinematic (re)presentation of the human face, especially of the face in close-up. Like the animal faces in the chaosmos of *Alice in Wonderland,* the cinematic face presents itself as the site of meaning and identity while simultaneously eluding, effacing its limits, and dissolving its signifying functions. Theoretically, I will work through this proposition with reference to, among other things, the Deleuzian distinction between the actual and the virtual, as well as his and Guattari's notion of faciality and the face in cinema. The chapter as a whole, however, is inspired by and generally organized around the work of Dutch filmmaker/photographer Johan van der Keuken (1938–2001), in particular his award-winning film, ironically yet appropriately entitled *Face Value* (1991).[1]

Before saying more about van der Keuken and his preoccupation with the face, let me try to approach the paradox of the visual reality of cinema and, more specifically, the ambivalence at the heart of documentary film, by exploring a notion we have come across but which I have not actually discussed before, that of the *"partage du sensible"* developed by Jacques Rancière. In French, the word *partage* has two, almost opposite meanings: to share, or to have in common, on one hand, and to divide, to portion out, on the other. This dual meaning gets lost in English translation, where *partage* usually appears as "distribution," which is also the word used by the author himself when he writes in English. In the opening chapter of *The Politics of Aesthetics,* titled "The Distribution of the Sensible," Rancière uses the original French phrase to define the "distribution of the sensible" as the "system of self-evident facts of sense perception that simultaneously discloses the existence of something in common and the delimitations that define the respective parts and positions within it."[2] In view of the centrality of the notion in his thought, it is nonetheless important to bear in mind that the *partage du sensible* is not just the way images, bodies, objects, and places are distributed across the field of sense perception, but that it is also the division of the sensible into that which is speakable, thinkable, visible, audible, and that which is not, that which is "portioned out." Indeed, it is for this reason that Rancière can insist that there is an "'aesthetics' at the core of politics," which should not be understood in Benjaminian terms, that is, as the "'aestheticization of politics,'" but rather in a post-Kantian sense, as the "system of *a priori* forms determining what presents itself to sense experience."[3]

In her recent book on documentary film, *Recording Reality, Desiring the Real* (2011), Elizabeth Cowie links Rancière's notion of the sensible with Deleuze's distinction between the actual and the virtual. She suggests that we "must apprehend the actual as a 'sensible,'" and furthermore "engage in a movement between a living and dwelling as the affectual, and a becoming a subject of knowledge that is constructed virtually in a transforming of the real into reality."[4] On this view, the notion of the *partage du sensible* would seem to capture, if not quite yet explain, the dual function of documentary film as both an extraction and organization of the real (representation/distribution) and an artistic creation (presentation/ division), and thus complicate a function that is more commonly defined in terms of the seemingly much more straightforward distinction between nonfiction and fiction. Deleuze's actual/virtual distinction adequately confuses such ostensible straightforwardness.

Deleuze sets up the distinction between the actual and the virtual in opposition to that between the possible and the real so as to conceptualize, in Constantin V. Boundas's gloss, "two mutually exclusive, yet jointly sufficient, characterisations of the real."[5] Deleuze begins to develop the notion of virtuality in relation to multiplicity as early as 1966, in his study of Bergson.[6] In this book, his main concern is to replace the Kantian notion of the conditions of possibility of representational knowledge with a notion of the condition of the genesis of the real. Bergson's critique of the possible is, in oversimplified terms, that the idea of reality as a realization of the possible suggests that the real is something more than possible, that it is a past possibility with real existence added to it. This is a false suggestion for Bergson because there is always more in the idea of the possible than there is in the idea of the real, just as there is always more in the idea of nonbeing than there is in the idea of being. For Deleuze this means that the condition of the genesis of the real is the virtual, which is fully real, for genesis is a process of actualization, not of realization (of past possibilities). As a radical or transcendental empiricist, Deleuze nonetheless insists on thinking the real through experience. He thus posits the virtual as the ground of individuation and personalization, but it is, crucially, a "ground that cannot resemble what it grounds"[7] and that must therefore be conceptualized as nonpersonal and pre-subjective. In the words of Daniel Smith and John Protevi:

> The virtual is the condition for real experience, but it has no identity; identities of the subject and the object are products of processes that resolve, integrate, or actualize (the three terms are synonymous for Deleuze) a differential field. The Deleuzean virtual is thus not the condition of possibility of any rational experience, but the condition of genesis of real experience.[8]

The importance of the distinction between the actual and the virtual in Deleuze's ontology may appear not only from the fact that it emerges in his earliest work and continues to inform all of his subsequent thought, but that he also devotes to this theme his last piece of writing, the essay "Immanence: A Life" (1995),[9] which he wrote, as John Rajchman puts it, in a "strange interval before his own death" (by suicide) and which is often considered as a testament of sorts "at a time of renewed difficulty and possibility for philosophy."[10] Moreover, Deleuze's very last text, published as an appendix to the second edition of *Dialogues II,* is literally titled "The Actual and the Virtual" (hereafter "A/V").[11] With their shared focus on the actual/virtual, these two short essays, which some Deleuze scholars believe to be chapters (drafts) of an unfinished project called "Ensembles and Multiplicities,"[12] simultaneously mark Deleuze's positioning as an empiricist and a philosopher of immanence[13] and testify to his significance for the study of the moving image, for it is in relation to cinema that the actual/virtual distinction, as Cowie also suggests, has proven to be particularly valuable.

As Boundas points out, in developing his notion of the virtual, Deleuze was not only influenced by Henri Bergson's critique of the possible, but also by Baruch Spinoza's idea of "differentiated substance" and by Nietzsche's concept of the "eternal return."[14] Philosophy, Deleuze posits, is the "theory of multiplicities," each of which is "composed of actual and virtual elements" ("A/V," 148). The virtual is not an image of the transcendental in a post-Kantian sense, but a purely differential field or multiplicity that cannot resemble the image of empirical experience, a ground that cannot appear as the figure of form to which it gives rise. Yet, since there is no such thing as a "purely actual" object, every actual, Deleuze insists, "surrounds itself with a cloud of virtual images" that constantly renew themselves, that produce other virtual images by which they are in turn surrounded, and that are both emitted and absorbed by actual images ("A/V," 148).

Virtual images, however, equally react upon the actual: as a consequence of their "mutual inextricability," virtual images are not "unreal," but a temporally distinct dimension of the real so that "virtual images are able to react upon actual objects" ("A/V," 149). The actual/virtual distinction thus replaces both the traditional divide between the true and the false and that between the real and the unreal.

Addressing the actual/virtual distinction in direct relation to film, in *Cinema 2: The Time-Image* (1985; hereafter *C2*),[15] Deleuze shows that in certain kinds of images, what he calls the "crystal-image," the distinction between actual and virtual becomes indiscernible. In the formation of such an image with two sides, an actual one and a virtual one, it becomes impossible to attribute actuality and virtuality as distinct aspects, in that each side can be seen to be "taking the other's role in a relation we must describe as reciprocal presupposition, or reversibility." The fact that there are images that are "by nature double," that is, images in which the real and the imaginary, the present and the past, the actual and the virtual cannot be discerned, leads Deleuze to the conclusion that there is "no virtual which does not become actual in relation to the actual, the latter becoming virtual through the same relation" (*C2*, 69).

It will be clear that Deleuze's replacement of the true/false and the real/unreal oppositions with the actual/ virtual distinction complicates the traditional terms in which documentary film has been defined and distinguished from feature or fiction film. Indeed, what his insistence on the actual and the virtual as reversible characterizations of the real entails is, first, that it becomes impossible to distinguish between real and unreal images (an urgent question in the age of digitization) and, second, that since the virtual is real insofar as it affects us, the evaluation of any image requires us to examine its intrinsic qualities, its actuals affecting us, on the perspective of the multiple forces it virtually contains. The latter inference explains why Cowie associates Rancière's notion of the "sensible" with Deleuze's "actual." It furthermore encourages us to take up Rancière's description of the "politics of aesthetics" as the "system of *a priori* forms determining what presents itself to sense experience" in order to consider the idea of the *partage du sensible* in relation to his writing about film.

While Rancière's concept of the *partage du sensible* and Deleuze's actual/virtual distinction are not quite the same, the similarities between them are nonetheless remarkable. It is therefore surprising to find Rancière, despite his insistence on the oppositional claims of the sensible, elsewhere, and with specific reference to film, maintain a clear difference between the fictional and the documentary function. To be sure, he admits, the distinction between fiction and nonfiction does not reside in any given text, but instead arises from differentiated forms of authorization in specific historical contexts. Fiction, Rancière argues, is not a "pretty story or evil lie," but designates the practice of "using the means of art to construct a 'system' of represented actions, assembled forms, and internally coherent designs." Hence, he continues, we "cannot think of 'documentary' film as the polar opposite of 'fiction' film simply because the former works with images from daily life and archive documents about events that obviously happened, and the latter with actors who act out an invented story." As a fabrication, a creation of a new reality—not a social or actual reality, but the reality of the film—the documentary is as fictional as any product of creative practice. The real difference between fiction and documentary film, Rancière submits, is that "instead of treating the real as an effect to be produced," documentary film "treats it as a fact to be understood."[16]

In our rapidly visualizing, increasingly digital cultural context, the understanding of seeing as believing, I have argued earlier, cannot possibly hold the purchase it traditionally may have had—and the scene from *Alice in Wonderland* cited at the beginning of this chapter underscores that it might never have been an adequate idea in the first place. Rancière's characterization of documentary film (not to mention the overall ocularcentrism that still largely prevails in other sociocultural practices, such as science and technology) indicates that the notion of vision as a site of understanding nevertheless remains compelling. Yet even Alice's response to the sight of the fish-footman and the frog-footman critically challenges the distinction between the cinematic presentation of the real as either an effect to be produced or as a fact to be understood, a challenge that at once points up the centrality of the visual in the fixing—and, as the case may be, the unfixing—of meaning, and that directs us to the other Deleuzian concept I have suggested to be of great significance to Johan van der Keuken's film practice, namely, the notion of the face or, more accurately, of "faciality." In order to adequately address the operations of van der Keuken's *Face Value,* I must first try to bring these two concerns, the documentary treatment of the real and the signification of the face, together.

For Deleuze and Guattari, the face, as it is first theorized in detail in *A Thousand Plateaus,* stands at the intersection of two semiotic systems, signifiance and subjectivation. Faciality is not the same thing as the face itself, but a function that operates in the form of what they call a *"white wall/black hole* system" (*TP,* 167). In this system, the "black hole" or unknown zone of the face, the zone in which affective energies may be invested, is correlated with subjectivation, while the "white wall," the surface upon which signs are projected and from which they are reflected, corresponds with signifiance. The face is "not an envelope exterior to the person who speaks, thinks, feels," Deleuze and Guattari write, for without guidance from the face, the "form of the signifier in language, even its units, would remain indeterminate" (*TP,* 167), that is, without the help of the face the listener would not be able to make her or his choices about meaning. They furthermore point out that the face is not "basically" individual, but rather "constructs the walls that the signifier needs in order to bounce off of" while simultaneously "dig[ging] the hole that subjectification needs in order to break through." The face is thus not something that simply exists, that comes "ready-made," but rather comes into being as the effect of an "abstract machine of faciality" (*TP*, 168). It is this "abstract machine" that engenders the face as surface: "Facial traits, lines, wrinkles; long face, square face, triangular face; the face is a map" (*TP*, 170).

From the understanding of the face as a "map" or "surface," Deleuze and Guattari infer that the head is included in the body, but the face is not. The face needs to be produced, is the product of a process, of *facialization,* the effect of the operation of an "abstract machine," an operation that is both "horrible and magnificent":

> The head, even the human head, is not necessarily a face. The face is produced
> only when the head ceases to be part of the body, when it ceases to be coded
> by the body, when it ceases to have a multidimensional, polyvocal corporeal
> code—when the body, head included, has been decoded and has to be *overcoded*
> by something that we shall call the Face. (*TP*, 170)

Deleuze and Guattari conclude that the face, standing at the crossroads of signifiance and subjectivation, is a production "in humanity," but the necessity by which it is produced "does not apply to human beings 'in general,'" nor is the face "animal." Rather, there is something inhuman about the face: "The inhuman in human beings: that is what the face is from the start" (*TP*, 171).

On this account of the face and its machinic production, Alice would appear not only to confuse the intelligible and the sensible in her encounter with the animal-faced footmen by privileging the socially legible, meaning bestowing uniforms covering their bodies over their faces, which, despite their perceptual immediacy, are reduced to significatory secondariness. She can also be seen to trigger, in her own lateral and nonsensical way, the abstract machine that produces the face. The faces of the footmen, the frog-face and the fish-face, do not appear to obtain within what Deleuze and Guattari designate the "black hole/ white wall" system. Instead, the footmen's entire bodies are facialized in Alice's willful reading practice: the liveried bodies are turned into legible surfaces or maps, while the footmen's heads, being (or having become) animal, appear to escape the process of facialization, to "dismantle the face and facializations, to become imperceptible" (*TP*, 171). As one among innumerable delightful instantiations of Carroll's ability to confront us with the many "paradoxes of sense,"[17] Alice's reading/seeing practice makes the ordinary operation of faciality and facialization palpable, not as something given or "basic," nor even as something necessarily human, but rather as a product of machinic operations. The paradox of her perception hence alerts us to the traditional model of the human face, a model that centers on its function in the process of communication.

It is in his later solo work, the first of his two books on cinema, *Cinema 1: The Movement Image* (1983; hereafter *CI*),[18] that we find the second locus of Deleuze's theorization of the face. Here, he describes the function of the human face as follows:

> Ordinarily, three roles of the face are recognizable: it is individuating (it distinguishes or characterizes each person); it is socialising (it manifests a social role); it is relational or communicating (it ensures not only communications between people, but also in a single person, the internal agreement between his character and his role). (*CI*, 99)

The puzzling appearance of the footmen's animal faces, perceptually recognizable to Alice yet displaced by the operations of the meanings of their socially legible bodies, throws this traditional communicational model into confusion. The apparent readability, the facialization of the liveried bodies, and the "quite special becomings-animal" of the footmen's heads, their escape from the "inhuman in human beings," conjures up Deleuze and Guattari's notion of the face as the "very special mechanism" at the intersection of significance and subjectivation (*TP*, 171, 167), in its resonance with and distinction from Emmanuel Levinas's concept of the human face as the "source from which all meaning appears."[19]

I evoke Levinas's reflections on the ambivalence of the human face at this point because his alternative theorizations allow me to do two things. First, they enable me to return to the question of the functioning of documentary film, in its simultaneous framing and unframing operations, to challenge Rancière's understanding of its organization of the real as a fact to be understood rather than as an actualization of the virtual to produce its reality as an actual effect. Second, Levinas's thought enables me to link up the actual/virtual distinction with Deleuze and Guattari's theorization of faciality in tandem with Deleuze's subsequent application of these ideas to the operation of the face in cinema in *Cinema 1,* especially to the function of the face in close-up. Both the question of the organization of the real and the cinematic operation of the face are central to van der Keuken's film *Face Value* (1991).

Born in Amsterdam in 1938, van der Keuken was originally trained as a photographer and published his first book of photo portraits, *We Are Seventeen* (1955), while still in high school.[20] Suggestive of his later work, the thirty pictures of his teenage friends collected in this publication are of a striking yet telling simplicity: all the photos appear to capture people doing essentially nothing, to present nothing much more than the experience of the moment itself. Van der Keuken's second book, *Behind Glass* (1957),[21] appeared while he was studying filmmaking in France, where other young Dutch filmmakers such as Joris Ivens, Louis van Gasteren, and Bert Haanstra were already enjoying growing critical acclaim. Though van der Keuken is primarily known today as one of the most illustrious and innovative independent filmmakers of the twentieth century, most of his work reveals his origins in photography.[22] In one of the very few scholarly writings devoted to the photographer-filmmaker's work, film critic Thomas Elsaesser contends, while placing him in a specifically Dutch tradition of filmmaking, that there is really no question of competition between the two media for van der Keuken: "He knew how to catch the instant (the gift of the photographer), while making us feel how this instant belonged in a continuum, a movement, a process."[23]

Most critics agree that van der Keuken is in the first instance an image maker, even if it is not always entirely clear what they mean by this. Film critic-historian and curator Bérénice Reynaud, for example, begins her reflections on the filmmaker's work by describing a range of "evocative, often disturbing images," which come to her mind when she thinks about his films.[24] "Powerful" and "often disturbing" as they may be, these images do not, for Reynaud, call forth memories of the films qua films: "Yet, only images. Images from which *something is missing.*" Reynaud associates the lack she perceives in these images with van der Keuken's "dialectical, playful and rigorous approach," which she suggests works against the grain of "memory-hoarding, nostalgia, hagiography." Despite her emphasis on the centrality of the image in van der Keuken's films, Reynaud unaccountably goes on to explain this approach by singling out cinema, as distinct from other forms of image making such as television or advertising, as a medium that is, and here she takes recourse to the words of French film scholar Marie Chevrie, "*not* the image, it is the recording of a moment."[25] Even apart from its blatant contradictions, I find this argument quite unpersuasive. Although Elsaesser's use of the word "image" is similarly undertheorized, his claim that what is "central" to van der Keuken's films is not so much their left-wing politics, their idiosyncratic themes, or unusual topics, but "the 'image' (which, of course, for him included sound, words and movement),"[26] is closer to my own viewing experience. For in my repeated encounters with van der Keuken's films—admittedly in the wake of and after embracing the affective turn—I do not perceive moments, or the recordings of moments, but on the contrary (as Reynaud herself initially appears to suggest) images, images in the dual sense proposed in previous chapters, as potentially significant but in the first place pictorial surfaces, artificial presences in their pure visibility, as aesthetic objects.

The function of the image, as I have maintained in relation to photographic or still images and as I am presently suggesting with respect to moving images as well, has not so much to do with representation, with the construction and distribution of knowledge, with treating reality as a fact to be understood. Any image, like everything else, may function as a sign, as a carrier of meaning, but they need not take on this function. Images, if they present themselves as objects of our concern, do so in our actual encounter, the occasion of our experience of them, in a prehension: they first and foremost affect us—in a powerful and potentially "disturbing" manner—in our embodied being, as organized aesthetic activity, prior to any act of interpretation and/or comprehension. Moreover, in its ineluctable depthlessness, as surface structure, the image may be argued to actively engage in the *partage du sensible* in the sense suggested by Rancière, that is, in the way bodies, objects, and places are distributed across the field of sense perception, and thus in the division of the sensible into that which is speakable, thinkable, visible, and audible and, at the same time, that which is not, that which is "portioned out" or excluded. But as the word *partage* itself indicates, such distribution does not constitute a differentiation between the possible and the real, or between the real and the imaginary, but rather defines the reversible relation between mutually exclusive yet inextricable characterizations of the real, the actual and the virtual. Images arising from the purely differential field, from the multiplicity of the virtual, affect us in the first instance largely unconsciously, precisely by presenting themselves in their actualization in the sensible, that is to say, aesthetically.

The *moving* image imposes its distributing operations in the sensible surreptitiously, and thus, I would argue, perhaps even more so than the still or photographic image, more violently, by appearing to offer us fluidity, sequentiality, continuity, and ostensible wholeness. Van der Keuken's background in photography made him fully aware of the singular operations of the moving image. As Reynaud points out, he turned to filmmaking "with the full acceptance of his new medium's double challenge: the passage of time—in which each image is 'annihilated' (his word) by the one just after it—and the constant necessity/desire/temptation to *reframe*."[27] This may be one of the reasons yet another French critic, Alain Bergala, characterizes van der Keuken's work as the "art of anxiety."[28] I will have more to say about the question of re/framing in a moment. For now, let me suggest that van der Keuken's keen awareness of the moving image's paradoxical capacity to simultaneously enact a certain sensual plenitude, to present an overabundance of visuality and to annihilate the image, to portion out, to exclude things from the field of vision, is acutely palpable in his films. While on one hand accounting for the fact that it is hard to remember these films as films rather than as images, it is on the other hand this "anxiety" over the medium's un/framing operations that explains the filmmaker's abiding fascination with the human face—apparent from his first published photographic work, through all of the fifty-five films he subsequently produced, culminating in *Face Value*.

On the sales website of Arte.TV, the main distribution center of European documentary films, *Face Value* is described as "an epic on humanity and cultural diversity in Europe through a multitude of appearances, a cartography of faces, the reflection of an imaginary Europe made up of London, Marseille, Prague and the Netherlands."[29] While to some extent illuminating (especially from a sales perspective), such a description situates van der Keuken and his film in the context of a politically engaged, if experimental, tradition of specifically *documentary* filmmaking. Van der Keuken himself objected to being classified as a documentary filmmaker, partly because he was also a photographer and writer and, in fact, a multitalented artist, but primarily because to him and his work, the distinction between fiction and documentary made no sense. Consequently, his films, socially engaged and most of the time politically dissident as they are, do not necessarily invite us to infer their underlying social meanings or ulterior, referential realities; they do not, as Rancière would have it, treat the real as a fact to be understood.

Van der Keuken's insight into the "filming process itself, and its physical aspects, the editing, the rhythm, etc." makes him reject any notion of film as a symbolic or symbolizing medium. In a short essay published in 1963, "Film Is Not a Language," he therefore dismisses any critical attempts to "read" his or any other films in significatory terms:

> Film is not, as is often assumed, a language in which certain combinations of signs refer to certain concepts and in which series of combinations of signs can be arranged into a syntaxis [*sic*]. Film has no sign and no significance. . . . People who refer to film as a language are essentially referring to a limited number of signals to which there are a limited number of conditional responses. . . . These signals have nothing to do with film itself. . . . The film is an instrument for the registration, reinforcement and distribution of the signal. All it can do is show, but it can show anything, in any way.[30]

Such insistence on the nonsignificatory operations of the film-image, its refusal to be captured within the closed terms of symbolic determination, marks film as the site of excess, a site where things can happen—film can show anything, in any way—but whatever happens in film cannot be reduced to concepts, to combinations of signs, or be brought under the order of syntax or of the signifier. Film as such, in other words, does not organize the real as an object of understanding.

Indeed, the very notion of the real is subject to van der Keuken's profound creative doubt. In her earlier-mentioned essay, Reynaud quotes a passage from one of the interviews she conducted with the filmmaker in which he gives particularly clear expression to such doubt:

> For me, the doubt about the Real of one's film has two causes. First, a belief that the Real is not a given, that it has to be suggested between the images; images are nothing but fragments, traces, bits of evidence, of something that has remained

elsewhere. Second, a process takes place in the spectator's mind, that consists of de-realizing these images from the Real to, paradoxically, prove their reality, or to the contrary, their artificiality.[31]

Van der Keuken's reflections on the Real in the first half of this passage recall Deleuze's distinction between the actual and the virtual as it plays out in terms of the founding concept of the plane of immanence. In *A Thousand Plateaus*, Deleuze and Guattari suggest that there may be "two planes" or "two ways of conceptualizing the plane":

> The plane can be a hidden principle, which makes visible what is seen and audible what is heard, etc., which at every instance causes the given to be given, in this state or that state, at this or that moment. But the plane itself is not given. It is by nature hidden. It can only be inferred, induced, concluded from that to which it gives rise (simultaneously or successively, synchronically or diachronically).
> (*TP*, 265)

What van der Keuken designates the Real is a hidden or organizational principle that cannot be perceived, is not given, and that can be described as "ungiven," as something that has "remained elsewhere," but which can be inferred from that to which it gives rise: the images or, rather, the images' in-between. The Real of his films is a compositional principle that is not itself visible but which serves to render visible, to bring into appearance, the "fragments, traces, bits of evidence" from which it stands aside and through which it can only be "suggested": the plane, in the words of Deleuze and Guattari, as the "development of forms" (*TP*, 265). The actual images that make up van der Keuken's films, the Real as the necessarily "ungiven," the plane of immanence developed and organized into forms, are the actuals in their inextricability from the "cloud of virtual images" that surrounds them and that are absorbed into them. In Deleuze's later formulation:

> The plane of immanence includes both the virtual and its actualization simultaneously, without there being any assignable limit between the two. The actual is the complement or the product, the object of actualization, which has nothing but the virtual as its subject. Actualization belongs to the virtual. The actualization of the virtual is singularity whereas the actual is individuality constituted. ("A/V," 149–50)

By confounding or, in effect, displacing the distinction between the real and the imaginary, the actual and the virtual, especially in the case of "crystal-images" in which the distinction cannot be discerned, the "evocative, often disturbing images" of van der Keuken's films fundamentally call into question, if they do not simply defy, any clear-cut distinction between fiction and documentary film.

Clearly, the many faces we see in *Face Value,* a film that revolves around the face and sight, can to some extent be connected to pre-existing social realities, dependent on whether one is (or thinks one is) familiar with the "typical" facial features of French, German, British, and Czech people, and or speaks or recognizes their respective languages. At the same time, however, the way these images of faces appear, actualize themselves, and thus operate on the viewer undercuts their function as signs. Some of the faces come oddly, sometimes awkwardly into view, for instance, the German-speaking construction worker whose face is gradually reduced to his moving mouth, then merely to one corner of his mouth, while the camera zooms in and moves unsteadily across its surface, as if it were mapping out its various parts until the image is all but fully abstract—an effect that is enhanced by the soundtrack in which the man's voice is struggling to be heard against the background noise of the machines working the site.

Or the toothless, smiling face of the older (French? Czech?) woman at a dance at what appears to be a local bar; shifting back and forth between her nimbly moving feet and close-ups of her face, the images do not so much reflect the lack of dental care in certain parts of Europe at a certain moment in history, or the ravaging effects of time on the human face, as they express joy, the intensity of movement, of sociality, of bodies moving together. *Face Value,* in the words of the filmmaker himself, is a "film which combines minute preparation with openness, thought with action. It presents a set of different positions within a field of relations, that could be called 'Europe,' an imaginary and partial Europe located between London, Marseille, Prague and the Netherlands."[32] The imaginary nature of this geographical location is equally strikingly perceptible in the sequence of the Dutch-speaking man talking about his childhood; the speaker is an ordinary-looking forty-something white man whose gaze is persistently turned away from the unmoving camera so that our gaze, too, appears to shift toward the imaginary winter landscape that he appears to envisage and that his words invoke.

The second aspect of van der Keuken's reflections upon the Real of his films compounds such defiance on the level at which Rancière addresses the distinction between fiction and documentary film, the level of the viewer or spectator. It thereby additionally evokes Wiesing's phenomenological celebration of the image, its singularity as the medium that alone can make the artificial presence of things possible. The filmmaker's insistence on the role of the viewer as an "active *subiectum*" (Bakhtin) in the process of aesthetic co-creation furthermore confirms that such images can only do their work, react upon the actual if they are subject to a process of derealization. These joint emphases, on the necessity for the derealization of images in order to prove their "reality" or their "artificiality," and the non- or asymbolic operation of film, are nowhere more pronounced (and disturbing) than in van der Keuken's treatment of the face, even if *Face Value* is "also a film about photography" in which the filmmaker has "portrayed not only faces, but also spaces and words."[33]

The human face can, according to Levinas, only signify, totally and exclusively, self-referentially. For even if the face for Levinas, we recall, is a "source from which all meaning appears," it is emphatically *not* the site of meaning itself. This self- or auto-referentiality means that expression is the signification of the face, but it is a signification that cannot be contained or possessed, captured in the chains of symbolization. Seen as such, the face as a site of expression rather than of meaning essentially breaks through the classic system of signification and thus focuses, par excellence, the inherent ambivalence of the visual organization of the real. As an aesthetic event, van der Keuken's *Face Value* does not so much show, but expresses such ambivalence.

For Levinas the face is a "living presence; it is expression."[34] In its unspeakable expressiveness, the face constitutes its own signification, but, as suggested, it is a signification that does not enter the familiar Peircian model of the sign as *representamen,* that is, the face is not "something that stands to somebody for something in some respect or capacity."[35] The face does not express itself by any measure or quality, but "καθ'αυτο," "in itself." The "face of the Other," Levinas hence proposes, "at each moment destroys and overflows the plastic image it leaves me, the idea existing to my own measure and the measure of its *ideatum*—the adequate idea." In other words, in breaking through "all the envelopings and generalities of Being," the face not only "expresses itself,"[36] but also, and this is what essentially defines it, escapes the power of the signifier: the face "resists possession" and is "present in its refusal to be contained."[37] Deleuze, too, describes the face as "expression, expression of affectivity or the emotional quality of a situation, a virtual disposition to act, potency waiting to become act."[38] The critical difference, however, between Levinas's and Deleuze's respective characterizations of the face in terms of expression is that the former addresses actual human faces, whereas Deleuze, having begun his detailed theorization of the human face, as we have seen, in his collaborative work with Guattari, in *Cinema One: The Movement-Image,* directs his (and thus our) attention to the face in cinema, the face framed, the face in close-up.

In his preface to the English edition of this book, his first on film, Deleuze explains that his main concern is neither to present a history of cinema nor to engage with technical, critical, or linguistic cinematographic concepts, but to "isolate" concepts that allow us to identify under what conditions certain "types of images" and the "signs which correspond to them" can be identified and defined. Assuming the image of the cinema generally to be "'automatic' and presented primarily as movement-image," he differentiates three types of cinematic movement-images: the perception-image, the affection-image, and the action-image. It is the second of these image types that Deleuze correlates with the close-up and the face; indeed, he opens his chapter on the affection-image as follows: *The affection-image is the close-up, and the close-up is the face.*" (*CI*, ix). Just as Levinas does with respect to the actual human face, Deleuze suggests that the face in/as close-up does not function within the terms of traditional signifying systems or forms of representation, which function according to a certain internal or intentional logic. The face/close-up does not hide some underlying meaning, nor does it function as a part for the whole: we cannot infer the entire person, or the meaning of the person, or even of the face itself from the image. The face/close-up expresses, but what it expresses is not something other than itself; it is not the visible/perceptual representation of something hidden or unseen, something it, in and of itself, is not. On the contrary, Deleuze maintains, the close-up of the face is not something that stands for something else, but rather abstracts something from all spatiotemporal coordinates, and that something is affect: "The affect is the entity, that is Power or Quality. It is something expressed." In the face/close-up, powers and qualities are not actualized, "embodied in states of things"—in which case we would be dealing with the action-image—but "considered for themselves, as expressed" (*CI*, 97).

In explaining the difference between these two opposed modalities of powers and qualities, Deleuze draws on C. S. Peirce's distinction between "firstness" and "secondness." The latter refers to what is in relation to something or someone else; it is the realm of the Real, of individuation, of actuality and existence, the domain "where the action-image is born." Firstness, in contrast, is a "totally different category, which refers to another type of image with other signs." Firstness is hard to define, because it primarily exists as something that is felt, not conceived, and it "concerns what is new in experience, what is fresh, fleeting and nevertheless eternal." Peirce's examples of firstness include, in Deleuze's gloss, "qualities or powers considered for themselves, without reference to anything else, independently of any question of their actualisation. It is that which it is for itself and in itself." Firstness is not, or not yet, a feeling or sensation, but the "quality of a possible sensation, feeling, or idea." As the category of the possible, firstness "expresses the possible without actualising it," and this is, for Deleuze, "exactly what the affection-image is: it is quality or power, it is potentiality considered for itself as expressed" (*CI*, 98).

To be sure, within this Peircian-Deleuzian model, any set of images is made up of "firstnesses, secondnesses and many other things besides," but it is the face/close-up—the affection-image "in the strict sense"—that "only refers to firstness"

(*CI*, 98). At this point, the difference between Levinas's focus on the human face and Deleuze's concern with the cinematic face in and as close-up, despite their shared emphasis on the face-sign as expression, becomes particularly relevant to my purposes here. As we have seen, Deleuze ascribes to the human face the three functions of individuation, socialization, and communication. In the case of the close-up, however, the face loses all three of these ordinary roles. The "primary originality and the distinctive quality of the cinema," in the words of director Ingmar Bergman, the master of close-ups whom Deleuze quotes approvingly, is the "possibility of drawing near to the human face,"[39] to the extent that the functions of the face in their secondness, their significance in the Real disappear; those aspects of the face that achieve actualization, and hence get caught up in the system of signification and that "presuppose a state of things where people act and perceive," dissolve, evaporate in the affection image (*CI*, 99).

In the close-up, the face is, but it has lost all its signifying functions; suspending individuation, socialization, and communication, the close-up transforms the face into a nothingness, a nakedness, a phantom, an expression of the possible without actualization. This quality, the *quale* of the face/close-up in cinema is what Deleuze calls "affection" or affect. And the affect, he maintains, is "impersonal and . . . distinct from every individuated state of things: it is nonetheless *singular*." In its singularity, which we recall is the "actualization of the virtual," but not the actual as "individually constituted" ("A/V," 150), the face/close-up confronts us with its firstness, with "what is new in experience" (*CI*, 98). It expresses a power considered for itself, "without reference to anything else," which is no less than to say that the paradox of the face in and as close-up finds its limit in the "effacement of faces in nothingness" (*CI*, 101). It is precisely this irreducible ambivalence at the heart of the image of the face, the cinematic production of the face as both the site of individuation (in the domain of the action-image) and of the face/close-up (the affection-image), with its singular power to efface, that van der Keuken, in all of his films but particularly in *Face Value*, is both haunted by, and relentlessly, perhaps obsessively, pursues.

As we have seen, van der Keuken is intensely aware of the "annihilating" operation of the sequential movement of images in film, which to some extent accounts for (and amplifies) his sense of the "necessity/desire/temptation to *reframe*" and for his films to qualify for Bergala as the "art of anxiety."[40] Deleuze's conceptualization of cinema as consisting of both movement-image and time-images and his elaboration on their different types allow me to think through the interconnections between the photographer/filmmaker's preoccupation with, on one hand, the human face and, on the other, the cinematic procedure of framing, deframing, and reframing.

Several critics have commented on van der Keuken's idiosyncratic framing practice. Bergala, for instance, suggests that in his "anxiety" to somehow "wrong" the visible world by arbitrarily sectioning it, by framing his images, and thus curtailing the infinity of the "body of reality," the filmmaker invented his "'unframed' pictures, which have since become famous." On Bergala's view, this deframing technique is a "relativization made visible of the act of framing," which allows van der Keuken to sidestep the authoritative act of imposing meaning, of impaling visual reality, and, therefore, of "doing violence to the world."[41] A similar approach to the filmmaker's deframing techniques is offered by Irish film scholar Des O'Rawe. In his essay "Cinema Lucida: Johan van der Keuken and the Meaning of Loss," O'Rawe claims that van der Keuken's "narrative patterns and deframing techniques, 'free-form' camera movement, and abstract colour and sound configurations" have less to do with conscious decisions than that they are a "more direct expression of his uncertainties about the possibility of ever framing and representing the world as it is, and was."[42] Although helpful in and of themselves, at least to the extent that one might try to make "sense" of van der Keuken's films, these approaches ultimately do not satisfy. This is partly because they inevitably land us back, if not in the world, then at least in the domain of representation and symbolization. This, it will be clear, would be an unaccountably reductive move, for as O'Rawe himself quite rightly submits, the filmmaker's use of "harsh contrasts of colour and sound . . . can unsettle a seemingly realistic representation and disturb the natural flatness of the image, accentuating movement, plasticity, and instability." Partly, and for me more importantly in view of my overall concerns in this chapter, because such approaches do not adequately account for the operation of the face, the face in and as close-up, in its specificity as the affection-image par excellence, and for the ways in which it is framed, deframed, and reframed, in the reality—or indeed the artificiality—of van der Keuken's films. To suggest a possible way to think the "problematic" of the framing of the affection-image, I return to Deleuze's concept of the time-image, or "crystal-image," as discussed in connection with the actual/virtual distinction, and I foreground its difference from and interrelations with the movement-image.

Deleuze associates the movement-image and its three types (action, perception, affection) primarily with prewar, classical (Hollywood) cinema as it is realized, following a sensory-motor schema, as montage: a perception is followed by an action. The movement-image functions within a certain (chrono)logical order, according to a clear narrative procession, and with linear references and incisions. Movement-images refer to each other and to the whole of spatial configuration, making a clear distinction between past and present, situation and response/action. Time-images, in contrast, which Deleuze relates to the introduction of new forms of postwar cinema (e.g., Italian neorealism and French *nouvelle vague*), do not proceed by any (chrono)logical order or by the narratological representation of actions and reactions. Breaking with the sensory-motor linkage of the movement-image, the time-image makes the distinction between the present and the past, and between the actual and the virtual, indiscernible. Various levels of duration coincide in the time-image, which thus dissolves the homogeneous structure of the movement-image and its linear spatiotemporal configuration to open onto the imaginary. Most films contain both general types of images, even if one of them may overdetermine the film as whole. What distinguishes the movement-image from the time-image is their respective spatial renderings of time. Yet whatever the nature of the image, and irrespective of its specific effects, every image is constituted by an in-between, an interval; in the movement-image, the interval is occupied by affection, "surg[ing] in the centre of indetermination" (*CI,* 65), between perception and action. In the time-image, it is something that comes from outside the narrational, linear set, a "coexistence of distinct dura-tions, or of levels of duration" (*CI,* xi) that are juxtaposed between images to form a nonrepresentable multiplicity, levels of duration that cannot be reconciled and that render the distinction between the actual and the virtual indiscernible.

Van der Keuken's *Face Value* presents us—or perhaps more accurately, violently and relentlessly confronts us—with the disruptive force of the interval, with the two types of interval specific to the two types of images Deleuze develops in his theory of cinema. In their primary function as affection-images, in-between the "two limit-facets, perceptive and active" of the movement-image, the faces/close-ups occupy the interval "without filling it in or filling it up" (*CI,* 65). Defying traditional frameworks of intelligibility and collapsing the Platonic dualisms of surface and depth, of appearances and reality, the face in and as close-up is present not as representation of something else, nor as expressions of another feeling or idea, but as expression in itself. The multiplicity of faces in *Face Value* are hence not to be "read" or *understood,* whether as, pace the Arte.TV sales department, an "epic on cultural diversity," or as, in van der Keuken's own words, a "certain combination of signs." As *images* in the broad sense suggested by Elsaesser, that is, including words, sound, and movement, they demand to be approached or experienced as pure quality or affect, as the expression of potentiality without actualization.

In its function as a kind of zero degree of signification per se—as an aesthetic event, the locus of a prehension—it is the face/close-up in the interval that is the affection-image. It "surges in the centre of indetermination," the effacement of faces in nothingness, that possesses the quality of "firstness," whose substance is what Deleuze calls the "compound affect of desire and astonishment" (*CI,* 65). It is this "compound affect," equally evoked by the frog-faced and fish-faced footmen in Alice and by van der Keuken's face/close-ups in us as spectators/perceivers, that renders Rancière's firm distinction between fiction and documentary—a distinction, we recall, that hinges on the genres' respective treatment of the real as an effect to be produced and as a fact to be understood—particularly unhelpful for an appreciation of van der Keuken's films, if it not altogether theoretically untenable. The faces populating van der Keuken's un/framed images, in their ultimate *indifférence,* which paradoxically gives them their life and their singularity, are not representations of something else, and they have no underlying depth or ulterior meaning. While extracted from and organizing reality, they are images, presenting things as exclusively visible: "All they can do is show." But what they can never show, what necessarily remains hidden, is the plane of immanence, that which the filmmaker himself calls the Real, the "hidden principle, which makes visible what is seen and audible what is heard," but which can only be "inferred, induced, concluded" from their in-betweens ("A/V," 49).

The other type of interval, the interval of the time-image, which occasionally converges with the interval constituted by the affection-image in *Face Value,* is equally crucial for the ways van der Keuken's films both warn us about taking what we see on the screen at face value and force us to feel, rather than conceive, the *dévisage,* the "effacement of faces in nothingness" (*C1,* 101). Defying the conventions of linear, narrative storytelling, juxtaposing sequences that "disrupt the texture of the film with sudden discontinuities, distractions, and detours"[43] and adopting a self-conscious method of (sometimes ludicrous) framing, pacing, and editing the faces of his subjects in their unspeakable expressiveness—as Bergala points out, the filmmaker "sometimes used the term 'excision' to describe what was in his eyes the ontologically aggressive nature of the act of framing"[44]—*Face Value* equally deploys "false continuity and irrational cuts" that define the interval of the time-image (*C2,* xi).

In the preface to the English edition of *Cinema 2: The Time-Image,* Deleuze states, "What is specific to the image, as soon as it is creative, is to make perceptible, to make visible, relationships of time which cannot be seen in the represented object and do not allow themselves to be reduced to the present" (*C2,* xii). This is, I think, what is essential to van der Keuken's idiosyncratic cinematic practice, as much as it explains and validates his rejection of the distinction between documentary and fiction film. Stripped of their three ordinary functions of individuation, socialization, and communication, the face-images in *Face Value* show rather than tell us something about the possibility of meaning and being, or indeed about nonmeaning and nonbeing. In their inherent ambivalence, their presentness as aesthetic events, as intervals, these face/close-ups do not so much document anything at all, but rather constitute a critique of that founding distinction between appearance and reality, between surface and depth, between animal-face and liveried body, between creation and understanding, between the real and the artificial: distinctions they at once inscribe and dissolve. As such, they simultaneously fix and transcend the limits of perceptible reality and restore that which has been "portioned out" in the *partage de sensible* to the "infinite equivalence of becoming." Opening onto the imaginative, van der Keuken's films enable the emergence of the "new" and expose us to what is "fresh, fleeting, and nevertheless eternal," and they can only do so in the event of our viewing experience, in the process of "derealization" that proves the image's reality, or its artificiality.

Experience is that mass of affects,
projects and memories that must perish
and be born for a subject to arrive
at the expression of what it is.

Jean-François Lyotard, *The Inhuman*

CONCLUSION

lines of flight and
the emergence of the new

I started this book by situating myself in a moment—a mood, a concatenation of events, with both theoretical and practical dimensions. The event, in a Deleuzian sense, is "unlimited becoming." This idea is one of the principal targets of Alain Badiou's (in)famous critique of Deleuze.[1] Rather than a philosopher of multiplicity, Badiou takes Deleuze's distinctly vitalist perspective, the importance of the category of "univocity" in his thinking, to mean that he is a philosopher of the One.[2] Acknowledging that the idea of the event is as central in his own "enterprise" as it is in Deleuze, Badiou considers the contrast between their respective conceptualizations of the event to be the direct result of the "original ambiguity of the idea [of the event] itself." He articulates this ambiguity and thus the contrast between his own and Deleuze's positions as follows: "In the first case, the event is disjoined from the One, it is separation, assumption of the void, pure non-sense. In the second case, it is the play of the one, composition, intensity of the plenum, the crystal (or logic) of sense."[3]

Badiou critiques Deleuze's idea of the event as "unlimited becoming" on two general grounds. First, because "like all philosophers of vital continuity," Deleuze does not allow for a division between "sense, the transcendental law of appearance, and truth, eternal exceptions." This, Badiou submits, leads to a certain dogmatism in his thought. Second, and more seriously, Badiou perceives a "latent religiosity" in Deleuze's "vitalist logic" that stems from his identification of "sense" with "truth." He writes, "If sense has in effect an eternal truth, then God exists, having never been anything other than the truth of sense." His counterclaims against Deleuze's empiricism and against his presumed dogmatism are that the event "must be thought as the advent of what is subtracted from all experience: the ontologically un-founded and the transcendentally discontinuous" and, furthermore, that it must be "released from every tie to the one . . . subtracted from Life in order to be released to the stars."[4] On one hand, Badiou accuses Deleuze, in his insistence on the univocity of being, of reinstalling transcendence, and, on the other, of an "aestheticisation of everything" by forging a "chimera, an inconsistent neologism: the 'sense-event.'" He thereby reverses, in the words of Mogens Laerke, the "practical dimension of Deleuze's philosophy" from being an "aggressive struggle on behalf of the chance event of the future and a joyful practice of the multiple into being a mnemonic ascesis of the virtual One."[5] While Badiou's critique is a serious one that should not be offhandedly dismissed, I would argue that it is precisely Deleuze's vitalism and his notion of the "sense-event" that render his ontology of crucial importance for the project of a neo-aesthetics, for a theoretically informed approach of the arts of the present in the wake of the affective turn.

In these, my concluding reflections on art and aesthetics after representation, I therefore wish to take up Badiou's dual challenge and use his "somewhat odd and . . . also rather severe"[6] accusations against Deleuze as a starting point to explore what I have called, in the introductory chapter, the political potential of affect in its unpredictable and at best ambivalent operations, especially in its specific, even privileged interconnection with art, with aesthetic experience as dynamic process or force field, the consequences of which are both equally powerful and equally variable and unforeseeable. I will do so by first returning to Deleuze's writings on the event, most prominent in his early work *The Logic of Sense* and in his later essay "What Is an Event?" in *The Fold: Leibniz and the Baroque* (1988; hereafter *F*).[7] Second, I will foreground the practical dimension of a Deleuzian-Whiteheadian ontology as an aesthetics of existence, by discussing, in tandem with these two affiliated thinkers, the central assumptions of Guattari's model of an ethico-aesthetics as articulated in his essay "The Three Ecologies" (1989; hereafter "TE") and in his earlier mentioned, posthumously published book *Chaosmosis: An Ethico-Aesthetic Paradigm* (hereafter *C*).[8] Guattari's radical "remodelization" of subjectivity, in its conscious as well as its unconscious operations, will allow me to revisit several of Whitehead's and Bakhtin's ideas on aesthetic activity and its object and to attempt to make good on my overall claim that art is not a Sunday afternoon activity but a "project" with both subjective and collective, both individual and sociopolitical implications.[9]

In previous chapters, I have not made much of a difference between the notion of the event in its everyday, common sense and in the philosophical sense that Badiou suggests has become a "common term for the greater number of contemporary philosophers."[10] It is a common term, that is to say, in the aftermath of, in Deleuze's words, Jean-Paul Sartre's proposal of the idea of an "impersonal transcendental field, not having the form of a synthetic personal consciousness or a subjective identity—with the subject, on the contrary, always being constituted" (LS, 98–99).[11] While philosophically unaccountable, my inclination thus far to not clearly theoretically define the idea of the event springs from my desire to maintain the practical, if not empirical, dimension of Deleuze's and Whitehead's, as well as Bakhtin's, respective uses of the term and to think with and through their various conceptualizations of it at different moments in my exploratory trajectory. Still, it is important to bear such distinctions in mind and to realize that, as Deleuze writes, the event is "not what occurs (an accident), it is rather inside what occurs, the purely expressed" (LS, 149).

For Deleuze, events are changes and transformations that are immanent to entities, forces that subsist over and beyond their actualization, virtualities. He defines events as by nature "ideal" and notes that this is what distinguishes them from their "realization in a state of affairs" (LS, 53), or, more simply, from accidents, in which they can nonetheless be expressed. He continues that the event "signals and awaits us . . . it is what must be understood, willed, and represented in that which occurs." This renders the question of the event an ethical one: "Either ethics makes no sense at all, or this is what it means and has nothing else to say: not to be unworthy of what happens to us" (LS, 149). The notion of the event as the "underlying" confluence of forces of an actualized state of affairs challenges the Platonic metaphysics of substance to "remove essences and substitute events in their place, as jets of singularities." The identity of a thing or the determination of a state of affairs cannot be ultimately distinguished from the forces and events that define it, even if the event can never be fully captured, remains unrelated to the material content of a thing, is "unlimited becoming" and hence without beginning or end. Deleuze's event is thus a dynamic concept that serves a dual philosophical and ethical purpose: "A double battle has the objective to thwart all dogmatic confusion between event and essence, and also every empiricist confusion between event and accident" (LS, 149–50). The point is to preserve the productive potential in every kind of force, to see events as potentialities, as moments that may generate new forces, to consider things anew, in short, to rise to the occasion of the chaos of life and to embrace the possibilities given in each moment. The event, in other words, is what Bakhtin's designates "unfinalizability," the idea that life is not only a "messy place, but also an open space."[12]

Deleuze's essay "What Is an Event?" constitutes his only extended engagement with Whitehead, whose concern with the question of the event is placed in the context of *The Fold*'s wider argument on the German mathematician and philosopher Gottfried Wilhelm Leibniz (or von Leibniz; 1646–1716) and on Deleuze's attempt to develop a neo-Leibnizian analytical model in terms of contemporary arts and science. Further pursuing the distinction between events and accidents presented in *The Logic of Sense,* Deleuze here follows Whitehead in maintaining that the world as such is made up of events, of happenings and processes, rather than of substances and essences: "An event does not just mean that 'a man has been run over.' The Great Pyramid is an event, and its duration for a period of one hour, thirty minutes, five minutes . . . a passage of Nature, of God, or a view of God." Instead of positing life as a chaotic multiplicity that needs to be embraced, as he repeatedly suggests in *The Logic of Sense,* this intonation of the idea of the event raises the question of what the conditions are that make an event possible. The answer Deleuze provides is that chaos "does not exist," that chaos is an "abstraction" that comes into being only through the intervention of "some sort of screen" placed between the One and the Many, a screen "that makes something" from the "purely disjunctive diversity" of the Many, and from which is it "inseparable." This screen functions like a "formless elastic membrane" and "makes something issue from chaos" (*F,* 76).

For Leibniz, the idea of the screen allows for different approximations to chaos. In a "cosmological approximation," Deleuze writes, chaos appears as the "sum of all possibles," whereas the screen "only allows compossibles—and only the best combination of compossibles—to be sifted through." From a psychic point of view, he goes on, "chaos would be a universal giddiness, the sum of all possible perceptions being infinitesimal or infinitely minute; but the screen would extract differentials that could be integrated in ordered perceptions." If the world appears chaotic to us, it is merely because our screening abilities are limited. If we cannot adequately follow the "infinite series of wholes and parts . . . each of which is extended over the following ones," it is because of the "insufficiency of our own screens." Referring directly to Whitehead, Deleuze subsequently attempts to offer a more precise definition of the event by describing it in terms of its four "components" or conditions: extension, intrinsic properties, individuals or prehensions, and eternal objects or "ingressions" (*F,* 77).

Extension exists when "one element is stretched over the following ones, such that it is a whole and the following elements are its parts." Forming an infinite series without final term or limit, the "event is a vibration with an infinity of harmonics or submultiples, such as an audible wave" or a "luminous wave." Extensive series have intrinsic properties (such as height, intensity, timbre, tint, color), which "enter on their own account in new infinite series, now converging toward limits, with the relation among limits establishing a conjunction." Once such conjunctions are formed, extensions no longer exist, but have become "intensities" or "degrees": "It is something rather than nothing, but also this rather than that: no longer the indefinite article, but the demonstrative pronoun." To move out of chaos from the mood of the indefinite and the demonstrative, the event requires the third component of the individual—that which Whitehead calls prehension—which is "creativity, the formation of a New" (*F*, 77). As we have seen, for Whitehead the subject emerges from the world in the prehension of its elements or data; prehension constitutes individual unity, which comes into being through the "how" of the prehension, the subjective form. In Deleuze's words, this occurs through the "form in which the datum is folded in the subject," so that the individual can be defined as a "concrescence of elements" that are given (*F*, 78).[13] The fourth and final component of the event Deleuze derives from Whitehead, eternal objects or "ingressions," requires a brief detour through the latter's theory of objects, presented as a published lecture in his less well-known book, *The Concept of Nature* (1920; hereafter *CN*).

An object, Whitehead submits, is an "ingredient in the character of some event."[14] The awkward term "ingression" serves more precisely to define the general relation of objects to events: "The ingression of an object into an event is the way the character of the event shapes itself in virtue of the being of the object . . . the event is what it is, because the object is what it is." The reverse holds equally true: "Objects are what they are because events are what they are" (*CN*, 145). Not all objects are the same, obviously, and even in the case of the same kind of objects, the ways they ingress into the event differ. Whitehead distinguishes three general kinds of object: sense-objects (colors, sounds, smells, feelings), perceptual objects (ordinary physical objects, such as garments, chairs, tables, trees), and scientific objects (electrons, etc.). The latter are primarily the result of the "endeavour to express in terms of physical objects the various roles of events as active ingredients in the ingression of sense-objects into nature" (*CN*, 158) and hence fall outside of his theory of objects.

In *Process and Reality,* significantly subtitled "An Essay in Cosmology," Whitehead expands on the concept of the object as an "ingredient in the character of some event" within the context of what he considers to be the task of European philosophy (which he characterizes as a "series of footnotes to Plato"), the necessity of the "construction of a philosophy of the organism" (*PR*, 39).[15] Sidestepping the idea that it is necessary to define reality, he proposes to conceive the "actualities constituting the process of the world" as "exemplifying the ingression (or 'participation') of other things which constitute the potentialities of definiteness for any actual existence" (*PR*, 39–40). Whatever is actualized is, in Deleuzian terms, arising from the realm of the virtual. Whitehead puts it thus: "The things which are temporal arise by their participation in the things which are eternal" (*PR*, 40).

The eternal (or the virtual) is timeless, but it is only in the actualization, in the "valuation of pure potentials," in which each "eternal object has a definite, effective relevance to each concrescent process," that novelty or creativity are possible. Actual entities allow us to generate ideas, to invent something new, to think and to create simultaneously, and without such actualizations there would be no life, no organism, no process, no novelty. In Whitehead's terms, the "ideal realization of potentialities in a primordial actual entity constitutes the metaphysical stability whereby the actual process exemplifies general principles of metaphysics, and attains the ends proper to specific types of emergent order" (*PR*, 40). Eternal objects for Whitehead evoke the notion of "Platonic form." In Deleuze they appear to transform into the notion of virtualities: "Any entity whose conceptual recognition does not involve a necessary reference to any definite actual entities of the temporal world is called an 'eternal object'" (*PR*, 44).

For Whitehead, then, "eternal objects" are possible forms of experience which "ingress" into the actual occasions of the event. Here it is helpful to recall that he makes a firm distinction between occasions and events. In Shaviro's gloss, an occasion, for Whitehead, is the "process by which anything becomes, and an 'event' . . . is an extensive set, or a temporal series of such occasions." Shaviro goes on to point out that the distinction is crucial for an understanding of Whitehead's metaphysics, in that an "actual occasion" never occurs "*ex nihilo,*" but rather "inherits its data from past occasions," while at the same time introducing something different, something new into the world, because every actual occasion is "also self-creating, or *causa sui,* by virtue of the novel way in which it treats these preexisting data or prior occasions" (*WC*, 19). This formulation recalls Bakhtin's assumption that creativity is immanent in ongoing processes that are not random interruptions, but the result of minute alterations that make up the continuous "event of being."[16] In Whitehead's own straightforward terms, "No thinker thinks twice; and, to put the matter more generally, no subject experiences twice" (*PR*, 29). Eternal objects are thus not actual objects or concrete existences in the form of sense-, perceptual- or scientific objects, but abstract potentialities for actual occasions. In other words, they constitute occasions in which they become what Deleuze calls the "purely expressed." As such, "eternal objects" are only available to us in their actualization, in the form of concrete events, but the way they become relevant to us, that is, the prehension of such data in their subjective form, is how they will generate or give birth to the new. Eternal objects are therefore not knowable in and of themselves, but they are nonetheless not ultimately different, though distinct in nature, from the actual occasions in which they are realized. While Deleuze does not discuss these aspects of the Whiteheadian idea of "eternal objects," he infers from the idea itself that the possibility for novelty and/or creation derives from the fact that the "best of all worlds is not the one that reproduces the eternal, but the one in which new creations are produced, the one endowed with a capacity for innovation or creativity" (*F*, 79).

As "pure Possibilities," eternal objects participate, ingress into the event, in the form of qualities, figures, or even things. They are virtualities that are actualized in experience, in prehensions, in moments or occasions of becoming. Their permanence, Deleuze writes, is thus not given in advance: they "gain permanence only in the limits of the flux" (of extensions) that "create them, or of the prehensions that actualize them" (*F*, 79–80). Since they are inseparable from the process of actualization, from their realization in the event, their "eternity is not opposed to creativity" (*F*, 79), but rather finds its conditions in the new, in new things, new figures, new qualities. Creativity, or the formation of the new, is thus, ostensibly paradoxically, a question of screening, of imposing limits, of delimiting the total multiplicity of pure possibility. It is on account of the latter aspect of Deleuze's conceptualization of the event as "unlimited becoming" that he can justifiably be "accused" of a certain vitalism. And so can Whitehead.

Vitalism, my online Merriam-Webster dictionary suggests, can designate two things: first, a doctrine that the functions of a living organism are due to a vital principle distinct from physicochemical forces; and second, a doctrine that the processes of life are not explicable by the laws of physics and chemistry alone and that life is in some part self-determining.[17] Underlying Whitehead's idea of the eternal object is his recognition that without the "actuality of [the] primordial valuation of pure potentials," that is, the fact that each eternal object has a "definite, effective relevance to each concrescent process," there would be a "complete disjunction of eternal objects unrealized in the temporal world" and hence no emergent order: "Novelty would be meaningless, and inconceivable" (*PR*, 40). Unlike rationalist models of thought, his "philosophy of organism" (now known as process philosophy) presupposes that not all elements in the universe are explicable by "theory," since "'theory' itself requires that there be 'given' elements so as to form the material for theorizing." There is no "givenness" that does not involve some screening, some kind of exclusion, for what is given is "separated off from what for that occasion is 'not given'" (*PR*, 42). The element of "givenness" in a thing is the result of a "decision," which can be but is usually not a question of conscious judgment and which is crucial for the actual occasion and the actual entity to emerge:

> The ontological principle asserts the relativity of decision; whereby every decision expresses the relation of the actual thing *for which* a decision is made, to an actual thing *by which* that decision is made. But "decision" cannot be construed as

a casual adjunct of an actual entity. It constitutes the very meaning of actuality. An actual entity arises from decision *for* it, and by its very existence provides decisions for other actual entities which supersede it. (*PR*, 43)

On Whitehead's view, actual entities or occasions are produced and produce themselves in their actualization, as discrete finite units of becoming. Rather than substances or essences, actual entities are what is given in experience, processes in their actual givenness, that are issued by being delimited from the total multiplicity of the universe. Eternal objects are not given as such, but acquire a limited givenness in each actual entity; the "determinate definiteness of each actuality is an expression of a selection" from the multiplicity of these objects (or forms). But the critical point is the "insistent particularity of things experienced and of the act of experiencing," an act which has no sooner "happened" when it is gone, to be "superseded" by other actual occasions of experience (*PR*, 43).

The fact that the eternal object is always a "potentiality for actual entities" means that the eternal object is, in itself, neutral. Only on meeting the third condition of the event, prehension or the individual, does the actual entity become "given." The concrescent feelings arising from the prehension of the actual entity converge with the "primary data" not to form a "mere multiplicity," however, but rather a "synthesis" the final unity of which is the actual entity, "another fact of 'givenness.'" This moment marks the limit of the occasion as a process of becoming: "The actual entity terminates its becoming in one complex feeling involving a completely determinate bond with every item in the universe, the bond being either a positive or a negative prehension. This termination is the 'satisfaction' of the actual entity." Since no subject experiences twice, every new prehension will bring some additional element or component to the actual entity's *synthetic* 'givenness'" (*PR*, 44), alter it, and thereby constitute the potential for the "formation of a New." This emphasis not only confirms what Shaviro describes as the "strictly limited scope" of occasions (*WC*, 19), it also explains why Deleuze defines the event, as an extensive set or series of occasions, in terms of "unlimited becoming," as a process of inevitable or necessary alteration—what Bakhtin designates the "unfinalizability" of the world as an ethical and phenomenal necessity. Finally, Whitehead's "doctrine of the emergent unity of the superject," that is, of the individual as both a subject "presiding over its own immediacy of becoming" and a "superject which is the atomic creature exercising its function of objective immortality," clarifies why his "philosophy of the organism" can be seen as a reversal of Kant's philosophy, in the sense that for the latter, the world emerges from the subject, while for the former, the subject emerges from the world.

It will be clear that in the orchestration of the subject-superject, eternal objects only appear as the "purely expressed" of actual occasions, as the forces immanent to entities as we experience them in their actualized, externalized condition. Whatever we define as an object (whether physical or mental) derives its quality of "being-an-object," its objectness, from its capacity to be prehended, to be experienced in perception. Moreover, since the final unity of subjective form, in Whitehead's words, is the "individual immediacy of an occasion," its "moment of sheer individuality," the occasion must be seen as an "absolute reality," which enjoys its decisive moment of "absolute self-attainment as emotional unity," only to perish "into the status of an object for other occasions" (*AI*, 177). This means that every occasion is sensitive to the existence of others, that actual entities take account of or "perceive" one another, and therefore that the subject-superject emerges from the total multiplicity of forms (or chaos) as a multicomponential process within the "throbbing emotion of the past hurling itself into a new transcendental fact" (*AI*, 177).

In order to bring all this "throbbing emotion" of the universe more down to earth, and to show the ways Whitehead's and Deleuze's vitalism does not so much, pace Badiou, issue in what Laerke unsurpassably calls a "mnemonic ascesis of the virtual One," but instead enables us to theorize the "sense-event" in its multiple, yet specific determinations on the level of the subject-superject, let me presently turn to Guattari's elaboration of subjectivity as a heterogeneous production in which the operation of art takes up a distinct, if not privileged, position. This in turn will allow me to restate my earlier claims about the significance of art in the processes of unlimited becoming and its actualization in everyday life, to reformulate the terms of the Whiteheadian/Deleuzian aesthetics of existence that it has been my purpose to unfold and explore in the foregoing pages.

The problem of subjectivity, or, rather, the question of subjectification, was of central concern for Guattari throughout his career not only as a philosopher but also as a social and political activist, as well as a practicing psychoanalyst. It is hence not surprising to find him return to this problem in the last two works published before his death in 1992. In the first of these, the deceptively concise essay "The Three Ecologies," Guattari assumes a generally ecological perspective in order to address the question of subjectivity beyond the terms of the traditional opposition between individual and society. The essay opens with a lengthy and incisive account of the ecological crises facing the contemporary world, culminating in the submission that traditional models of thought are inadequate to the task of generating effective responses to them. Guattari subsequently sets out to outline an experimental conceptual framework for which he adopts the neologist term "ecosophy" (a contraction of the phrase ecological philosophy) to rectify the shortcomings of traditional environmentalist perspectives, which obscure the complexity of the relationship between humans and their natural environment by maintaining a dualistic separation of human (cultural) and nonhuman (natural) systems. Insisting on the necessity to broaden our views of ecology to include not only the natural environment, but also the social and subjective ecosystems within which human existence evolves, Guattari intends the term "ecosophy" to designate an ethico-political framework of articulation in which the three ecological registers of existence—the environment, social relations, and human subjectivity—are thoroughly integrated. But here, as in his earlier collaborative work with Deleuze, Guattari privileges difference and heterogeneity, assemblages and multiplicities, rather than embracing a "holistic" point of view on these interrelated systems. He introduces the mathematical term "transverse," a line that intersects a system of other lines, to further qualify his paradigm and to foreground his concern with the variable intersections among these three complexly connected, parallel systems, or "ecologies."

Guattari justifies the need for such a "transversal" perspective by pointing up the paradox of postmodernity, that a variety of new technoscientific developments have opened up an equally expanding range of possibilities for solving major ecological problems as well as for the reconstruction of sustainable social relations, while existing social and subjective formations as yet do not seem capable of productively using these resources. Our lifeworlds are in the process of being fundamentally reconfigured by revolutionary technoscientific developments. The various ecological, social, and cultural consequences of such transformations do not ask for purely technocratic responses, but rather for an "authentic political, social, and cultural revolution . . . on a global scale." This revolution should, Guattari writes, not merely address "relations of force on a grand scale," but also take into account "molecular domains of sensibility, intelligence and desire" ("TE," 28).

By emphasizing the importance of the "molecular" level on which global changes critically take effect, Guattari seeks to underline that the increasing decentralization and fragmentation of a postindustrial world reigned by what he calls "Integrated World Capitalism" ("TE," 47) definitively mark what Daniel Bell has termed "the end of ideology."[18] Since all the grand humanistic ideologies derived from the nineteenth and early twentieth centuries are exhausted, any attempt to create similarly normativizing, "unequivocal" worldviews/political models is not only unfeasible but also downright unhelpful. What is called for instead, Guattari suggests, is to use the "ecosophical example" to trace the lines along which a "reconstruction of human praxis in the most varied domains" can be effected ("TE," 33), that is, to explore, on a multiplicity of levels at once, possibilities for new sociopolitical and cultural arrangements that will lead to new forms of individual and/or collective "resingularization"—as distinct from modes of being manufactured by the mass media or merely considered in terms of facts, statistics, and general predictions. Such resingularization would incorporate affective change, multiple modes of nondiscursive signification, and the proliferation of sense, as much as it would require the development of specific practices that would help us to reinvent the ways we live, on interpersonal and community levels, as well as on global levels.[19]

Boldly claiming that its overall problematic is the "production of human existence itself in new historical contexts" ("TE," 34), Guattari projects the ecosophic project simultaneously to evolve on the three ecological planes (natural, social, subjective) it centrally involves. Taking the first, the environment, as self-evident, he continues by developing his ideas in relation to the two remaining ecologies, especially important in their interrelated operations. He foresees social ecosophy to involve experimentations with new modalities of "'group-being' [*l'être-en-group*]," both through institutional interventions and through "existential mutations driven by the motor of subjectivity" ("TE," 34). These experimentations should help us to respond to such variegated problems as racism, phallocentrism, market-driven art practices, a technocratic and equally market-oriented educational system, as well as impoverished systems of town planning, commercialized recreational systems, and the power of military-industrial complexes. Alongside these practices of experimentation on a microsocial and institutional level, mental ecosophy should seek remedies against the standardization of human existence through the mass media, new information and communications technologies, and the fashion and advertising industries, as well as to the manipulation of opinion through media politics, social surveys, and "charismatic" public figures. New forms of being-with-others will serve to "reinvent the relation of the subject to the body, to phantasm, to the passage of time, to the 'mysteries' of life and death." Rather than resembling the *modus operandi* of psychiatrists ("always haunted by an outmoded ideal of scientificity"), the ways of functioning of mental ecosophy will be more like the "operations of an artist" ("TE," 35).

Guattari's integrational or "transversalist" perspective on human existence evidently entails a highly different conception of subjectivity than either the traditional Cartesian subject as the center of rational consciousness, or the poststructuralist subject, fatally caught in the grips of the alienating systems—of discourse, of power—that already exist and predetermine its coming into being. Just as Whitehead contends that the subject as such does not exist, but is something that must be constantly renewed since it does not outlive the feelings that bring it to life at any given moment, Guattari urges us to abandon any idea of the "subject" and redirect our focus to the "*components of subjectification*," to the various forces or "vectors" of its becoming, each of which can be seen to be "working more or less on its own" ("TE," 36). Additionally, where Whitehead posits the subject as always a subject-superject whose individuality constitutes the moment of creativity, Guattari, though using a different terminology, similarly argues that a transversalist perspective on human existence requires first of all a reconsideration of the relation between the concepts of the individual and subjectivity to the extent that the two should be clearly distinguished from each other.

The individual, Guattari submits, should not be regarded as a site through which all vectors of subjectification necessarily pass; instead, he posits the individual as "something like a 'terminal' for processes that involve human groups, socio-economic ensembles, data-processing machines, etc." ("TE," 36). This means that it makes little sense to assume individual interiority in opposition to and split off from different layers or modalities of exteriority. Rather, we should conceive of interiority as something that is constituted "at the crossroads of multiple components, each relatively autonomous in relation to the other, and, if need be, in open conflict" ("TE," 36). Countering poststructuralist notions of the subject as the mere product of, or as that which is spoken by, larger structures of discourse and power, he nonetheless follows Whitehead (to be sure, without mentioning him) in stipulating the creative potential of the self as it comes into being in the moment of its singularity, the actual occasion of its discontinuous transformation, in its encounter with that which is given. In other words, like Whitehead's subject-superject, Guattari's individual subject is in a process of "unlimited" becoming, not *ex nihilo,* but in its active interrelations with the multiple "components" that make up its equally heterogeneous ecosphere. Any concept of subjectivity that rests on the exclusive operations of exterior systems or structures in producing subjective interiority hence misses precisely what is crucial to the process of subjectification as such, which is its "intrinsically progressive, creative and auto-positioning dimensions" ("TE," 36).

Although he does not articulate his transversalist model in terms of an "aesthetics of existence" (Whitehead), Guattari implicitly indicates, by describing the operations of mental ecosophy with reference to artistic practices and by foregrounding the creative aspects of subjectivation, that the projected ecosophic paradigm is not merely ethicopolitical, but also profoundly aesthetic in inspiration. What he will later come to define as "chaosmosis," a contraction of "chaos" (not in the general sense of formless matter, but with reference to dynamic systems whose extreme sensitivity to small changes makes their behavior, although determined by initial conditions, so unpredictable as to appear random) and "osmosis" (the process whereby molecules pass through a semipermeable membrane from a less concentrated solution in a more concentrated one in order to equalize the solute concentration of the two sides), is as much an ethical as it is an aesthetic paradigm. His joint concern in "The Three Ecologies" with "aesthetic creation and with ethical implications" hence leads him to a reassessment of the psyche and of psychoanalytic thought beyond its pseudo-scientific aspirations overall, in order to highlight instead this reconfigured psyche's aesthetic components ("TE," 37).

Rejecting phenomenological analysis ("handicapped by a systematic 'reduction-ism' that leads it to reduce the objects under consideration to a pure intentional transparency") as a viable alternative to classic psychoanalysis, Guattari starts from the assumption that a "psychical fact" is "inseparable from the assemblage of enunciation that engenders it." He additionally refuses to make a clear distinction between, on one hand, cognitive or conceptual understanding and, on the other, affective or perceptive comprehension, regarding the two as "entirely complementary." He nonetheless maintains that there is a "kind of relationship of uncertainty between the apprehension [*la saisie*] of the object and the apprehension of the subject." To account for this differential, i.e., for the spatiotemporal gap between object and subject without returning to the traditional opposition between rational and intuitive modes of understanding, Guattari gestures toward what will become a central aspect of the more fully elaborated concept of subjectification delineated in *Chaosmosis*—to which I will turn shortly—which is its self-creative or *autopoietic* dimensions. In "The Three Ecologies," he restricts himself to the view that the articulation of both the apprehension of the subject and that of the object requires a "*pseudo-narrative* detour" through the stories, myths, and "supposedly scientific accounts" that make up a culture and that have as their aim to produce jointly a "discursive intelligibility" ("TE," 37). He additionally suggests that the repetitions deployed by this pseudo-narrative detour, in their infinite permutations, form the "very supports of existence," in that discourse becomes the "bearer of a non-discursivity" that cancels out the "play of distinctive oppositions" at both the formal and content levels of expression. Such repetitions, functioning through an endless range of "rhythms and refrains," enable the regeneration of "incorporeal Universes of reference, whose singular events punctuate the process of individual and collective historicity" ("TE," 38).

In *Chaosmosis,* Guattari will increasingly connect such punctuating events to the incorporeal frames of reference as those relative to music and art. Within the ecosophical paradigm, they primarily function to counter visions of the world—associated with structuralism and postmodernism—in which micropolitical forms of human intervention are no longer granted any significance. In trying to safeguard, or to rediscover and rekindle, the creative and constructive dimensions of subjective processes, it is necessary, Guattari writes, to acknowledge that the three ecologies are not so much governed by the logic of ordinary communication and discursive intelligibility as they are by a different logic—or "eco-logic"—that consists in "intensities" and "auto-referential existential assemblages engaging in irreversible durations" ("TE," 44). Being only concerned with the "movement and intensity of evolutive processes," ecological praxes, what Whitehead and Deleuze refer to as actual occasions and events, involve that which runs counter to the normal order of things, that invoke alternative intensities to those of established discursive sets, in order to forge "new existential configurations" ("TE," 45).

Guattari frankly acknowledges the risks involved in the "deterritorializations" effected by such "dissident" vectors of subjectification, which in their most violent manifestations might bring about the destruction of the assemblage of subjectivity per se. He nonetheless insists that more gentle forms of deterritorialization, "processual lines of flight" breaking through referential frames of expression and enunciation to operate as "decorporealized existential materials" ("TE," 45), are necessary to escape from the huge subjective void produced by "Integrated World Capitalism" so as to forge new productive subjective assemblages, as well as to gear emancipatory struggles toward such micropolitical and microsocial interventions as might lead to a "rebuilding of human relations at every level of the socius" ("TE," 49).

Whereas the overall net of Guattari's ecosophical logic is cast across the three existential territories of the environment, social relations, and subjectivity, its implications for these three ecological registers are, as already indicated, consistently inferred from the disruptive, deterritorializing potential of modes of creative expression most commonly associated with art. Indeed, by locating an expressive "a-signifying rupture" at the heart of all forms of ecological praxis, Guattari appears to suggest that it is in the first place certain forms of aesthetic practice (if not quite in the Whiteheadian, overarching sense, then definitely in the slightly more narrow sense suggested by Bakhtin) that may be capable of bringing about scenarios of processual assemblage that break with the dead-end logic of contemporary power formations and postindustrial consumerism. In experimenting with suspending referential meaning and disrupting established chains of signification, artistic creation would thus seem most closely to resemble the operations of the new ecosophical logic by opening up the fields of virtuality that will allow for a more constructive and sustainable individual and collective future. For even if, Guattari explains, "ethical paradigms" must be invoked in order to "underline the responsibility and necessary 'engagement' required not only of psychiatrists but also of all those in the fields of education, health, culture, sport, the arts, the media, fashion, who are in a position to intervene in individual and collective psychical proceedings," aesthetic paradigms must be foregrounded in order to "emphasize that everything . . . has to be continually reinvented, started again from scratch, otherwise processes become trapped in a cycle of deathly repetition [*répétition mortifère*]" ("TE," 39). Existing models of subjectivity fail precisely on this count; they remain "closed to the possibility of creative proliferation" ("TE," 55).

To assess the relevance of certain "theoretical bodies" to mental ecology, Guattari writes, two criteria are of critical importance: first, that they have the "capacity to recognize discursive chains at the point when they break with meaning," and second, that they utilize "concepts that allow for a theoretical and practical auto-constructability" ("TE," 55). As we have seen, Whitehead disputes the subject's self-perpetuating capacity, in the sense that it needs to be continually re-constituted, to be animated by ever more actual occasions, ever more new feelings. It is Guattari's major concern, however, to illuminate the *poietic* power of the subject in the face of the larger structures of sociodiscursive power. What the two philosophers hence (or nonetheless) share is their emphasis on the importance of aesthetic activity in the production of a self as creativity, of a subjectivity not "trapped in a cycle of deathly repetition." Although he concedes that the "assemblage of enunciation" from which the subject emerges is "composed of heterogeneous elements that take on a mutual consistency and persistence as they cross the thresholds that constitute one world at the expense of the other," Guattari insists that the "operators of this crystallization are fragments of a-signifying chains of the type that Schlegel likens to works of art" ("TE," 54–55).[20]

The suggestion that aesthetic practice assumes a special role in the ecosophic paradigm is furthermore corroborated by the fact that in trying to grasp these "a-signifying points of rupture," Guattari takes recourse to the psychoanalytic notion of partial objects, or what Winnicott calls "transitional" objects.[21] Freud recognized the existence of vectors of subjectification that elude the "mastery of the Self; partial subjectivity, complexual, taking shape around objects in the rupture of meaning," but restricted their reality and operation to instinctual and corporeal levels. Guattari, in contrast, claims that "other institutional objects, be they architectural, economic, or Cosmic, have an equal right to the functioning of existential production" ("TE," 56). Composing themselves around objects in the disruption of meaning, such "generators of a breakaway or 'dissident' subjectivity," he argues, "constitute vectors of subjectification that hence escape not only the mastery of the ego, but also the logic of discursive sets, as well as that of ordinary existence," and are, as such, unrepresentable. By expanding the range of such components beyond the inaccessibility of the Freudian unconscious, Guattari posits these proto-subjective elements as the focal points of creative subjectification, which may be impossible to represent but which, in their transversal connections with other objects contributing to the subjective production, are accessible nonetheless, if only by the "detour of a phantasmatic economy" ("TE," 56). That is to say, just as for Whitehead as for Deleuze, "eternal objects" are accessible only in the actual occasion by which they are "screened" off and emerge from chaos in the expressive event.

When he returns to the question of subjectivity in the first chapter of *Chaosmosis,* it is this rereading of the notion of the "transitional" partial object, or indeed the (Lacanian) *objet petit a,* via Bakhtin's concept of the aesthetic object, that enables Guattari to further elaborate and clarify the function of *aesthesis,* affect, and fantasy in processes of "dissident" modes of becoming. At the same time, the call for an "ecology of the imaginary" with which he concludes "The Three Ecologies," in the later book becomes the starting point for a remodelization of the unconscious itself.

Anticipating the "hyperindividualization" and "hyperconsumption" characteristic of our own "hypermodern times" (Lipovetsky), in *Chaosmosis,* Guattari situates his continued reflections on subjectivity in the context of the historical transformations of late twentieth-century postmodernity, marked by the disintegration of larger sociopolitical and institutional structures and the increasing prominence of subjective factors in current events. He numbers, among other things, the "global diffusion of the mass media" as well as rising demands for conservative modes of "subjective singularity" in the form of neonationalism, religious fundamentalism, and technoscientific determinism among the major causes for this shift (c, 2, 5). As before, Guattari does not see technological innovation as good or bad in and of itself. What he is primarily worried about are the uses to which such new, sophisticated technological resources are put and about their potentially impoverishing effects on human existence if they are not deployed to create new "Universes of reference" (c, 5) and used to counter the stultifying effects of, among other things, the mass media and commercial communication technologies in their current, pervasive operations.

Rather than addressing these issues in the more general, institutional terms in which Lipovetsky casts his analysis,[22] Guattari insists, from his perspective as a practicing psychoanalyst, on the necessity of acknowledging that the "semiotic productions of the mass media, informatics, telematics and robotics" cannot be separated from psychological subjectivity, but that they form constitutive components within the subject's variegated production. Borrowing an expression from Bakhtin, he defines the plural and heterogeneous nature of subjectivity in postindustrial societies as "polyphonic," so as to underline that there are "a-signifying semiological dimensions" to the subject's production that run alongside (and often independently from) the significatory effects of linguistic semiotics (c, 4). Affective, sense-perceptual, and corporeal in nature, this "a-signifying regime," he argues, find its origins in the "pre-verbal subjective formations of the infant," which, contrary to what Freud believed, do not constitute determinate stages in psychic development, but rather make up levels of subjectivation that "maintain themselves in parallel throughout life" (c, 6). This explains why both social "machines," as well as new information and communication technologies, not only operate at the levels of memory and intelligence, but also at those of sensibility, affect, and phantasy.

Drawing on contemporary ethological research, Guattari further suggests that even the earliest experiences of the infant are not so much purely individual, but instead are of a thoroughly interpersonal or "trans-subjective" nature. The feeling of self cannot be separated from the feeling of the other: a "dialectic between 'sharable affects' and 'non-sharable affects'" runs through and structures the "emergent phases of subjectivity," even in its most "nascent" stages (c, 6). As a relatively open, discontinuous process of constitutive encounters—"occasions," in Whitehead's terms, or "singularities," in Deleuze's terms—subjectivation is thus a multicomponential production in which "multiple exchanges between individual-group-machine" offer possibilities for the recomposition of both corporeal and incorporeal realities. Within the inevitably shifting and changing complexes of subjectivation, the individual is capable of realizing a certain autonomy or *auto-poiesis,* similar to what Whitehead calls the "subjective form" of prehensions, by forging ever more new relations with others, objects both mental and physical, animate and non-animate. Rather than issuing from "ready-made dimensions," processes of subjectivation can thus be seen to involve a "creation which in itself indicates a kind of aesthetic paradigm" (c, 7), just as Deleuze's individual is the moment of "creativity, the formation of a New" (F, 77).

In line with his argument in "The Three Ecologies," Guattari privileges, throughout *Chaosmosis,* the "incorporeal frames of reference as those relative to music and the plastic arts" when it comes to the most creative and heterogeneous components of subjectivity, that is to say, aesthetic activity as critical counterforce to the conservative and controlling or reterritorializing effects of nationalistic, phallocratic, ethnic, religious, political, economic, technological, and other systems of resingularization. The fact that he compares the creation of new modalities of subjectivity to the creation of new forms by "an artist . . . from the palette" (c, 7) partly derives from his need to stipulate the intrinsically transversal relations among the various machines that form the conditions of the subject's emergence. The comparison furthermore allows him to incorporate the preverbal levels of "nascent" subjectivity into the complex assemblages of enunciation that produce adult subjectivity in individualized as well as collective forms, rather than restricting their operations to the primordial realm of early infancy. The term "collective" in this context therefore does not mean "exclusively social," but should rather be understood as a "multiplicity that deploys itself as much beyond the individual, on the side of the socius, as before the person, on the side of preverbal intensities, indicating a logic of affect rather than a logic of delimited sets" (c, 9). The latter emphasis on the logic of affect as "man's nonhuman becoming" (WP, 173), in tandem with his persistent foregrounding of the *autopoietic* potential of aesthetic practices, at once aligns Guattari's ethico-aesthetic paradigm with Whitehead's critique of pure feeling as not merely an aesthetics, but also an ethics of existence, and hence it underscores the critical function of art in the process of "sensory becoming," as the "action by which something or someone is ceaselessly becoming-other (while continuing to be what they are)" (*WP*, 177).

To substantiate his claim that it is from artistic frames of reference that the most heterogeneous aspects of subjectivity can develop and yet maintain his psychoanalytical perspective, Guattari must establish the place of the Freudian unconscious within the larger frame of the proposed ethico-aesthetic paradigm. Since the unconscious has since its invention come to function as an "institution, 'Collective Equipment' in the broadest sense," there is no escaping being "rigged out" with one, even in our post-Freudian, post-Lacanian times, a fact we become aware of as soon as we make a slip of the tongue, dream, or forget (*C*, 10). Stripping this most elusive and initially decidedly radical concept of Freudian psychoanalysis of all of its pseudo-scientific trappings, Guattari resituates the unconscious within the "multiplicity of cartographies" in relation to which every individual and social group positions itself, alongside all other technical, institutional, social, and familial apparatuses that go into their making. Within his "multicomponent cartographic" model, the unconscious thus assumes its place as one among many aspects of subjectivation, "superposing . . . heterogeneous strata of variable extension and consistency." This "schizo Unconscious" has lost its inextricable ties to familial and childhood trauma, being geared more toward actual praxis and future becomings than toward "fixations on, and regressions to, the past." As an "Unconscious of Flux and of abstract machines" (*C*, 12), rather than of structure and language, the concept of the unconscious can thus be reappropriated as a "partial instrument" for understanding the operations of subjectivity in its heterogeneity and complexity, especially the existential registers that "involve a dimension of an aesthetic order" as a dimension of "processual creativity" (*C*, 13), which is indispensable for the regeneration of new existential territories, of progressive forms of subjective resingularization.

As a practice of everyday life, Guattari's linking of the aesthetic event with the operations of the unconscious—albeit a "schizo" unconscious—indicates that aesthetic activity involves a manner of engaging reality that is distinct from modes of perception and understanding informed by cognition or rational thought. This is borne out by his subsequent attempt to clarify what he has earlier described as the "a-signifying rupture" brought about by certain forms of artistic creation. Within the ecosophical paradigm, aesthetic experiments with the suspension of referential meaning and the disruption of significatory chains lead, we have seen, to the construction of partial objects, which, remaining unrepresentable and inaccessible to rational thought, may yet be approached through the detour of a phantasmatic economy. The question Guattari now finds himself confronted with is how to explain the deterritorializing and disruptive effects ascribed to these partial objects; how do proto-subjective elements "insert" themselves into the psyche and "start to work for themselves . . . to secrete new fields of reference?" (C, 13).

As mentioned above, it is Bakhtin's notion of the aesthetic object that helps Guattari to elucidate the function and effects of the partial object, of what he himself will call a "partial enunciator." His primary purpose is to build a bridge between the concept of the partial object that marks on one hand the "autonomisation" of unconscious components, and on the other the "subjective autonomisation relative to the aesthetic object" (C, 13). Guattari therefore seeks to draw the partial object of psychoanalysis toward a "partial enunciation" by expanding the notion of the *objet petit a* beyond the voice and the gaze, which Lacan had already included in it, so as to cover the "full range of-nuclei [*sic*] of subjective autonomisation" (C, 14), including those produced within group and machinic complexes of enunciation. Bakhtin's assumption of aesthetic activity as an act of "co-creation" that escapes both a work of art's material and its significatory determination becomes, in Guattari's psychoanalytical terms, a certain transference of subjectivation between the author and the reader/spectator of a work of art.

Guattari links Bakhtin's "aesthetic object" to the psychoanalytic partial object by defining the content of the former as something that "detaches itself from its connotations that are as much cognitive as aesthetic." There is, he argues, a "certain type of fragment of content that 'takes possession of the author' to engender a certain mode of aesthetic enunciation" (C, 14). In detaching itself from the artistic material, this type of fragment is the event of striving, in Bakhtin's words the "axiological tension," which is both "fictively irreversible" and "in its essence, ethical" ("CMF," 267). The irreversibility of the aesthetic object, and "implicitly the idea of autopoiesis," lead Guattari to the proposition that it is such partial enunciators, fragments detached from form, material, and ordinary signification, that form "existential 'motif[s],'" which in turn arrange themselves into "existential refrains" that couple "them to the existential Territory of my self" (C, 15, 17). Emerging from within the larger constellation of complexes of subjectivation, these incorporeal domains are given only in the creative moment, so that we can only "detect [them] at the same time that we produce them." As "nuclei of eternity lodged between instants," they elude situational elements and discursive time, opening up "lines of virtuality" that only emerge in the event of their appearance (C, 17). In Whitehead's/Deleuze's terms, they are eternal objects that only appear as the "purely expressed" of actual occasions.

His detour through psychoanalysis and Bakhtinian aesthetics allows Guattari to define the "poetic function"—what I have been referring to as aesthetic activity or artistic creation—as that which breaks through established territorializing systems so as to "recompose artificially rarefied, resingularised Universes of subjectivation." In describing its task in such terms, Guattari not only points up the function of artworks ("blocs of sensation") as "catalysing existential operators," but also underlines the distinction between the operation of "ordinary," utilitarian objects and whatever counts as art in a given society at a given moment in history. Although the "poetic function" is thus to rupture, to break through, and to destratify controlling/conservative subjective singularities, its productive force lies in its potential to enable new "armatures of existence" within the context of alternative, affirmative assemblages of enunciation. The "efficiency" of the poetic function, Guattari hence maintains, lies in its capacity to "promote active, processual ruptures within semiotically structured, significational and denotative networks" and to "put emergent subjectivity to work" (c, 19).

The crux of Guattari's ethico-aesthetic paradigm is, on one hand, that it helps us to think the function of affect in both its prepersonal and presubjective operations and to reflect critically upon its effects—which, again, are neither pregiven nor unambivalent—on the transversally interconnected levels of subjective and collective modes of un/becoming. Furthermore, in unfolding his notion of the "poetic function" on the side of both socius and psyche, and by enlarging its operations to include the multiple and heterogeneous existential registers with which the incorporeal domains as those relative to literature and art are transversally interconnected, he allows us to posit, in line with both Bakhtin and Whitehead, aesthetic practice as a practice of everyday life, instead of confining it to a domain separated from the more ordinary realms of meaning and being. Instead of resigning ourselves to the controlling operations or merely rejecting the "delimited sets" of prevailing power formations and symbolic structures, we may thus learn actively to use the asignifying, transformational potential of art for the actualization of new modalities of being—more precisely, of becoming—in the world. Rather than a "privileged 'way out' of the perceived impasse in cultural studies," to evoke Hemmings' earlier cited phrase, Guattari's ethico-aesthetic paradigm, as a critical part of what Massumi calls an "asignifying philosophy of affect," provides a theoretical grounding to what so-called minority studies have been acutely aware of since their inception—the inextricable links between the subjective and the social, of the transversal interrelations between the personal and the political—and thus offers possibilities for concrete micro-social, "eco-sophical" practices.

On the other hand, however, Guattari's multicomponential model of subjectification indicates that in order for such practices not merely to bring about change, but to bring about change for the better, that is, to generate new existential configurations that effectively enrich our relations with the world and with one another, some form of ethical reflection, or even active intervention in the process of creative desingularization, is nonetheless required. In "The Three Ecologies," Guattari warns against the most violent manifestations of deterritorialization effected by "dissident" vectors of subjectification, which might lead to the destruction of the subjective assemblage as such. In *Chaosmosis,* too, he cautions against the more neurotic or obsessive forms of deterritorialization that may cause the whole personality or a whole society to implode. In other words, the escape from the subjective void produced by postindustrial capitalism and consumerism cannot be dislodged from its immediate and ultimate aim: to generate new planes of consistency—sustainable lifeworlds—that allow for more meaningful, valuable, and enriching modes of being, on the social, interpersonal, and individual levels.

As an embodied/embedded practice, projecting worlds and selves that are yet to come, art, in its *differentia specifica,* constitutes one of the assemblages of enunciation defined by Guattari as "living auto-poietic machines' *par excellence*" (*c,* 61). At the same time, in its irreversible connections with the objective world, and precisely because of its ability to "'imaginarize' the various manifestations of violence" (*c,* 58), aesthetic activity cannot merely be or remain a question of random deterritorialization. Fueled by the need to recompose oppressive sociopolitical formations and to reconfigure the positions of collective as well as individual subjectivities within them, an affirmative approach to art and aesthetics, that is, a neo-aesthetics that I have described as a critical and theoretical project in the wake of the affective turn, must find its destination in actively and effectively exploiting its possibilities for ethico-aesthetic intervention in the enlarged sense outlined above. Visual culture, or aesthetic practice more generally, will continue to function as one of the most powerful resources for generating both potentially violent and more gentle forms of deterritorialization, for such "processual lines of flight" as open up onto imaginary worlds, onto future virtualities. Art, as a "sense-event" par excellence, is not, pace Badiou, the "advent of what is subtracted from all experience." On the contrary, in its actualization (of the virtual as the condition of real experience), the event of art is a happening within the ongoing yet discontinuous process that forms the occasion for deterritorialization as much as it is for what Deleuze calls the "formation of a New" and for what Bakhtin describes as a "completely new ontic formation." Provided that we develop sufficient "screens" that make something issue from its "disjunctive diversity," any attempt at avoiding art's violent embrace is simply not an option—neither phenomenally, nor ontologically or ethically.

In the sense that we must always and inevitably respond to the world, interact with our environment in a continuous yet variegated series of encounters, the possibility for novelty, for a New, for fresh selves to emerge, is simply given. The fact that the world is, to recall Bakhtin, not only a messy place but also an open space leaves us no option but to allow ourselves to be taken up in its embrace: the "unfinalizability" of both the world and our selves guarantees the possibility of innovation, for the genuinely new, for potentiality and creativity. But Bakhtin importantly adds to this that the openness and messiness of the world provides "no alibi for being." We are also always answerable, accountable for our responses to the environment in their distinctiveness and particularity. Such accountability, I have suggested, includes our ethical obligation to seek encounters that allow for the creation or generation of something new that will enrich, rather than diminish, our relation to the world and to one another. The point is to preserve the productive potential in every kind of force, to see events as potentialities, as moments that may generate new forces, to consider things anew, in short, to rise to the occasion of the chaos of life and to embrace the possibilities given in each moment. Such possibilities, I believe with Whitehead, have less to do with understanding, cognition, or with language and representation, but are primarily, and prior to any stabilization in systems or categories, a question of feeling, their actualization a direct result of our ability to affect and being affected. Artistic experience, aesthetic events we seek out—whether reluctantly, unwittingly, passionately or eagerly—offer us occasions for new forms of feeling. It is art, in its essential artificiality, its simultaneous adventurousness and finiteness that, par excellence, may offer us such "screens" as enable the freedom to feel differently, to experience anew. Therein lie both its truth and its uncontrollable beauty.

notes

INTRODUCTION

1. Rita Felski, "From Literary Theory to Critical Method," *Profession* (2008): 114.

2. Clare Hemmings, "Invoking Affect: Cultural Theory and the Ontological Turn," *Cultural Studies* 19.5 (2005): 550.

3. Rosi Braidotti, *Metamorphoses: Towards a Materialist Theory of Becoming* (Cambridge UK: Polity Press, 2002), 1.

4. Hemmings, "Invoking Affect," 549.

5. Nicholas Mirzoeff's work on three editions of *The Visual Culture Reader* for Routledge has been a major influence on the demarcation of the (non)field (1998, 1998, 2013). See also, inter alia, Jessica Evans and Stuart Hall, eds., *Visual Culture: The Reader* (London: SAGE, 1999); Margaret Dikovitskaya, *Visual Culture: The Study of the Visual after the Cultural Turn* (Cambridge, Mass.: The MIT Press, 2006); Richard Howells, *Visual Culture* (Cambridge, UK: Polity, 2006); Whitney Davis, *A General Theory of Visual Culture* (Princeton, N.J.: Princeton University Press, 2011).

6. A mode of analysis in which I have a longstanding investment, as will be clear from, inter alia, the critical readings of literary texts and films in renée c. hoogland, *Lesbian Configurations* (Cambridge, UK: Polity Press; New York: Columbia University Press, 1997).

7. See, for example, my essays "The Matter of Culture: Aesthetic Experience and Corporeal Being," *Mosaic: A Journal for the Interdisciplinary Study of Literature* 36.3 (2003): 1–18; "Fact and Fantasy: The Body of Desire in the Age of Posthumanism," *Journal of Gender Studies* 11.3 (2002): 213–31; and "'First Things First': Fantasy and the Question of Gendered Sexuality," *Journal of Gender Studies* 8.1 (1999): 43–56.

8. Marita Sturken and Lisa Cartwright, *Practices of Looking: An Introduction to Visual Culture,* 2nd ed. (Oxford: Oxford University Press, 2009).

9. Laura Mulvey, "Visual Pleasure and Narrative Cinema," *Screen* 16:3 (1975): 6–18.

10. Sturken and Cartwright, *Practices of Looking,* 5.

11. Ibid., 6.

12. See, e.g., Jay David Bolter and Richard Grusin, *Remediation: Understanding New Media* (Cambridge, Mass.: The MIT Press, 2000); Henry Jenkins, *Convergence Culture: Where Old and New Media Collide* (New York: New York University Press, 2006).

13. Mark Hansen, "The Time of Affect, Bearing Witness to Life," *Critical Inquiry* 30.3 (2004): 591.

14. Ibid., 589.

15. Ibid., 594.

16. Patricia T. Clough, "The Affective Turn: Political Economy, Biomedia and Bodies," *Theory, Culture & Society* 25.1 (2008): 5–6.

17. Brian Massumi, *Parables for the Virtual: Movement, Affect, and Sensation* (Durham, N.C.: Duke University Press, 2002).

18. Ibid., 24.

19. "Intensity" is central to Deleuze's critique of nineteenth-century scientific thought and is first elaborately explored in chapter 5 of his book *Difference and Repetition,* trans. Paul Patton (New York: Columbia University Press, 1994), 222–61.

20. Massumi, *Parables,* 25.

21. Félix Guattari, *Chaosmosis: An Ethico-Aesthetic Paradigm,* trans. Paul Bains and Julian Pefanis (Sydney: Power Publications, 1995), 4.

22. Massumi, *Parables,* 27.

23. Braidotti, *Metamorphoses,* 2.

24. Ibid., 104.

25. Massumi, *Parables,* 27.

26. Cf. Rei Terada's challenging study *Feeling in Theory: Emotion after the "Death of the Subject"* (Cambridge, Mass.: Harvard University Press, 2001) for an argument that challenges these assertions.

27. Hemmings, "Invoking Affect," 551.

28. For a compelling examination of minor negative affects, such as envy, anxiety, or irritation, and their significance for the nature of late modernity, see Sianne Ngai's *Ugly Feelings* (Cambridge, Mass.: Harvard University Press, 2005). For a reconceptualization of an earlier prevalent mode of negative affect, melancholia, see Jonathan Flatley, *Affective Mapping: Melancholia and the Politics of Modernity* (Cambridge, Mass.: Harvard University Press, 2008).

29. Clough, "The Affective Turn," 5.

30. Braidotti, *Metamorphoses,* 2.

31. Massumi, *Parables,* 27.

32. In the following chapters, I will nonetheless be using these terms interchangeably, depending on and determined by their usage in the works of my various theoretical interlocutors.

ONE. ARTISTIC ACTIVITY

1. M. M. Bakhtin, "Supplement: The Problem of Content, Material, and Form in Verbal Art," in *Art and Answerability: Early Philosophical Essays by M. M. Bakhtin,* ed. Michael Holquist and Vadim Liapunov, trans. Vadim Liapunov; supplement trans. Kenneth Brostrom (Austin: University of Texas Press, 1990).

2. This is a different line than the one running from Sylvan S. Tomkins through, inter alia, Eve Sedgwick and Sianne Ngai—quite rightly distinguished, yet equally debunked, by Ruth Leys in her essay "The Turn to Affect: A Critique," *Critical Inquiry* 37 (2011): 434–72. Cf. Sylvan S. Tomkins, *Affect, Imagery, Consciousness / Vol. II: The Negative Affects* (New York: Springer Publishing, 1963); Ngai, *Ugly Feelings;* Eve Kosofsky Sedgwick, *Touching Feeling: Affect, Pedagogy, Performativity* (Durham, N.C.: Duke University Press, 2003).

3. These are the respective titles of two books representative of the renewed interest in

aesthetics, which emerged in the early years of the present century, following, and breaking with, what Hal Foster famously defined as postmodernism's "anti-aestheticism," in *The Anti-Aesthetic: Essays on Postmodern Culture* (Port Townsend, Wash.: Bay Press, 1983). See Isobel Armstrong's *The Radical Aesthetic* (Oxford: Blackwell Publishers, 2000); and *The New Aestheticism,* ed. John J. Joughin and Simon Malpas (Manchester: Manchester University Press, 2003).

4. Another often rebuked term, "neo-aesthetics" was, I believe, first used in 2001, in the title of a conference jointly organized by Tate Modern (London) and Staffordshire University (UK), Immanent Choreographies: Deleuze and Neo-Aesthetics. For a review of the event, see Jon Beasley-Murray, "Rearguard Action," *Radical Philosophy* 111 (2002): 51–53.

5. Arthur C. Danto, *After the End of Art: Contemporary Art and the Pale of History* (Princeton, N.J.: Princeton University Press, 1997).

6. For a helpful introduction to Bakhtinian dialogism and its wider implications, see Michael Holquist, *Dialogism,* 2nd ed. (London: Routledge, 2002).

7. On Bakhtin's investment in and contribution to neo-Kantianism, see Michael F. Bernard-Donals, *Mikhail Bakhtin: Between Phenomenology and Marxism* (Cambridge, UK: Cambridge University Press, 1994), especially chapter 2, "Neo-Kantianism and Bakhtin's Phenomenology," 18–46.

8. In ostensible conflict with Massumi's pertinent distinction between the terms "affect" and "emotion" as discussed in the introduction, in this and the following chapters I will use these terms, as well as "feeling," pretty much interchangeably, since this is the way they appear in the theoretical texts (Bakhtin, Whitehead, Deleuze) under discussion. It is clear, however, that the respective terms "emotion" and "feeling" in these works more or less coincide with what Massumi designates "affect."

9. I am referring to and loosely paraphrasing from Immanuel Kant, *Critique of Judgment,* trans. Werner S. Pluhar (Indianapolis: Hackett, 1987), to which I will return in more detail in the next chapter. For helpful discussions of Kant's aesthetic theory, see, e.g., Douglas Burnham, *An Introduction to Kant's Critique of Judgment* (Edinburgh: Edinburgh University Press, 2000); Salim Kemal, *Kant's Aesthetic Theory* (London: St. Martin's Press, 1992), and Mary McCloskey, *Kant's Aesthetic* (London: Macmillan, 1987).

10. Katerina Clark and Michael Holquist, *Mikhail Bakhtin* (Cambridge, Mass.: Harvard University Press, 1986), 58.

11. Gary Saul Morson and Caryl Emerson, *Mikhail Bakhtin: Creation of a Prosaics* (Stanford, Calif.: Stanford University Press, 1990), 79.

12. Ibid.

13. Ibid., 89.

14. Ibid., 79.

15. Ibid., 36.

16. Clark and Holquist, *Mikhail Bakhtin,* 76.

17. Morson and Emerson, *Mikhail Bakhtin,* 40.

18. Steven Shaviro, *Without Criteria: Kant, Whitehead, Deleuze, and Aesthetics* (Cambridge, Mass.: The MIT Press, 2009), 66, 47.

19. I will discuss phenomenology at more length in chapter 5, where I take up Lambert

Wiesing's and Vilém Flusser's respective theories of the mediated/technical image in relation to so-called ruin porn.

20. Alfred North Whitehead, *Process and Reality* (New York: The Free Press, 1985), 113. Cited in Shaviro (*wc*, 51).

21. Shaviro clarifies the differences by pointing out that, for Whitehead, prehension need not be conscious, and, most of the time is not; plus, neither subject nor datum pre-exist their encounter, but are produced in and by it (*wc*, 55, n. 9).

22. Alfred North Whitehead, *Adventures of Ideas* (New York: The Free Press, 1967), 176.

23. See note 1 in this chapter.

24. As much as un- or de-forming/-formed aspects do, as I shall argue in the next chapter.

25. Again, both theoretical models are obviously much broader in their implications than I am able to suggest or account for here.

26. I am referring to its difference from, for example, the work of Marina Abramović, whose recent retrospective exhibition "Marina Abramović: The Artist is Present" (2010), at the Museum of Modern Art in New York, clearly produced intense affective experiences in viewers/visitors, but whose interaction with the work did not include actual physical touch. For an impression of the nonetheless profoundly affectively dis/organizing *poietic* effects of the art/performance—the artist's longest performance to date, see MOMA's semipermanent multimedia website: http://www.moma.org/interactives/exhibitions/2010 /marinaabramovic/, accessed March 16, 2012.

27. See note 12 in this chapter.

TWO. VIOLENT BECOMINGS

1. Various slightly different versions of the statement have since appeared in English translation, the most common being the one used here, and the alternative phrase, the "greatest work of art in the entire cosmos." I am relying on the German version as quoted in *Die Zeit*, which is "*das Grösste Kunstwerk, das es je gegeben hat.*" Cited by Robert Hilferty, *Andante: Everything Classical* (September 2001), http://andante.com, a site that appears at the time of this writing (March 21, 2012) to have become defunct.

2. Julia Spinola, "Monstrous Art," *Frankfurter Allgemeine Zeitung,* September 25, 2001.

3. E.g., Lee Harris, *Civilization and Its Enemies: The Next Stage of History* (New York: The Free Press, 2004).

4. Moritz Gaede, "The Hijacking of Terrorism," *Theatrum Mundi: 911,* http://www .drivedrive.com/moritz_gaede/theatrum_mundi_911.html, accessed March 22, 2012.

5. These are words lifted from the introduction to one of several volumes of essays engaging the so-called ethical turn that were published around the turn of the present century, inter alia, Marjorie Garber, Beatrice Hanssen, and Rebecca L. Walkowitz, eds., *The Turn to Ethics* (New York and London: Routledge, 2000), viii. See also, e.g., Edith Wyschorod and Gerald P. Kennedy, eds., *The Ethical* (Malden, Mass.: Blackwell, 2003); Todd F. Davis and Kenneth Womack, eds., *Mapping the Ethical Turn: A Reader in Ethics,*

Culture, and Literary Theory (Charlottesville and London: University Press of Virginia, 2001).

6. An association suggested, for example, by the titles of and contributions to Jerrold Levinson, ed., *Aesthetics and Ethics: Essays at the Intersection* (Cambridge, UK: Cambridge University Press, 1998); and Dorota Glowacka and Stephen Boos, eds., *Between Ethics and Aesthetics: Crossing the Boundaries* (Albany: State University of New York Press, 2002). For a highly critical view on the turn to ethics, see Jacques Rancière, "The Ethical Turn of Aesthetics and Politics," *Critical Horizons* 7.1 (2006): 1–20.

7. This irresistible phrase is the title of a collection of essays edited by Bill Beckley, with David Shapiro, *Uncontrollable Beauty: Toward a New Aesthetics* (New York: Allworth Press, 1998).

8. Kant, *Critique of Judgment,* 115.

9. I am using "un/pleasant" here in a very different sense from the way Ngai does in her study of variously distinct "ugly feelings." Cf. Ngai, *Ugly Feelings.*

10. "Hylomorphism" is the theory derived from Aristotle that every physical object is composed of two principles, an unchanging prime matter and a form deprived of actuality with every substantial change of the object. Hylomorphism is rejected by Deleuze and Guattari, who follow the French philosopher Gilbert Simondon in exposing the "technological insufficiency of the matter-form model, in that it assumes a fixed form and a matter deemed homogeneous" (inert, passive) and thus denies the incipient energetic forces, and the *"variable intensive affects,"* contained in matter. Gilles Deleuze and Félix Guattari, *A Thousand Plateaus: Capitalism and Schizophrenia,* trans. Brian Massumi (Minneapolis: University of Minnesota Press, 2003), 408.

11. Peter Kivy, ed., *The Blackwell Guide to Aesthetics* (Oxford, UK: Blackwell, 2004).

12. Ludwig Wittgenstein, *Tractatus Logico-Philosophicus,* trans. David Pears and Brian McGuinness (London and New York: Routledge, 1961), 6.421.

13. See, inter alia, Hans-Georg Gadamer, *Truth and Method,* 2nd rev. ed., trans. J. Weinsheimer and D. G. Marshall (New York: Crossroad, 2004); *Philosophical Hermeneutics,* trans. and ed. David Linge (Berkeley: University of California Press, 1976).

14. Gabrielle Starr, "Ethics, Meaning, and the Work of Beauty," *Eighteenth-Century Studies* 35.3 (2002): 362.

15. Ibid., 367.

16. Shlomith Rimmon-Kenan, "Concepts of Narrative," *COLLeGIUM: Studies Across Disciplines in the Humanities and the Social Sciences* (2006), Vol. 1: The Travelling Concept of Narrative, 10.

17. Shlomith Rimmon-Kenan, *Narrative Fiction: Contemporary Poetics* (London: Methuen, 1983), 2.

18. Rimmon-Kenan, "Concepts of Narrative," 12.

19. Ibid., 11.

20. The distinction refers to the raw material of a narrative (*fabula*), its constituting (narrative) "events," as distinct from the way these materials are organized, the way they are narrated (*suzjet*). It is interesting to note that we only ever have access to the latter.

21. Rimmon-Kenan, "Concepts of Narrative," 13.

22. Ibid., 14.

23. Ludwig Wittgenstein, *Philosophical Investigations,* trans. G. E. M. Anscombe (1953; Oxford: Blackwell, 1978), 32. Cited in ibid., 16.

24. Rimmon-Kenan, "Concepts of Narrative," 16.

25. Mieke Bal, "Narrative Inside Out: Louise Bourgeois' Spider as Theoretical Object," *Oxford Art Journal* 22.2 (1999): 101.

26. Ibid.

27. Ibid., 110.

28. Ibid., 112. To be sure, Bal's project in this essay, as well in her subsequent work on visual art, is very different from what Patrick Colm Hogan, for example, attempts to do in his recent study *Affective Narratology: The Emotional Structure of Stories* (Lincoln: University of Nebraska Press, 2001). Rather than "applying" narratological methods to visual objects, Hogan links insights on emotion, largely taken from cognitive science, to narratology in order to explore the ways in which emotions organize and orient stories and, vice versa, how stories inform the development of our emotional lives.

29. Bal, "Narrative Inside Out," 109.

30. Marie-Laure Ryan, "Media and Narrative," entry for the *Routledge Encyclopedia of Narrative,* http://lamar.colostate.edu/pwryan/mediaentry.html, accessed February 12, 2007.

31. Bal, "Narrative Inside Out," 113.

32. Ibid., 105.

33. Ibid., 128.

34. Bal would further develop this undertaking in a book she wrote a few years later in collaboration with Norman Bryson. See Mieke Bal and Norman Bryson, *Looking In: The Art of Viewing* (London: Routledge, 2001).

35. Armstrong, *The Radical Aesthetic,* 59.

36. In the context of Whitehead's metaphysics, this is actually a misnomer, for, as Shaviro explains, Whitehead makes a strict distinction between "occasions" and "events," where the former term refers to the "process by which anything becomes," and the latter is an "extensive set, or a temporal series of such occasions." Shaviro infers from this that an occasion is "something like what Deleuze calls a *singularity:* a point of inflection or of discontinuous transformation" (*wc,* 18–19).

37. William Hogarth, *The Analysis of Beauty* [1753], ed. Ronald Paulson (New Haven, Conn.: Yale University Press, 1997).

38. Julia Kristeva, *Powers of Horror: An Essay on Abjection,* trans. Léon S. Roudiez (New York: Columbia University Press, 1982), 1.

39. Mary Douglas, *Purity and Danger: An Analysis of Concepts of Pollution and Taboo* (London: Routledge, 2002).

40. Judith Butler, *Bodies That Matter: On the Discursive Limits of "Sex"* (London: Routledge, 1993).

41. See Craig Houser, Leslie C. Jones, Simon Taylor, and Jack Ben-Levi, *Abject Art: Repulsion and Desire in American Art* [ISP Papers, No. 3] (New York: Whitney Museum of American Art, 1993).

42. Georges Bataille, "Informe," in *Documents* 7 (December 1929), 382. Rpt. in *Visions of Excess: Selected Writings, 1927–1939,* ed. and intro. Allan Stoekl; trans. Allan Stoekl, with Carl R. Lovitt and Donald M. Leslie, Jr. (Minneapolis: University of Minnesota Press, 1985), 217.

43. Rosalind Krauss, "*Informe* without Conclusion," *October* 78 (1996): 99.

44. Immanuel Kant, *Observations on the Feeling of the Beautiful and the Sublime,* 2nd paperback ed., trans. John T. Goldthwait (Berkeley: University of California Press, 2003), 48.

45. Also cited in Shaviro (*wc,* 3).

46. William Hogarth, *The Analysis of Beauty,* http://books.google.com/books, accessed March 24, 2012.

47. Starr, "Ethics, Meaning, and the Work of Beauty," 374.

48. "Untimely," in the sense that, as Claire Colebrook explains, art and philosophy have the power to create new "lines" of becoming, where "mutations and differences produce not just the progression of history but disruptions, breaks, new beginnings and 'monstrous' births." See Claire Colebrook, *Gilles Deleuze* (London and New York: Routledge, 2002), 57.

49. I am drawing here on Tamsin Lorraine's pithy and concise discussion of "lines of flight" in *The Deleuze Dictionary,* ed. Adrian Parr (New York: Columbia University Press, 2005), 144–46.

THREE. NEO-AESTHETICS AND THE STUDY OF THE ARTS OF THE PRESENT

1. Gilles Deleuze, *The Logic of Sense,* ed. Constantin V. Boundas, trans. Mark Lester with Charles Stivale (New York: Columbia University Press, 1990), 260. For extensive explorations of this "wrenching duality," see Daniel W. Smith, "Deleuze's Theory of Sensation: Overcoming the Kantian Duality," in *Deleuze: A Critical Reader,* ed. Paul Patton (Oxford, UK: Blackwell Publishers, 1996), 29–56; Shaviro, *Without Criteria,* 67–68; and Stephen Zepke, "The Artist-Philosopher: Deleuze, Nietzsche, and the Critical Art of Affirmation," in *Art as Abstract Machine: Ontology and Aesthetics in Deleuze and Guattari* (New York: Routledge, 2005), 11–39.

2. See William James, *Essays in Radical Empiricism* (Radford, Va.: Wilders Publications, 2007).

3. Deleuze, *Difference and Repetition,* 56–57.

4. Daniel Smith and John Protevi, "Gilles Deleuze," in *The Stanford Encyclopedia of Philosophy* (Winter 2011 Edition), ed. Edward N. Zalta, http://plato.stanford.edu/archives/win2011/entries/deleuze, accessed July 3, 2012.

5. The "present" here thus explicitly pertains to the postmodern moment at and after which George Marcus and Michael Fischer coined the phrase "crisis of representation" to refer to the uncertainty in the human sciences about adequate means of describing social reality. Deconstructive postmodernism, as is commonly known, argues that "reality" is grounded in language and that the "natural" world, taken for granted by empirical positivist science as an object for study, could, after the "linguistic turn," no longer be simply assumed. The world is never known directly, but is constructed, or given meaning, through discourse. Such meanings are historically and culturally contingent, dependent upon the legitimation processes of dominant discourses embodied in differing

communities of practice. See George Marcus and Michael Fischer, *Anthropology as Cultural Critique* (Chicago: University of Chicago Press, 1986), chapter 1.

6. Gilles Deleuze and Claire Parnet, *Dialogues II,* trans. Hugh Tomlinson and Barbara Habberjam, rev. ed. (New York: Columbia University Press, 2007), 6.

7. Ibid., 7.

8. See, for example, Charles J. Stivale, *Gilles Deleuze's ABCs: The Folds of Friendship* (Baltimore: The Johns Hopkins University Press, 2008).

9. *L'Abécédaire de Gilles Deleuze* is a French television program produced by Pierre-André Boutang in 1988–1989. It consists of an eight-hour series of interviews between Gilles Deleuze and Claire Parnet. Available online at http://video.google.com/videoplay?do cid+438091653681675611, accessed April 16, 2012.

10. This is also the subtitle of Deleuze's book on the painter Francis Bacon: *Francis Bacon: The Logic of Sensation,* trans. and intro. Daniel W. Smith, afterword by Tom Conley (Minneapolis: University of Minnesota Press, 2004).

11. Deleuze, ABC: "C as in Culture," helpfully transcribed by Charles S. Stivale at www. langlab.wayne.edu/cstivale/d-g/abc1.html, accessed April 17, 2012.

12. In their final collaborative work, Deleuze and Guattari make a point of describing these two aspects of philosophy as "qualitatively different," yet "complementary," in that concepts, always fragmentary elements that do not fit together, need a "plane of immanence" that "rolls them up and unrolls them." Concepts are "events," but the plane is the "horizon of events," that which holds the concepts together, without losing its openness. See Gilles Deleuze and Félix Guattari, *What Is Philosophy?*, trans. Hugh Tomlinson and Graham Burchell (New York: Columbia University Press, 1994), 35.

13. Gilles Deleuze, "On Philosophy," in *Negotiations 1972–1990,* trans. Martin Joughin (New York: Columbia University Press, 1995), 137.

14. Deleuze and Guattari, *A Thousand Plateaus,* 343–44.

15. Deleuze and Guattari distinguish "sensory becoming" as "otherness caught in expression," from "conceptual becoming," in the sense that the latter is "heterogeneity grasped in an absolute form," the action by which the "common event itself eludes what is" (*WP, 177*).

16. On Deleuze's philosophy as a form of art itself, as an art of fabulation, see Gregory Flaxman, *Gilles Deleuze and the Fabulation of Philosophy* (Minneapolis: University of Minnesota Press, 2012).

17. See, for example, Hemmings, *Invoking Affect,* and Leys, *The Turn to Affect.*

18. It is not my interest here to launch an overall defense of the two philosophers, but the fact that Deleuze's concepts are put to use by scholars in architecture, urban studies, geography, film studies, musicology, anthropology, gender studies, literary studies, as well as philosophy, and that Guattari, even though his solo writings are less well known, hence still relatively unmined, has been widely recognized for his contributions to fields as diverse as economics, ecology, pragmatics, linguistics, and media theory, and his radical ideas are always grounded in the practical contexts of global politics and materialist social critique, adequately proves such accusations ungrounded. For a helpful and thorough assessment of the latter's work, see Eric Alliez and Andre Goffey, eds., *The Guattari Effect* (London: Continuum, 2011).

19. See, for instance, Hal Foster, *Recodings: Art, Spectacle, Cultural Politics* (New York: The New Press, 1985); *Compulsive Beauty* (Cambridge, Mass.: MIT Press, 1993); *The Return of the Real: The Avant-Garde at the End of the Century* (Cambridge, Mass.: MIT Press, 1996); *Prosthetic Gods* (Cambridge, Mass.: MIT Press, 2006).

20. Hal Foster, "Post-Critical," *October* 139 (Winter 2012): 14.

21. *L'Abécédaire de Gilles Deleuze.* Transcript, see http://www.langlab.wayne.edu/cstivale /d-g/abcs.html, accessed March 22, 2013.

22. Sturken and Cartwright, *Practices of Looking,* 5.

23. Hal Foster, "The Medium Is the Market," *London Review of Books* 30.19 (October 9, 2008): 23–24.

24. Marshall McLuhan, "The Medium Is the Message," in *Understanding Media,* rpt. (London and New York: Routledge, 2003), 7–23.

25. Foster, "The Medium Is the Market," 23.

26. Gilles Lipovetsky, *Hypermodern Times,* trans. Andrew Brown (Cambridge UK: Polity, 2005).

27. Foster, "The Medium Is the Market," 24.

28. Andy Warhol, *The Philosophy of Andy Warhol (From A to B and Back Again)* (Orlando, Fla.: Harcourt, Inc., 1977), 92.

29. Foster, "Post-Critical," 4, 6.

30. The latter phrase is, of course, a reference to Jacques Rancière's *The Politics of Aesthetics,* whose subtitle reads "the distribution of the sensible."

31. Foster, "Post-Critical," 3.

32. Gilles Deleuze, *Nietzsche and Philosophy,* trans. Hugh Tomlinson (New York: Columbia University Press, 1995) 2, 3.

33. Hal Foster, *The First Pop Age: Painting and Subjectivity in the Art of Hamilton, Lichtenstein, Warhol, Richter, and Ruscha* (Princeton, N.J.: Princeton University Press, 2012), 109–71.

34. Ibid., 109.

35. Ibid., 122–23.

36. An impressive body of work to which I am not even trying to do justice; see, inter alia, Arthur C. Danto, *The Abuse of Beauty: Aesthetics and the Concept of Art,* 3rd. rpt. (Chicago and La Salle, Ill.: Open Court, 2005); *Andy Warhol* (New Haven, Conn.: Yale University Press, 2009). Danto separates "aesthetics" from his "philosophy of art" because of the former's conventional domination by the "idea of beauty"—a very different notion of aesthetics than that I have so far been employing.

37. Zepke, *Art as Abstract Machine,* 32. This (1962) is the same year in which Warhol began his first celebrity portraits—of, among others, the recently widowed Jackie Kennedy, Elizabeth Taylor, Marilyn Monroe (started immediately after her suicide), and Elvis— and the two sets are often considered companion pieces; the "death and disaster" series includes *Red Car Crash, Purple Jumping Man,* and *Orange Disaster,* as well as *Tunafish Disaster,* various suicides (including the famous one of the young woman lying on top of a car after her jump off of the Empire State Building), and the first *Electric Chair* works.

38. Friedrich Nietzsche, *The Will to Power,* trans. W. Kaufmann and R. J. Hollingdale (New York: Vintage, 1967) 853; cited in Zepke, *Art as Abstract Machine,* 14.

39. Ibid.

40. Ibid., 24.

41. Ibid., 30.

42. Ibid., 31.

43. Gary Shapiro, *Archaeologies of Vision: Foucault and Nietzsche on Seeing and Saying* (Chicago: University of Chicago Press, 2003), 9.

44. Ibid., 358.

45. Michel Foucault, "Theatrum Philosophicum," in *Language, Counter-Memory, Practice: Selected Essays and Interviews by Michel Foucault,* ed. and introd. Donald F. Bouchard (Ithaca, N.Y.: Cornell University Press, 1977), 182.

46. Shapiro, *Archeologies of Vision,* 362.

47. Zepke, *Art as Abstract Machine,* 31.

48. Ibid., 29.

49. I am using "sadness" here in the ethical sense suggested by Deleuze's reading of Spinoza, as one of the modes of feeling by which our power to act (a power that is "inseparable from a capacity for being affected") is diminished or restrained, whereas it "increases or is enhanced by affections of joy." Gilles Deleuze, *Spinoza: Practical Philosophy,* trans. Robert Hurley (San Francisco: City Light Books, 1988), 97, 101.

50. The exhibition "Animal Logic: Photography by Richard Barnes" ran at the temporary location of the Cranbrook Art Museum (then under construction) from October 4, 2009, through January 3, 2010. A monograph of the same title, containing four related series of Barnes' photographic work, appeared in 2009. See Richard Barnes, *Animal Logic* (New York: Princeton Architectural Press, 2009).

51. The exhibition, curated by Nina Katchadourian, ran from September 12 through October 9, 2008, in the Drawing Room Gallery, drawingcenter.org. A catalogue of the same title (Drawing Papers 80), with a conversation between artist and curator, accompanied the show. See Kathleen Henderson, *What if I Could Draw a Bird That Could Change the World?* (New York: The Drawing Center, 2008).

FOUR. THE GROUNDLESS REALITIES OF ART PHOTOGRAPHY

1. W. K. Wimsatt, Jr., and Monroe C. Beardsley, "The Intentional Fallacy," in *The Verbal Icon: Studies in the Meaning of Poetry,* 3–18 (Lexington: University of Kentucky Press, 1954).

2. Fred W. McDarrah, Gloria S. McDarrah, and Timothy S. McDarrah, eds., *Photography Encyclopedia* (Farmington Hills, Mich.: Cengage Gale, 1998).

3. Bernard E. Jones, *Cassell's Cyclopaedia of Photography* (New York: Arno, 1973).

4. New World Encyclopedia contributors, "Fine art photography," in *New World Encyclopedia,* http://newworldencyclopedia.org, accessed January 27, 2012.

5. Jacques Rancière, *The Future of the Image,* trans. Gregory Elliott (London: Verso, 2009).

6. The Solomon R. Guggenheim Museum and the San Francisco Museum of Modern Art recently jointly organized a comprehensive mid-career survey, featuring more than

seventy color photographs and five video installations by Rineke Dijkstra (June 29–October 3, 2012); http://www.sfmoma.org and http://www.guggenheim.org, accessed April 27, 2012. An accompanying catalogue appeared under the title *Rineke Dijkstra: A Retrospective* (New York: Guggenheim Museum Publications, 2012).

7. Works in the exhibition were collected and published in Rineke Dijkstra, *Portraits* (Muenchen: Schirmer/Mosel, 2004).

8. Jean Baudrillard, *Simulacra and Simulation,* trans. Sheila Faria Glaser (Ann Arbor: University of Michigan Press, 1994). As indicated in the previous chapter, this is a very different notion of the simulacrum from Deleuze's use of the term with reference to art.

9. Guy Debord, *The Society of the Spectacle,* trans. Donald Nicholson-Smith (New York: Zone Books, 1995), 26.

10. Susan Sontag, *On Photography* (New York: Picador, 1977), 153–80.

11. Charles Baudelaire, "The Salon of 1859," trans. Jonathan Mayne, in *Photography in Print,* ed. Vicki Goldberg (Albuquerque: University of New Mexico Press, 1988), 125.

12. Walter Benjamin, "The Work of Art in the Age of Mechanical Reproduction," in *Illuminations,* trans. Harry Zohn (New York: Schocken Books, 2007), 226.

13. Rosalind E. Krauss, "Reinventing the Medium," *Critical Inquiry* 25.2 (1999): 292.

14. Ibid., 292–93.

15. Jacques Rancière, "Notes on the Photographic Image," *Radical Philosophy* 156 (2009): 8.

16. Walter Benjamin, "Little History of Photography," in *Selected Writings Vol. 2 1927–1934,* trans. Rodney Livingstone and others (Cambridge, Mass.: The Belknap Press of Harvard University, 1999), 518.

17. Benjamin, "The Work of Art," 226.

18. Krauss borrowed this term from Benjamin to use it as the title of her noteworthy study of modernism, *The Optical Unconscious* (Cambridge, Mass.: MIT Press, 1994).

19. Benjamin, "Little History," 512.

20. Edward Steichen, *The Family of Man* (New York: The Museum of Modern Art, 2003).

21. Ibid., n.p.

22. First published in 1961, Barthes' essay "The Photographic Message" appeared in English, trans. Stephen Heath, in *Image-Music-Text* (New York: Hill and Wang, 1978). I am citing from its reprint in *A Barthes Reader,* ed. and introd. Susan Sontag (New York: Hill and Wang, 1982), 194.

23. Roland Barthes, "The Great Family of Man," in *Mythologies,* trans. Annette Lavers (New York: Hill and Wang, 1972), 101.

24. These are Krauss's words, paraphrasing Benjamin's initial (1931) position. Krauss, "Reinventing," 291.

25. Krauss, "Reinventing," 293.

26. Roland Barthes, *Camera Lucida: Reflections on Photography,* trans. Richard Howard (New York: Hill and Wang, 1981).

27. Rancière, "Notes," 8–9.

28. Sontag, *On Photography,* 163, 167. In view of her ruthlessly negative take on the medium, it is curious to realize that Sontag spent some fifteen years of her life in a close romantic relationship with celebrated photographer Annie Leibovitz.

29. The term *objet petit a* in Lacan stands for the unattainable object of desire. The "*a*" refers to the French word for "other" [*autre*]. The small "a" differentiates the object from the "*grand Autre,*" or the capitalized "Other." The origins of the term may be traced to Freud's concept of the "lost object," while it reappears in Melanie Klein's notion of the "partial object." Lacan, his translator suggests, "insists that '*objet petit a*' should remain untranslated, thus acquiring, as it were, the status of an algebraic sign." "Translator's Note" in Jacques Lacan, *The Four Fundamental Concepts of Psycho-analysis,* ed. Jacques-Alain Miller; trans. Alan Sheridan (Norton and Co.: New York and London, 1981), 282. I will return to the notion of the "partial object" in my concluding chapter.

30. Rancière, "Notes," 9.

31. Geoffrey Batchen, *Each Wild Idea: Writing Photography History* (Cambridge, Mass.: MIT Press, 2002), 109.

32. James Elkins, "Critical Response: What Do We Want Photography to Be? A Response to Michael Fried," *Critical Inquiry* 31 (2005): 347.

33. Krauss, "Reinventing," 293.

34. This is in fact the central question in Elkins' debate with Michael Fried referred to above.

35. Sontag, *On Photography,* 166–67.

36. Rancière, "Notes," 8–9.

37. Ibid., 15.

38. Thérèse St.-Gelais, "Rineke Dijkstra: Une communauté de solitudes," *Parachute* 102 (2001): 18.

39. Ibid., 29.

40. Jean-Luc Nancy, *The Ground of the Image,* trans. Jeff Fort (New York: Fordham University Press, 2005), 1.

41. Images of these works are, alas, not available for reproduction in any but Rineke Dijkstra's own books; see, therefore, the earlier mentioned catalogues *Portraits* and *A Retrospective.*

FIVE. THE RUSE OF THE RUINS

1. John Huey, "Assignment Detroit: Why Time Inc. Is in Motown," *Time,* September 24, 2009, http://www.time.com/time/magazine, accessed May 10, 2012.

2. http://detroit.blogs.time.com/.

3. As a counter statement, cf. the documentary film *Urban Roots* (2011), directed by Mark MacInnis, which follows the urban farming phenomenon in Detroit. More info at the Tree Media website: http://UrbanRootsAmerica.com/home.html, accessed May 11, 2012.

4. Lambert Wiesing, *Artificial Presence: Philosophical Studies in Image Theory,* trans. Nils F. Schott (Stanford, Calif.: Stanford University Press, 2010), back cover.

5. For such more serious and well-balanced arguments, see, e.g., John Patrick Leary's online publications in *Guernica: A Magazine of Art and Politics,* "Detroitism" (January 15, 2011), and "Can't Forget the People of the Motor City" (April 6, 2011), http://www .Guernicamag.com/features/leary_1_15_11/ and http://Guernicamag.com/blog/john _patrick_leary/, both accessed May 10, 2012.

6. The conference, titled "Detroit, Global City: The Motor City in the World," took place September 22–24, 2011. There is no website, but the organizers did launch a Facebook page, http://www.facebook.com/events/249657375079101/?ref=nf, accessed May 10, 2012.

7. See, e.g., Kyle Chayka's blog, "Detroit Ruin Porn and the Fetish for Decay" (January 13, 2011) on *Hyperallergic: Sensitive to Arts and its Discontents*, http://hyperallergic.com/16596 /detroit-ruin-porn/; or "The Ruin Porn Post," by bfp (September 15, 2011) on *Feministe: In Defense of the Sanctimonious Women's Studies Set,* http://www.feministe.us/blog /archives/2011/09/15/the-ruin-porn-post, accessed May 10, 2012.

8. Andrew Moore, *Detroit Disassembled* (Akron, Ohio: Akron Art Museum, 2010), published on the occasion of the exhibition Detroit Disassembled: Photographs by Andrew Moore, at the Akron Museum, June 5–October 10, 2010; Yves Marchand and Romain Meffre, *The Ruins of Detroit* (Göttingen: Steidl, 2010). For an extensive gallery of the French duo's photographs, see their website http://www.MarchandandMeffre.com/detroit/index. html, accessed May 11, 2012. Selected works of both Moore and Marchand/Meffre, along with those of half a dozen other photographers, both local and nonlocal, were included in the exhibition Detroit Revealed: Photographs, 2000–2010, at the Detroit Institute of Arts, October 16–April 8, 2012. A catalogue of the same title appeared in conjunction with the exhibition, published by the DIA, featuring essays by art critics/historians Nancy W. Barr, John Gallagher, and Carlo McCormick.

9. Born in Prague, Flusser emigrated to London in 1939, and after he had lost all of his family in the Nazi concentration camps, he went to Brazil, where he taught philosophy and worked as a journalist. He left Brazil in 1972 and spent the rest of his life alternately in Germany and the south of France. His works are written in several different languages, but the ones I am drawing on were both originally published in German.

10. See note 7 in this chapter.

11. Julia Reyes Taubman, *Detroit: 138 Square Miles,* foreword by Elmore Leonard (Detroit: Museum of Contemporary Art, 2011). I will not discuss any of the photographs reprinted here in any detail. They primarily serve as an illustration of my theoretical observations, and, unlike the photos discussed in previous chapters, not as objects of examination themselves.

12. Vilém Flusser, *Towards a Philosophy of Photography,* trans. Anthony Mathews (London: Reaktion Books, 2000, reprinted 2007). *Into the Universe of Technical Images,* trans. Nancy Ann Roth, intro. Mark Poster (Minneapolis: University of Minnesota Press, 2011).

13. Mark Poster, Introduction to Flusser, *Into the Universe,* xix. Poster numbers Foucault, Lacan, and Deleuze among such media-negligent theorists.

14. See, for example, such recent collections of essays as Antony Bryan and Griselda Pollock, eds., *Digital and Other Virtualities: Renegotiating the Image* (London and New York: I. B. Tauris, 2010); Jacques Khalip and Robert Mitchell, eds., *Releasing the Image: From Literature to New Media* (Stanford, Calif.: Stanford University Press, 2011); Oliver Grau, with Thomas Veigl, eds., *Imagery in the 21st Century* (Cambridge, Mass.: The MIT Press, 2011).

15. Edmund Husserl, "Phantasy and Image Consciousness," in *Phantasy, Image Consciousness, and Memory (1898–1925),* trans. John B. Brough (Dordrecht: Springer, 2005) § 26.59 [modified], cited in Wiesing, *Artificial Presence,* 81.

16. Ron Williams, "Green Detroit: Why the City Is Ground Zero for the Sustainability

Movement," on *Alternet* (April 22, 2010), http://www.alternet.org/environment/146577/green_detroit:_why_the_city_is_ground_zero_for_the_sustainability_movement, accessed May 14, 2012. According to the *Alternet* website, Ron Williams is president of 3rdWhaleMobile and Chair of the Free Speech TV board of directors. He is the founder and former editor and publisher of *Metro Times* (Detroit), founder of Dragonfly Media, former board chair of the Independent Media Institute (AlterNet), and founder of happyfrog.ca.

17. Andreas Huyssen, "Nostalgia for Ruins," *Grey Room* 23 (2006): 7.

18. Ibid., 11.

19. Brian Dillon, "Fragments from a History of Ruin," *Cabinet* 20 (2006): 1.

20. Brian Dillon, "Introduction: A Short History of Decay," in *Ruins* (London: Whitechapel Gallery Ventures Ltd./Cambridge, Mass.: The MIT Press, 2011), 12.

21. Huyssen, "Nostalgia for Ruins," 7.

22. Ibid., 11.

23. Ibid.

24. Ibid., 12, 13.

25. Dillon, "Fragments from a History of Ruins," 2, 5, 8.

26. Ibid., 8.

27. Ibid., 8–9.

28. Huyssen, "Nostalgia for Ruins," 8.

29. Ibid., 9.

30. Husserl, "Phantasy and Image Consciousness," § 38.86; cited in Wiesing, *Artificial Presence*, 37.

SIX. VISUALIZING THE FACE

1. Unlike previous ones, the current chapter, sadly, does not contain any images of its main subject's work. The sole copyright holder of Johan van der Keuken's oeuvre, his widow Nosh van der Lely, refused to grant me permission to reproduce some of the photographer/filmmaker's photographs and still images. She let me know that this would not serve her and her current husband's interests, since they are preparing an exhibition and a new book of previously published and unpublished materials by her deceased husband. I have not been offered further information on this project. For a limited yet helpful resource on Johan van der Keuken's films, see the interactive exhibition/website of the Museum of Modern Art in New York, http://www.moma.org/interactives/exhibitions/2001/jvdk/.

2. Jacques Rancière, *The Politics of Aesthetics: The Distribution of the Visible,* trans. Gabriel Rockhill (London and New York: Continuum, 2008), 12.

3. Ibid., 13.

4. Elizabeth Cowie, *Recording Reality, Desiring the Real* (Minneapolis: University of Minnesota Press, 2011), 3.

5. Constantin V. Boundas, "Virtual/Virtuality," in *The Deleuze Dictionary,* ed. Adrian Parr (New York: Columbia University Press, 2005), 296.

6. Gilles Deleuze, *Bergsonism,* trans. Hugh Tomlinson and Barbara Habberjam (New York: Zone Books, 1988). In my brief discussion of this concise but complex book, I am

gratefully drawing on Daniel Smith and John Protevi, "Gilles Deleuze," in *The Stanford Encyclopedia of Philosophy* (Winter 2011 Edition), ed. Edward N. Zalta, http://plato.stanford.edu/archives/win2011/entries/deleuze/, accessed May 17, 2012.

7. Ibid., n.p.

8. Ibid., n.p.

9. Gilles Deleuze, "Immanence: A Life," in *Pure Immanence: Essays on A Life,* trans. Anne Boyman (New York: Zone Books, 2005), 25–33.

10. John Rajchman, introduction to *Pure Immanence,* 20.

11. Gilles Deleuze, "The Actual and the Virtual," trans. Elliot Ross Albert, in Gilles Deleuze and Claire Parnet, *Dialogues II,* rev. ed., trans. Hugh Tomlinson and Barbara Habberjam (New York: Columbia University Press, 2007), 149–52.

12. In a translator's note, Eliot Ross Albert accounts for the stylistic oddity of the latter text by suggesting that, "rather than a finished paper, 'L'actuel et la virtuel' is a series of notes, drafts, or *aides-mémoires* for a paper," in *Dialogues II,* 171.

13. Immanence, meaning "existing or remaining within" is a founding concept in Deleuze's ontology in its general opposition to transcendence, or a metaphysical beyond or outside. The term "plane of immanence" appears as "pure immanence," in the short work of the same title, as an unqualified immersion or embeddedness, an infinite field or "smooth space" without substantial or constitutive division. See note 8 in this chapter.

14. Boundas, "Virtual/Virtuality," 297.

15. Gilles Deleuze, *Cinema 2: The Time-Image,* trans. Hugh Tomlinson and Robert Galeta (Minneapolis: University of Minnesota Press, 2010).

16. Jacques Rancière, *Film Fables,* trans. Emiliano Battista (Oxford and New York: Berg, 2006), 158.

17. In his preface to *The Logic of Sense,* Deleuze assigns Carroll a "privileged place," because he has provided the "first great *mise en scène* of the paradoxes of sense" (*The Logic of Sense,* xiii).

18. Gilles Deleuze, *Cinema 1: The Movement-Image,* trans. Hugh Tomlinson and Barbara Habberjam (Minneapolis: University of Minnesota Press, 2009), 99.

19. Emmanuel Levinas, *Totality and Infinity: An Essay on Exteriority,* trans. Alphonso Lingis (Pittsburgh: Duquesne University Press, 1969), 297.

20. Joan van der Keuken, *Wij Zijn 17 [We Are Seventeen],* introd. Simon Carmiggelt (Bussum: van Dishoeck, 1955).

21. Joan van der Keuken (photos), and Remco Campert (text), *Achter Glas [Behind Glass]* (Hilversum: Uitgeverij v.h. C. De Boer Jr., 1961), n.p.

22. After intermittently showing them as parts of larger exhibitions, van der Keuken collected the photos taken in the course of a career that spanned forty-six years in *The Lucid Eye: The Photographic Work 1953–2000* (Amsterdam: De Verbeelding, 2001).

23. Thomas Elsaesser, "The Body as Perceptual Surface: The Films of Johan van der Keuken," in *European Cinema: Face to Face with Hollywood* (Amsterdam: Amsterdam University Press, 2005), 197.

24. Bérénice Reynaud, "Johan van der Keuken: Fragments for a Reflection," in

BorderCrossing: The Cinema of Johan van der Keuken (Ithaca, N.Y.: Herbert F. Johnson Museum of Art and Cornell Cinema, Cornell University, 1990), 11.

25. Marie Chevrie, "Le cinéma contre l'image (suite): Il était une fois," *Cahiers du Cinéma* 397 (1987), cited in ibid.

26. Elsaesser, "The Body as Perceptual Surface," 200.

27. Reynaud, citing from an unpublished text delivered by the photographer/filmmaker at the "Cinéma du Réel" in Paris, 1987, in "Johan van der Keuken," 12.

28. Alain Bergala, "On Photography as the Art of Anxiety," introduction to Johan van der Keuken, *The Lucid Eye,* trans. Babette Cillekens/Vertaalcentrum VU. 3–18, http://czarabox. blogspot.com/2011/12/on-photography-as-art-of-anxiety-by.html, accessed August 6, 2012.

29. Arte.Sales, "Johan van der Keuken," http://sales.arte.tv/detailFiche. action?programId=1020, accessed January 18, 2012.

30. Johan van der Keuken, "Film Is Not a Language," *Art From Now* [*Kunst van Nu*], MOMA Interactive Exhibitions, 2001, http://www.moma.org/interactives/ exhibitions/2001/jvdk/essays/essays.html, accessed January 18, 2012.

31. Reynaud, "Johan van der Keuken," 12.

32. Johan van der Keuken, on *Wallonie Image Production,* http://www.wip.be/index. php?l=en&p=movie:700002, accessed February 1, 2013.

33. Ibid.

34. Levinas, *Totality and Infinity,* 66.

35. Charles Sanders Peirce, *Collected Papers* (Cambridge, Mass.: Harvard University Press, 1931), 228.

36. Levinas, *Totality and Infinity,* 51.

37. Ibid., 197, 194.

38. Gabriele Buzzi, "Expression and Dévisage: The Face's Signification from Art to Reality," on VJTheory.net, 2007, http://www.vjtheory.net/web_texts/text_buzzi.htm, accessed January 18, 2012.

39. Ingmar Bergman, *Cahiers du Cinema,* October 1959 cited in Deleuze, *Cinema 1,* 99.

40. The subtitle of Bergala's essay on Johan van der Keuken's photography is "the art of anxiety."

41. Bergala, "On Photography as the Art of Anxiety." 12.

42. Des O'Raw, "Cinema Lucida: Johan van der Keuken and the Meaning of Loss." *Screening the Past: An International, Refereed, Electronic Journal of Screen History* (November 17, 2010), http://www.latrobe.edu.au/screeningthepast/29/johan-van-der-keuken.html, accessed February 12, 2012.

43. Ibid., n.p.

44. Bergala, "On Photography as the Art of Anxiety," 11.

CONCLUSION

1. Badiou unfolds his critique of Deleuze in two texts: Alain Badiou, *La clameur de l'Être* (Paris: Hachette, 1997), and *Court traité d'ontologie transitoire* (Paris: Seuil, 1998). For a thoughtful appreciation of Badiou's respectful yet fundamental critique, see Mogens

Laerke, "The Voice and the Name: Spinoza in the Badioudian Critique of Deleuze," *Pli* 8 (1999): 86–99, http://web.warwick.ac.uk/philosophy/pli_journal/pdfs/laerke_pli_8.pdf, accessed May 27, 2012.

2. Against the "equivocity" of Platonism, that is, the supposition that only one being truly is, while all other beings are derivative, Deleuze adopts the concept of "univocity" from John Duns Scotus, Baruch Spinoza, and Nietzsche, to suggest that no being is more real than any other and therefore that being is, univocally, difference. "With univocity, however, it is not the differences which are and must be: it is being which is Difference, in the sense that it is said of difference. Moreover, it is not we who are univocal in a Being which is not; it is we and our individuality which remains equivocal in and for a univocal Being" (*DR,* 39). Contra Badiou, there is thus, for Deleuze, no one substance, only an always differentiating process, folding, unfolding, refolding. See, e.g., Claire Colebrook, "Univocal," in Adrian Parr, ed., *The Deleuze Dictionary,* 291–93 (New York: Columbia University Press, 2005).

3. Alain Badiou, "The Event in Deleuze," trans. Jon Roffe, *Parrhesia: A Journal of Critical Philosophy*, n.p., http://www.lacan.com/baddel.htm, accessed May 27, 2012. The original French text is "L'événement selon Deleuze," in Alain Badiou, *Logiques des mondes* (Paris: Seuil, 2006).

4. Ibid., n.p.

5. Laerke, "The Voice and the Name," 87.

6. Ibid., 86.

7. Gilles Deleuze, *The Fold: Leibniz and the Baroque,* trans. Tom Conley (Minneapolis: University of Minnesota Press, 1993), 79–82.

8. Félix Guattari, *The Three Ecologies,* trans. Ian Pindar and Paul Sutton (London and New Brunswick, N.J.: The Athlone Press, 2000); Guattari, *Chaosmosis.*

9. The second half of this chapter finds its origins in earlier work on the critical role of art in the actualization of embodied subjectivity, as explored in, among others, my essay "The Matter of Culture." That I find myself returning to these ideas so many years later suggests, in a reassuring yet startling way, that in any "adventure of ideas" somehow inheres a distinct desire for harmony, for a narrative circularity. The only explanation is the pull of the forces of the universe.

10. Badiou, "The Event in Deleuze," n.p.

11. In Badiou's essay cited above, the phrase appears slightly differently, but it is not clear if this is Badiou misquoting or a result of the translation of Badiou's text; since the latter does not provide references, there is no way of determining who is to "blame" for the misquotation/deviation from an English translation of the original French text.

12. See chapter 1, note 14.

13. This is, accidentally, the reason why Whitehead's subject is always a "subject-superject." As he stipulates in *Process and Reality:* "An actual entity is at once the subject experiencing and the superject of its experiences. It is the subject-superject, and neither half of this description can for a moment be lost sight of" (*PR,* 29).

14. Alfred North Whitehead, *The Concept of Nature* (Amherst, N.Y.: Prometheus Books, 2004), 143.

15. Just as the *The Concept of Nature* is made up of a series of lectures given in London

in the early 1920s, *Process and Reality* consists of a series of lectures delivered as the Gifford Lectures at the University of Edinburgh during the session of 1927–28.

16. See chapter 1, note 16.

17. http://www.merriam-webster.com/dictionary/vitalism, accessed May 27, 2012.

18. Daniel Bell, *The End of Ideology: On the Exhaustion of Political Ideas in the Fifties,* 2nd ed. (Cambridge, Mass.: Harvard University Press, 2000).

19. It appears these insights have since made their way into a widening range of social scientific and other socioeconomic domains and are beginning to take concrete, material effect: while I was finishing this chapter, I came across a blog post by Daniel Isenberg, professor of management practice, Babson Global, and founding executive director of the Babson Entrepreneurship Ecosystem Project, on the rebirth of inner cities in recent years. While formerly primarily evoking images of destruction, dereliction, and decay, "inner cities" today, he suggests, are "in"—"innovative, hip hotbeds of convenient culture, commerce and connection." Literally echoing Guattari, Isenberg defines today's inner cities as "holistic entrepreneurship ecosystems," which flourish as a result of an emphasis on "best processes" rather than "best practices," inventing time, rather than money, and "experimentation," rather than protocol. Examples include the Boston Innovation District and similar "platforms" (rather than programs) for innovation in London, Buenos Aires, and Barcelona. I would like to add Detroit to this list of urban ecosystems whose "centripetal force . . . is pulling the ambitious and educated back in, and [is] increasing cities' innovative capacity, without sacrificing (at least some would argue) their inclusiveness." See Daniel Isenberg, "Planting Entrepreneurial Innovation in Inner Cities," Harvard Business Review/HBR Blog Network, June 5, 2012, http://blogs.hbr.org/cs/2012/06/planting_entrepreneurial_innov.html, accessed June 6, 2012.

20. Guattari's reference to Schlegel, according to a footnote in *The Three Ecologies,* can be traced to Phillippe Lacoue-Labarthe and Jean-Luc Nancy, in *L'absolu littéraire: théorie de la littérature du romantisme allemand* (Paris: Editions de Seuil, 1978), 126. A translator's note indicates that the reference to Friedrich von Schlegel's famous Fragment 206 from *The Athenaeum* can additionally be found in Maurice Blanchot's *The Infinite Conversation,* trans. Susan Hanson (Minneapolis: University Minnesota Press, 1993), 352–59 (*The Three Ecologies,* 94 n. 58).

21. Transitional objects find their origins in an early stage of infant development, with the child's emerging awareness of the difference between inner and outer reality. They are at once "me" and "not-me," and are transitional in that they facilitate the transition from the baby for whom external objects have not yet separated to the capacity to relate to "objectively perceived" objects. See Donald Winnicott, "Transitional Objects and Transitional Phenomena," in *International Journal of Psycho-Analysis* 34 (1953), 89–97; additional material was added to the paper in Winnicott's *Playing and Reality* (London: Tavistock, 1971), 1–30.

22. Cf., Lipovetsky, *Hypermodern Times.*

bibliography

Alliez, Eric, and Andre Goffey, eds. *The Guattari Effect.* London: Continuum, 2011.

Armstrong, Isobel. *The Radical Aesthetic.* Oxford: Blackwell Publishers, 2000.

Arte.Sales. "Johan van der Keuken." http://sales.arte.tv/detailFiche.action?programId=1020. Accessed January 18, 2012.

Badiou, Alain. *La clameur de l'Être.* Paris: Hachette, 1997.

———. *Court traité d'ontologie transitoire.* Paris: Seuil, 1998.

———. "The Event in Deleuze." Translated by Jon Roffe. *Parrhesia: A Journal of Critical Philosophy.* http://www.lacan.com/baddel.htm. Accessed May 27, 2012.

Bakhtin, M. M. "Supplement: The Problem of Content, Material, and Form in Verbal Art." In *Art and Answerability: Early Philosophical Essays by M. M. Bakhtin.* Edited by Michael Holquist and Vadim Liapunov. Translated by Vadim Liapunov. Supplement translated by Kenneth Brostrom. Austin: University of Texas Press, 1990.

Bal, Mieke. "Narrative Inside Out: Louise Bourgeois' Spider as Theoretical Object." *Oxford Art Journal* 22.2 (1999): 103–26.

Bal, Mieke, and Norman Bryson. *Looking In: The Art of Viewing.* London: Routledge, 2001.

Barnes, Richard. *Animal Logic.* New York: Princeton Architectural Press, 2009.

Barthes, Roland. *Camera Lucida: Reflections on Photography.* Translated by Richard Howard. New York: Hill and Wang, 1981.

———. "The Great Family of Man." In *Mythologies.* Translated by Annette Lavers. New York: Hill and Wang, 1972, 100–102.

———. "The Photographic Message." In *A Barthes Reader.* Edited and with an introduction by Susan Sontag. New York: Hill and Wang, 1982, 194–210.

Bataille, Georges. "Informe." In *Documents* 1 (Paris 1929). Rpt. in Georges Bataille, *Vision of Excess: Selected Writings, 1927–1939.* Translated by Allan Stoekl, with Carl R. Lovitt and Donald M. Leslie Jr. Minneapolis: University of Minnesota Press, 1985, 31.

Batchen, Geoffrey. *Each Wild Idea: Writing Photography History.* Cambridge, Mass.: MIT Press, 2002.

Baudelaire, Charles. "The Salon of 1859." Translated by Jonathan Mayne. In *Photography in Print,* ed. Vicki Goldberg. Albuquerque: University of New Mexico Press, 1988, 123–26.

Baudrillard, Jean. *Simulacra and Simulation.* Translated by Sheila Faria Glaser. Ann Arbor: University of Michigan Press, 1994.

Beasley-Murray, Jon. "Rearguard Action." *Radical Philosophy* 111 (2002): 51–53.

Beckley, Bill, with David Shapiro, eds. *Uncontrollable Beauty: Toward a New Aesthetics.* New York: Allworth Press, 1998.

Bell, Daniel. *The End of Ideology: On the Exhaustion of Political Ideas in the Fifties.* 2nd ed. Cambridge, Mass.: Harvard University Press, 2000.

Benjamin, Walter. "Little History of Photography." In *Selected Writings Vol. 2 1927–1934.* Translated by Rodney Livingstone and others. Cambridge, Mass.: The Belknap Press of Harvard University, 1999, 507–30.

———. "The Work of Art in the Age of Mechanical Reproduction." In *Illuminations.* Translated by Harry Zohn. New York: Schocken Books, 2007, 217–51.

Bergala, Alain. "On Photography as the Art of Anxiety." Introduction to Johan van der Keuken, *The Lucid Eye.* Translated by Babette Cillekens/Vertaalcentrum VU. 3–18. http://czarabox.blogspot.com/2011/12/on-photography-as-art-of-anxiety-by.html. Accessed August 6, 2012.

Bernard-Donals, Michael F. *Mikhail Bakhtin: Between Phenomenology and Marxism.* Cambridge, UK: Cambridge University Press, 1994.

Bolter, Jay David, and Richard Grusin. *Remediation: Understanding New Media.* Cambridge, Mass.: MIT Press, 2000.

Boundas, Constantin V. "Virtual/Virtuality." In *The Deleuze Dictionary,* ed. Adrian Parr. New York: Columbia University Press, 2005, 296–98.

Braidotti, Rosi. *Metamorphoses: Towards a Materialist Theory of Becoming.* Cambridge, UK: Polity Press, 2002.

Bryan, Antony, and Griselda Pollock, eds. *Digital and Other Virtualities: Renegotiating the Image.* London and New York: I. B. Tauris, 2010.

Butler, Judith. *Bodies That Matter: On the Discursive Limits of "Sex."* London: Routledge, 1993.

Buzzi, Gabriele. "Expression and Dévisage: The Face's Signification from Art to Reality." VJTheory.net, 2007. http://www.vjtheory.net/web_texts/text_buzzi.htm. Accessed January 18, 2012.

Carroll, Lewis [1865]. *Alice's Adventures in Wonderland.* Project Gutenberg. http://www.gutenberg.org/ebooks/11. Accessed January 18, 2012.

Clark, Katerina, and Michael Holquist. *Mikhail Bakhtin.* Cambridge, Mass.: Harvard University Press, 1986.

Clough, Patricia T. "The Affective Turn: Political Economy, Biomedia, and Bodies." *Theory, Culture & Society* 25.1 (2008): 1–22.

Colebrook, Claire. *Gilles Deleuze.* London and New York: Routledge, 2002.

———. "Univocal." In *The Deleuze Dictionary,* ed. Adrian Parr. New York: Columbia University Press, 2005, 291–93.

Cowie, Elizabeth. *Recording Reality, Desiring the Real.* Minneapolis: University of Minnesota Press, 2011.

Danto, Arthur C. *The Abuse of Beauty: Aesthetics and the Concept of Art.* 3rd rpt. Chicago and La Salle, Ill.: Open Court, 2005.

———. *After the End of Art: Contemporary Art and the Pale of History.* Princeton, N.J.: Princeton University Press, 1997.

———. *Andy Warhol.* New Haven, Conn. Yale University Press, 2009.

Davis, Todd F., and Kenneth Womack, eds. *Mapping the Ethical Turn: A Reader in Ethics, Culture, and Literary Theory.* Charlottesville and London: University Press of Virginia, 2001.

Davis, Whitney. *A General Theory of Visual Culture.* Princeton, N.J.: Princeton University Press, 2011.

Debord, Guy. *The Society of the Spectacle.* Translated by Donald Nicholson-Smith. New York: Zone Books, 1995.

Deleuze, Gilles. "The Actual and the Virtual." Translated by Elliot Ross Albert. In Gilles Deleuze and Claire Parnet, *Dialogues II.* Translated by Hugh Tomlinson and Barbara Habberjam. Rev. ed. New York: Columbia University Press, 2007, 149–52.

———. *Bergsonism.* Translated by Hugh Tomlinson and Barbara Habberjam. New York: Zone Books, 1988.

———. *Cinema 1: The Movement-Image.* Translated by Hugh Tomlinson and Barbara Habberjam. Minneapolis: University of Minnesota Press, 2009.

———. *Cinema 2: The Time-Image.* Translated by Hugh Tomlinson and Robert Galeta. Minneapolis: University of Minnesota Press, 2010.

———. *Desert Islands and Other Texts 1953–1974.* Edited by David Lapoujade. Translated by Michael Taormina. Los Angeles and New York: Semiotext(e), 2004.

———. *Difference and Repetition.* Translated by Paul Patton. New York: Columbia University Press, 1994.

———. *The Fold: Leibniz and the Baroque.* Translated by Tom Conley. Minneapolis: University of Minnesota Press, 1993.

———. *Francis Bacon: The Logic of Sensation.* Translated and with an introduction by Daniel W. Smith. Afterword by Tom Conley. Minneapolis: University of Minnesota Press, 2004.

———. "Immanence: A Life." In *Pure Immanence: Essays on A Life.* Translated by Anne Boyman. New York: Zone Books, 2005, 25–33.

———. *The Logic of Sense.* Edited by Constantin V. Boundas. Translated by Mark Lester with Charles Stivale. New York: Columbia University Press, 1990.

———. *Negotiations 1972–1990.* Translated by Martin Joughin. New York: Columbia University Press, 1995.

———. *Nietzsche and Philosophy.* Translated by Hugh Tomlinson. New York: Columbia University Press, 1995.

———. *Spinoza: Practical Philosophy.* Translated by Robert Hurley. San Francisco: City Light Books, 1988.

Deleuze, Gilles, and Félix Guattari. *A Thousand Plateaus: Capitalism and Schizophrenia.* Translated by Brian Massumi. Minneapolis: University of Minnesota Press, 2003.

———. *What Is Philosophy?* Translated by Hugh Tomlinson and Graham Burchell. New York: Columbia University Press, 1994.

Deleuze, Gilles, and Claire Parnet. *Dialogues II.* Translated by Hugh Tomlinson and Barbara Habberjam. Rev. ed. New York: Columbia University Press, 2007.

Dijkstra, Rineke. *Portraits.* Muenchen: Schirmer/Mosel, 2004.

———. *Rineke Dijkstra: A Retrospective.* New York: Guggenheim Museum Publications, 2012.

Derrida, Jacques. *Memoirs of the Blind: The Self-portrait and Other Ruins.* Translated by

Pascale-Anne Brault and Michael Naas. Chicago and London: University of Chicago Press, 2007.

Dillon, Brian. "Fragments from a History of Ruin." *Cabinet* 20 (2006): 1–10.

———. "Introduction: A Short History of Decay." In *Ruins*. London: Whitechapel Gallery Ventures Ltd.; Cambridge, Mass.: MIT Press, 2011, 10–19.

Dikovitskaya, Margaret. *Visual Culture: The Study of the Visual after the Cultural Turn.* Cambridge, Mass.: MIT Press, 2006.

Douglas, Mary. *Purity and Danger: An Analysis of Concepts of Pollution and Taboo.* London: Routledge, 2002.

Elkins, James. "Critical Response: What Do We Want Photography to Be? A Response to Michael Fried." *Critical Inquiry* 31 (2005): 338–56.

Elsaesser, Thomas. "The Body as Perceptual Surface: The Films of Johan van der Keuken." In *European Cinema: Face to Face with Hollywood.* Amsterdam: Amsterdam University Press, 2005.

Evans, Jessica, and Stuart Hall, eds. *Visual Culture: The Reader.* London: SAGE, 1999.

Felski, Rita. "From Literary Theory to Critical Method." *Profession* (2008): 108–16.

Flatley, Jonathan. *Affective Mapping: Melancholia and the Politics of Modernity.* Cambridge, Mass.: Harvard University Press, 2008.

Flaxman, Gregory. *Gilles Deleuze and the Fabulation of Philosophy.* Minneapolis: University of Minnesota Press, 2012.

Flusser, Vilém. *Into the Universe of Technical Images.* Translated by Nancy Ann Roth. Introduction by Mark Poster. Minneapolis: University of Minnesota Press, 2011.

———. *Towards a Philosophy of Photography.* Translated by Anthony Mathews. London: Reaktion Books, 2000. Reprint 2007.

Foster, Hal. *The Anti-Aesthetic: Essays on Postmodern Culture.* Port Townsend, Wash.: Bay Press, 1983.

———. *Compulsive Beauty.* Cambridge, Mass.: MIT Press, 1993.

———. *The First Pop Age: Painting and Subjectivity in the Art of Hamilton, Lichtenstein, Warhol, Richter, and Ruscha.* Princeton, N.J.: Princeton University Press, 2012.

———. "The Medium Is the Market." *London Review of Books* 30.19 (October 9, 2008): 23–24.

———. "Post-Critical." *October* 139 (Winter 2012): 3–8.

———. *Prosthetic Gods.* Cambridge, Mass.: MIT Press, 2006.

———. *Recodings: Art, Spectacle, Cultural Politics.* New York: The New Press, 1985.

———. *The Return of the Real: The Avant-Garde at the End of the Century.* Cambridge, Mass.: MIT Press, 1996.

Foucault, Michel. "Theatrum Philosophicum." In *Language, Counter-Memory, Practice: Selected Essays and Interviews by Michel Foucault.* Edited and with an introduction by Donald F. Bouchard. Ithaca, N.Y.: Cornell University Press, 1977, 165–95.

Gadamer, Hans-Georg. *Philosophical Hermeneutics.* Translated and edited by David Linge. Berkeley: University of California Press, 1976.

———. *Truth and Method.* Translated by J. Weinsheimer and D. G. Marshall. 2nd rev. ed. New York: Crossroad, 2004.

Gaede, Moritz. "The Hijacking of Terrorism. *Theatrum Mundi: 911.* www.archive.org/ details/Theatrum_Mundi_911. Accessed March 28, 2012.

Garber, Marjorie, Beatrice Hanssen, and Rebecca L. Walkowitz, eds. *The Turn to Ethics.* New York and London: Routledge, 2000.

Glowacka, Dorota, and Stephen Boos, eds. *Between Ethics and Aesthetics.* Albany: State University of New York Press, 2002.

Grau, Oliver, with Thomas Veigl, eds. *Imagery in the 21st Century.* Cambridge, Mass.: MIT Press, 2011.

Guattari, Félix. *Chaosmosis: An Ethico-Aesthetic Paradigm.* Translated by Paul Bains and Julian Pefanis. Sydney: Power Publications, 1995.

———. *The Three Ecologies.* Translated by Ian Pindar and Paul Sutton. London and New Brunswick, N.J.: The Athlone Press, 2000.

Hansen, Mark. "The Time of Affect, Bearing Witness to Life." *Critical Inquiry* 30.3 (2004): 585–626.

Harris, Lee. *Civilization and Its Enemies: The Next Stage of History.* New York: The Free Press, 2004.

Hemmings, Clare. "Invoking Affect: Cultural Theory and the Ontological Turn." *Cultural Studies* 19.5 (2005): 548–67.

Henderson, Kathleen. *What if I Could Draw a Bird That Could Change the World?* New York: The Drawing Center, 2008.

Hogan, Patrick Colm. *Affective Narratology: The Emotional Structure of Stories.* Lincoln: University of Nebraska Press, 2011.

Hogarth, William. *The Analysis of Beauty.* Edited by Ronald Paulson. New Haven, Conn.: Yale University Press, 1997.

Holquist, Michael. *Dialogism.* 2nd ed. London: Routledge, 2002.

hoogland, renée c. "Fact and Fantasy: The Body of Desire in the Age of Posthumanism. *Journal of Gender Studies* 11.3 (2002): 213–31.

———. "'First Things First': Fantasy and the Question of Gendered Sexuality." *Journal of Gender Studies* 8.1 (1999): 43–56.

———. *Lesbian Configurations.* Cambridge, UK: Polity Press; New York: Columbia University Press, 1997.

———. "The Matter of Culture: Aesthetic Experiences and Corporeal Being." *Mosaic: A Journal for the Interdisciplinary Study of Literature* 36.3 (2003): 1–18.

Houser, Craig, Leslie C. Jones, Simon Taylor, and Jack Ben-Levi. *Abject Art: Repulsion and Desire in American Art.* New York: Whitney Museum of American Art, 1993.

Howells, Richard. *Visual Culture.* Cambridge, UK: Polity, 2006.

Huey, John. "Assignment Detroit: Why Time Inc. Is in Motown." *Time,* September 24, 2009. http://www.time.com/time/magazine/article/0.9171.1926008.00.html. Accessed July 3, 2012.

Huyssen, Andreas. "Nostalgia for Ruins. *Grey Room* 23 (2006): 6–21.

James, William. *Essays in Radical Empiricism.* Radford, Va.: Wilders Publications, 2007.

Jenkins, Henry. *Convergence Culture: Where Old and New Media Collide.* New York: New York University Press, 2006.

Jones, Bernard E. *Cassell's Cyclopaedia of Photography.* New York: Arno, 1973.

Joughin, John J., and Simon Malpas, eds. *The New Aestheticism.* Manchester and New York: Manchester University Press, 2003.

Khalip, Jacques, and Robert Mitchell, eds. *Releasing the Image: From Literature to New Media.* Stanford, Calif.: Stanford University Press, 2011.

Kant, Immanuel. *The Critique of Judgment.* Translated by Werner S. Pluhar. Indianapolis: Hackett, 1987.

——— . *Observations on the Feeling of the Beautiful and the Sublime.* 2nd paperback ed. Translated by John T. Goldthwait. Berkeley: University of California Press, 2003.

Kivy, Peter, ed. *The Blackwell Guide to Aesthetics.* Oxford, UK: Blackwell, 2004.

Krauss, Rosalind. "*Informe* without Conclusion." *October* 78 (1996): 89–105.

——— . *The Optical Unconscious.* Cambridge, Mass.: MIT Press, 1994.

——— . "Reinventing the Medium." *Critical Inquiry* 25.2 (1999): 289–305.

Kristeva, Julia. *Powers of Horror: An Essay on Abjection.* Translated by Léon S. Roudiez. New York: Columbia University Press, 1982.

Lacan, Jacques. *The Four Fundamental Concepts of Psycho-Analysis.* Edited by Jacques-Alain Miller. Translated by Alan Sheridan. New York and London: W. W. Norton & Company, 1981.

Laerke, Mogens. "The Voice and the Name: Spinoza in the Badioudian Critique of Deleuze." *Pli* 8 (1999): 86–99. http://web.warwick.ac.uk/philosophy/pli_journal/pdfs/laerke_pli_8.pdf. Accessed July 3, 2012.

Leary, John Patrick. "Can't Forget the People of the Motor City." *Guernica: A Magazine of Art and Politics,* April 6, 2011. http://www.guernicamag.com/blog/john_patrick_leary/. Accessed July 3, 2012.

——— . "Detroitism." *Guernica: A Magazine of Art and Politics,* January 15, 2011. http://www.guernicamag.com/features/leary_1_15_11/. Accessed July 3, 2012.

Levinas, Emmanuel. *Totality and Infinity: An Essay on Exteriority.* Translated by Alphonso Lingis. Pittsburgh: Duquesne University Press, 1969.

Levinson, Jerrold, ed. *Aesthetics and Ethics: Essays at the Intersection.* Cambridge, UK: Cambridge University Press, 1998.

Leys, Ruth. "The Turn to Affect: A Critique." *Critical Inquiry* 37 (2011): 434–72.

Lipovetsky, Gilles. *Hypermodern Times.* Translated by Andrew Brown. Cambridge, UK: Polity, 2005.

Lorraine, Tamsin. "Lines of Flight." In *The Deleuze Dictionary,* ed. Adrian Parr. New York: Columbia University Press, 2005, 144–46.

Lyotard, Jean-François. *The Inhuman.* Translated by Geoffrey Bennington and Rachel Bowlby. Stanford, Calif.: Stanford University Press, 1991.

Marchand, Yves, and Romain Meffre. *The Ruins of Detroit.* Göttingen: Steidl, 2010.

Marcus, George, and Michael Fischer. *Anthropology as Cultural Critique.* Chicago: University of Chicago Press, 1986.

Massumi, Brian. *Parables for the Virtual: Movement, Affect, and Sensation.* Durham, N.C.: Duke University Press, 2002.

McDarrah, Fred W., Gloria S. McDarrah, and Timothy S. McDarrah. *Photography Encyclopedia.* Farmington Hills, Mich.: Cengage Gale, 1998.

McLuhan, Marshall. *Understanding Media.* Reprint, London and New York: Routledge, 2003.

Mirzoeff, Nicholas, ed. *The Visual Culture Reader.* 1st ed. New York and London: Routledge, 1998.

———. *The Visual Culture Reader.* 2nd edition. New York and London: Routledge, 1998.

———. *The Visual Culture Reader.* 3rd edition. New York and London: Routledge, 2013.

Moore, Andrew. *Detroit Disassembled.* Akron, Ohio: Akron Art Museum, 2010.

Morson, Gary Saul, and Caryl Emerson. *Mikhail Bakhtin: Creation of a Prosaics.* Stanford, Calif.: Stanford University Press, 1990.

Mulvey, Laura. "Visual Pleasure and Narrative Cinema." *Screen* 16.3 (1975): 6–18.

Nancy, Jean-Luc. *The Ground of the Image.* Translated by Jeff Fort. New York: Fordham University Press, 2005.

Ngai, Sianne. *Ugly Feelings.* Cambridge, Mass.: Harvard University Press, 2005.

O'Raw, Des. "Cinema Lucida: Johan van der Keuken and the Meaning of Loss." *Screening the Past: An International, Refereed, Electronic Journal of Screen History* (November 17, 2010). http://www/latrobe.edu.au/screeningthepast/29/johan-van-der-keuken.html. Accessed February 12, 2012.

Nietzsche, Friedrich. *Twilight of the Idols: or How to Philosophize with a Hammer.* Translated by Duncan Large. New York: Oxford USA, 1998.

Parr, Adrian, ed. *The Deleuze Dictionary*. New York: Columbia University Press, 2005.

Peirce, Charles Sanders. *Collected Papers.* Cambridge, Mass.: Harvard University Press, 1931.

Poster, Mark. Introduction. In Vilém Flusser, *Into the Universe of Technical Images.* Translated by Nancy Ann Roth. Minneapolis: University of Minnesota Press, 2011, ix–xxvii.

Proust, Marcel. *Contre Sainte Beuve.* Paris: Editions Flammarion, 1987.

Rajchman, John. Introduction. In Gilles Deleuze, *Pure Immanence: Essays on A Life.* Translated by Anne Boyman. New York: Zone Books, 2005, 7–23.

Rancière, Jacques. "The Ethical Turn of Aesthetics and Politics." *Critical Horizons* 7.1 (2006): 1–20.

———. *Film Fables.* Translated by Emiliano Battista. Oxford and New York: Berg, 2006.

———. *The Future of the Image.* Translated by Gregory Elliott. London: Verso, 2009.

———. "Notes on the Photographic Image." *Radical Philosophy* 156 (2009): 8–15.

———. *The Politics of Aesthetics: The Distribution of the Visible.* Translated by Gabriel Rockhill. London and New York: Continuum, 2004.

Reynaud, Bérénice. "Johan van der Keuken: Fragments for a Reflection." In *BorderCrossing: The Cinema of Johan van der Keuken.* Ithaca, N.Y.: Herbert F. Johnson Museum of Art and Cornell Cinema, Cornell University, 1990, 11–14.

Rimmon-Kenan, Shlomith. "Concepts of Narrative." *COLLeGIUM: Studies Across Disciplines in the Humanities and the Social Sciences.* Vol. 1: The Travelling Concept of Narrative (2006): 1–20.

———. *Narrative Fiction: Contemporary Poetics.* London: Methuen, 1983.

Ryan, Marie-Laure. "Media and Narrative." In *Routledge Encyclopedia of Narrative Theory.* http://lamar.colostate.edu/pwryan/mediaentry.html. Accessed February 12, 2007.

Sedgwick, Eve Kosofsky. *Touching Feeling: Affect, Pedagogy, Performativity.* Durham, N.C.: Duke University Press, 2003.

Shapiro, Gary. *Archaeologies of Vision: Foucault and Nietzsche on Seeing and Saying.* Chicago: University of Chicago Press, 2003.

Shaviro, Steven. *Without Criteria: Kant, Whitehead, Deleuze, and Aesthetics.* Cambridge, Mass.: MIT Press, 2009.

Smith, Daniel W. "Deleuze's Theory of Sensation: Overcoming the Kantian Duality." In *Deleuze: A Critical Reader,* ed. Paul Patton. Oxford, UK: Blackwell Publishers, 1996, 29–56.

Smith, Daniel W., and John Protevi. "Gilles Deleuze." In *The Stanford Encyclopedia of Philosophy* (Winter 2011 Edition), ed. Edward N. Zalta. http://plato.stanford.edu /archives/win2011/entries/deleuze. Accessed July 3, 2012.

Sontag, Susan. *On Photography.* New York: Picador, 1977.

Spinola, Julia. "Monstrous Art." In *Frankfurter Allgemeine Zeitung.* English Language Edition. September 25, 2001.

St.-Gelais, Thérèse. "Rineke Dijkstra: Une communauté de solitudes. *Parachute* 102 (2001): 14–31.

Starr, Gabrielle. "Ethics, Meaning, and the Work of Beauty." *Eighteenth-Century Studies* 35.3 (2002): 361–78.

Steichen, Edward. *The Family of Man.* New York: The Museum of Modern Art, 2003.

Stivale, Charles J. *Gilles Deleuze's ABCs: The Folds of Friendship.* Baltimore: Johns Hopkins University Press, 2008.

Sturken, Marita, and Lisa Cartwright. *Practices of Looking: An Introduction to Visual Culture.* 2nd ed., Oxford: Oxford University Press, 2009.

Taubman, Julia Reyes. *Detroit: 138 Square Miles.* Foreword by Elmore Leonard. Detroit: Museum of Contemporary Art, 2011.

Terada, Rei. *Feeling in Theory: Emotion and the "Death of the Subject."* Cambridge, Mass.: Harvard University Press, 2001.

Tomkins, Sylvan S. *Affect, Imagery, Consciousness / Vol. II: The Negative Affects.* New York: Springer Publishing, 1963.

Van der Keuken, Joan. *Wij Zijn 17* [*We Are Seventeen*]. Introduction by Simon Carmiggelt. Bussum: van Dishoeck, 1955.

Van der Keuken, Joan (photos), and Remco Campert (text). *Achter Glas* [*Behind Glass*]. Hilversum: Uitgeverij v.h. C. De Boer Jr., 1961.

Van der Keuken, Johan. "Film Is Not a Language." In *Art From Now* [*Kunst van Nu*]. MOMA Interactive Exhibitions, 2001. http://www.moma.org/interactives/exhibitions/2001/jvdk /essays/essays.html. Accessed February 6, 2012.

———. *The Lucid Eye—The Photographic Work 1953–2000.* Amsterdam: De Verbeelding, 2001.

Warhol, Andy. *The Philosophy of Andy Warhol (From A to B and Back Again).* Orlando, Fla.: Harcourt, Inc., 1977.

Whitehead, Alfred North. *Adventures of Ideas.* 1933. New York: The Free Press, 1967.

———. *The Concept of Nature.* 1920. Amherst: N.Y.: Prometheus Books, 2004.

———. *Process and Reality.* 1929. New York: The Free Press, 1985.

Wiesing, Lambert. *Artificial Presence: Philosophical Studies in Image Theory.* Translated by Nils F. Scott. Stanford, Calif.: Stanford University Press, 2010.

Wimsatt, W. K., Jr., and Monroe C. Beardsley. "The Intentional Fallacy." In *The Verbal Icon: Studies in the Meaning of Poetry,* 3–18. Lexington: University of Kentucky Press, 1954.

Winnicott, Donald. *Playing and Reality.* London: Tavistock, 1971.

———. "Transitional Objects and Transitional Phenomena." *International Journal of Psycho-Analysis* 34 (1953): 89–97.

Winterson, Jeanette. *Why Be Happy When You Could Be Normal?* New York: Grove Press, 2012.

Wittgenstein, Ludwig. *Philosophical Investigations.* Translated by G. E. M. Anscombe. Oxford: Blackwell, 1978.

———. *Tractatus Logico-Philosophicus.* Translated by David Pears and Brian McGuinness. London and New York: Routledge, 1961.

Wyschorod, Edith, and Gerald P. Kennedy, eds. *The Ethical.* Malden, Mass.: Blackwell, 2003.

Zepke, Stephen. *Art as Abstract Machine: Ontology and Aesthetics in Deleuze and Guattari.* New York: Routledge, 2005.

index